I0795914

IMAGES
of America

THE KESWICK THEATRE

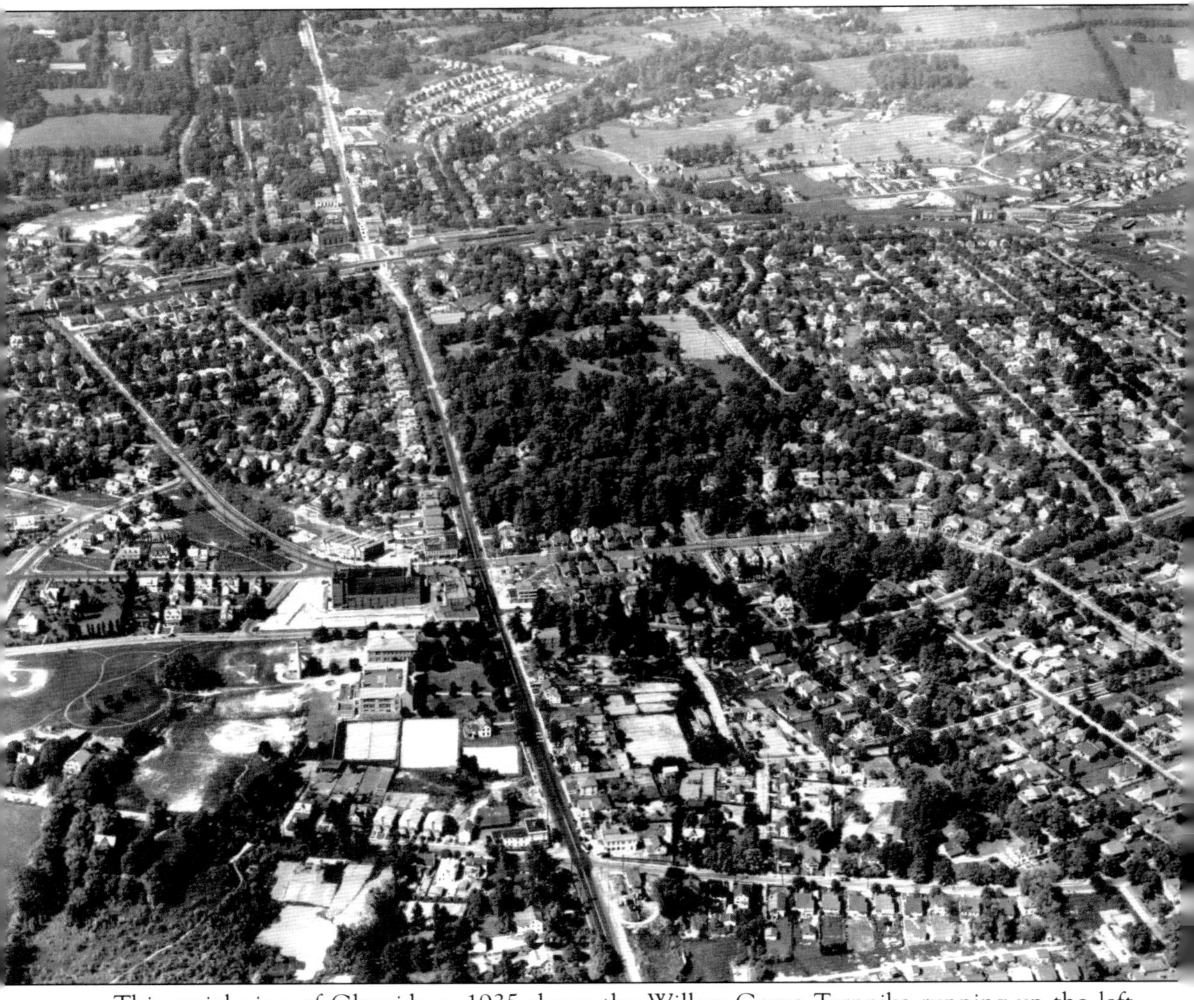

This aerial view of Glenside *c.* 1935 shows the Willow Grove Turnpike running up the left center. The turnpike was renamed Easton Road. The theater plant is shown in the mid-left quadrant. This area was just beginning to be developed.

IMAGES
of America

THE KESWICK THEATRE

Judith Katherine Herbst

ARCADIA
PUBLISHING

ISBN 978-0-7385-3561-6

Published by Arcadia Publishing
Charleston, South Carolina

Printed in the United States of America

Library of Congress Catalog Card Number: 2004100479

For all general information contact Arcadia Publishing at:
Telephone 843-853-2070
Fax 843-853-0044
E-mail sales@arcadiapublishing.com
For customer service and orders:
Toll-Free 1-888-313-2665

Visit us on the Internet at www.arcadiapublishing.com

The pleasure of your presence
is requested at the opening of the

-: Keswick Theatre :-

Easton Road, Wharton Avenue and Keswick Ave.

GREATER GLENSIDE

Thursday Evening, December 27, 1928

EDWIN N. JOHNSON

Doors open - 7.15 P. M. - - Show begins - 8.15 P. M.

ADMIT ONE

Welcome to the Keswick Theatre! Edwin Johnson's opening night invitation reflects the level of patronage that was desired in this new venue in the Philadelphia area. The opening was heavily publicized in both the local and regional press.

CONTENTS

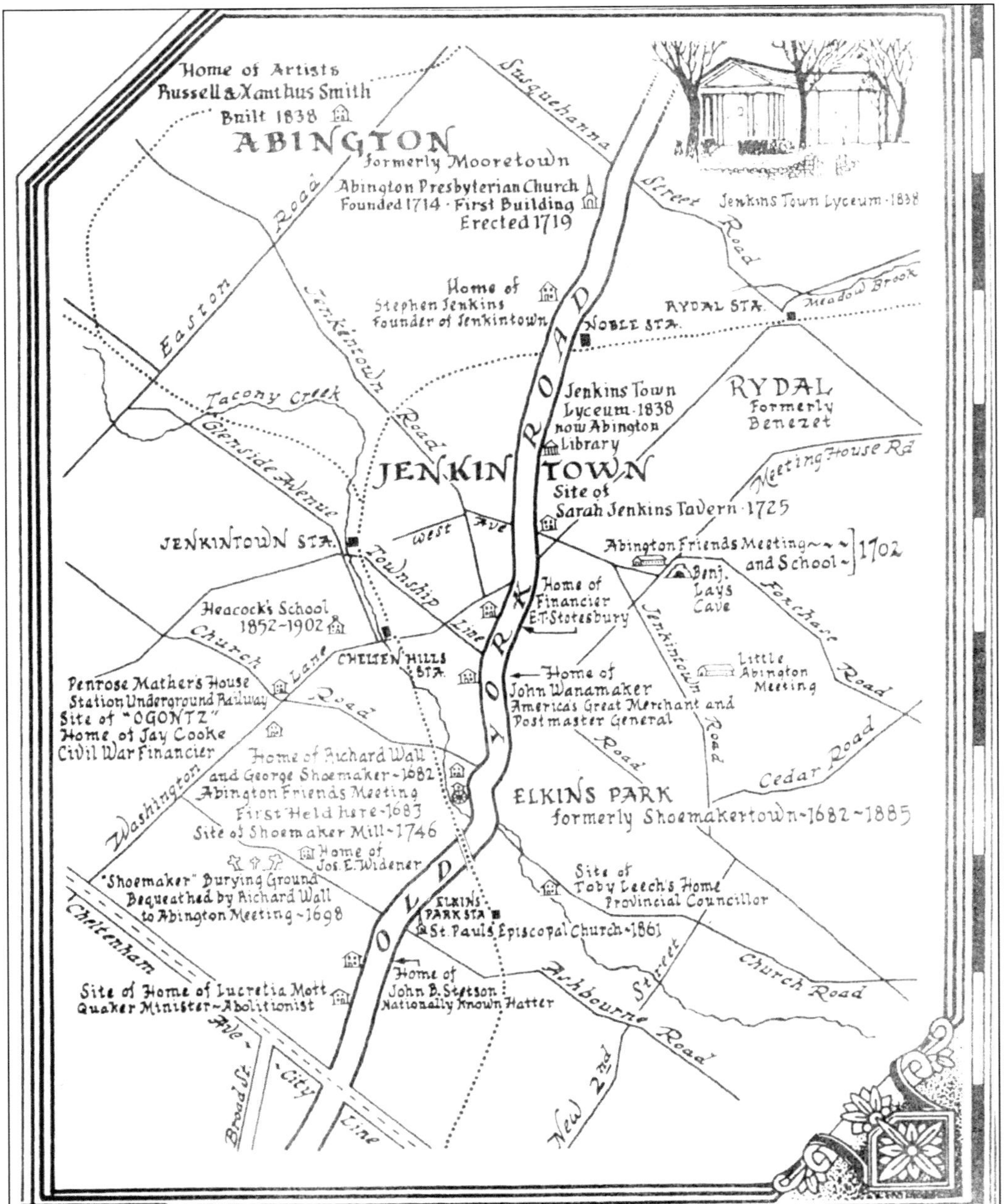

This map was uncovered in the archives of the local Weldon Fire Company. Although its origins are unknown, it is a rich source of historical and cultural information about the Abington area. The Keswick Theatre is not listed on the original map.

Introduction

The stories of Keswick Village, Weldon, or even greater Glenside do not reside specifically in the building of the Keswick Theatre. The word "building" indicates a work in progress as well as a place. Therefore, not only do the walls of a building gain coverings and fixtures but also the place perhaps absorbs some of the life that passes through it. For a moment, let's pretend that the same building not only is seen but also sees and mirrors our past, weathering both good times and bad. Keeping the Keswick Theatre vital reflects the historic and economic times of the community.

Beginning its history at the end of the vaudeville era, the Keswick encompasses a community on the brink of growth. In the 1920s, the Glenside area was changing from rural to suburban at a rate reflective of the period's economic prosperity. The community leaders envisioned keeping a "small-town flavor" to the area. This vision remains 75 years later. Less than two miles from the city limits of Philadelphia, in the township of Abington, Glenside remains community oriented and retains much of the same identity that it had at the beginning of the 20th century, when Abington was made up of villages connected by turnpikes. Moreover, a small-town community is celebrated.

Recently, I attended a local talk given by a member of the Pennsylvania Economic Development Department. This talk mentioned the concept of creating communities that would attract young adults to stay in the state. Ideal communities would include commerce, such as shops or a mall area; good housing, such as new homes or older ones that had weathered the test of time and had some character to set them apart; good schools and resources for families; and cultural opportunities for these young adults and their families as they grew. Just after 1900, community leaders envisioned the same for Glenside. The Keswick Theatre was part of that initiative.

Glenside has welcomed many people to its community over the years: people who decided to live here, who chose to work here, or who came just to perform here. Harry Brackinridge is one such person. He came here to work as the first stage manager at the Keswick Theatre. His daughter still calls the area home. Whether he was sending performers to the Casi Conte Hotel so they would not have to commute from the city when performing, or taking them to see his gardens for a little relaxation, Harry Brackinridge typified the Glenside welcome.

It is not uncommon, at the back lot of the Keswick Theatre, to see tour buses and school buses lined up side by side, carrying schoolchildren and performers such as Kenny Rogers, Etta James, David Lee Roth, B.B. King, and Willie Nelson. Glenside residents are as proud of these performers visiting Glenside as they are of the children who continue to dance in recitals on the same stage that was graced with the Marx Brothers, Fanny Brice, and Mae West. Performers and guests are all treated with warmth.

The Keswick Theatre is here because the residents wished for it—and fought for it. Many of the people who fought for the theater in the 1980s were the first patrons of the venue in the 1920s; many were those patrons' children. The building was kept open through the Depression, through movie shortages and strikes, through fire, flood, and financial problems. This book is a tribute to the many who supported the Keswick Theatre over the years, whether by making donations to the Glenside Landmarks Society or by handing over their hard-earned 25¢ for the Saturday matinee. They are too many to number individually. They are too important to not remember.

The Keswick story reveals that the venue remained a commercial enterprise for most of its history. It struggled through vaudeville and the Depression; it struggled into the 1950s and was remade with Hollywood; and though saved by a not-for-profit entity, the building was soon a commercial enterprise once again. Today, it maintains that status of an independent commercial enterprise. Proof of its success is that *Pollstar Magazine* includes the Keswick Theatre on its list of the top 50 venues with a capacity of 5,000 or fewer. Others on the list include giants such as Atlanta's Fox Theatre and the Chicago Theatre—venues three times the size of the Keswick.

This is a story of records lost and of how important it is for communities to retain those records for future communities. As this project was undertaken, it was discovered that records, photographs, programs, and memories were lost. No true history is a comfortable history; there are always tales of sorrow, conflicting interests, slights, and hurts. This book prefers to focus on the tales of vision, hard work, and humor, as they are what saved the venue and made it vital.

The Old York Road Historical Society, located in neighboring Jenkintown, collects such history, and the theater has become committed to giving these records to such organizations for the future. Many families have contributed to the success of this book, including the Brackinridges, the DeMarcos, the Contis, and the Clarks. The Weldon Fire Company, celebrating its centennial, opened up its collection to this effort. Compiling this book would not have been possible without this community assistance. This is a part of the current history that can be used by other communities who are struggling to save historic properties.

The fact that this building is an architectural treasure won the day in many ways, but it is the art that is found here that spurred the imagination of those who worked to save the theater and to retain it several times over. This art includes the entertainment, both amateur and professional, that was performed on its stage. It includes the richness of the work that went into the building, which has become as much of a signature as the entertainers are: the plaster, the flooring, and the artwork all inspired people to support the effort. Furthermore, it includes the talent that poured from the theater—vaudeville, vitaphone, film, music, humor, and drama—and was received by a community both near and far.

The architecture is accentuated by the engineering wonders of the building. Horace Trumbauer and Turner Construction turned a creek bed into a heating and cooling system, complete with pump house. The construction team turned airways into organ chambers, mounted the organ on an elevator so that it could rise from the pit, and hid 80 rooms behind ornate walls designed to entrance the public. Meanwhile, the show would go on, smoothly, from those hidden spaces.

The Keswick's story is the story of children. Children attended the first vaudeville matinees and, later, allowed their own children to attend the Kiddie Corner matinees of the 1940s through the 1960s. From the 1930s until today, several generations have danced upon the stage. There were those who became community firefighters after the fires of the 1950s. Perhaps children who played pranks became police officers. Some young people became enthralled with architecture or engineering thanks to their Saturday morning visits, when they watched the magic brass mushrooms rise from the floor. Certainly, there were those who dreamed of becoming movie stars, concert performers, comedians, and magicians; if they did not realize those dreams as professionals, perhaps they did so as amateurs or as teachers, or today, they send their children here to spur the same dreams. The children come—and they return, generation after generation. In 1928, they were served by the *Kiwanis Follies*; today, the children are still welcome, regardless of circumstances.

Bond drives and food drives were held during the world wars. Today, coat drives, toy drives, and food drives continue, as communities, made up of both locals and artists, come together in an outpouring of generosity. The theater has served the Protestant, Catholic, Jewish, and Buddhist communities, to name a few, including serving as "St. Keswick's" while the sanctuary of the local Catholic church, St. Luke's, was refurbished. Each time artists, professional or amateur, perform on the stage of the Keswick Theatre, they lengthen its history. Each year that it remains a part of the community, local and national, the building lends itself to the continuing history of entertainment and community. Every time the doors open and people enter, the theater keeps building.

One

Vaude-Film 1928–1951

The early days of the Keswick Theatre were ripe with possibility and disappointment. Real-estate developer Edwin Johnson took a swampy piece of land and literally sunk a theater into it. Building a theater was not a new concept. There were to be at least five other venues in the local area before the peak of movie venues ended in eastern Montgomery County. These were to include venues in Jenkintown, Willow Grove, Ambler, and Hatboro. In fact, less than four blocks away, also in Glenside, the Nixon Theatre had already been doing business since 1922.

The Keswick Theatre was ornate and most likely overpriced, and in the end, Edwin Johnson had to develop an escrow deal to recoup the investment. By 1936, he was bankrupt.

The marketing plans were not always successful, and the building had mechanical issues from its opening day. By the early 1930s, the venue was offering children's matinees for 10¢ and giving away products to attract patrons. A letter was discovered from the 1930s, thanking a benefactor for a contribution to the auditorium fund. In the 1940s, ferrets were unleashed in the tunnels to fix a rodent problem.

At one point, advertisements all but disappeared from the local paper and began to be seen in the more powerful city newspapers, such as the *Philadelphia Inquirer*. This was a clear indicator that the venue was looking for a broader reach. Many patrons recall the trolley ride to the Keswick Theatre clearly, indicating that competition called patrons from farther away to the venue.

The vaudeville names were famous ones, but films were difficult to get for an independent theater. Despite the fact that Our Gang, Fanny Brice, the Marx Brothers, and, if oral history is accurate, even the big band leaders such as Duke Wellington, appeared on the stage side by side with the lesser-known heroes of the vaudeville era, the theater found itself in economic troubles by the 1940s.

Yet the building endeared itself to the local residents, and something about attending an event at the Keswick Theatre was viewed as special, out of the ordinary. Was it the spirit of Albert Fischer, also known as "Mr. Hollywood"? Was it the fact that Ted Rouston also gave dance lessons and tried to produce films from the venue? Was it something in the makeup of the venue? Or was it all of these things put together?

As other venues suffered the fate of time and, though still cherished as historical sites with emotive history, struggled on as not-for-profit organizations, the Keswick Theatre managed to remain a commercial enterprise through its turbulent beginnings. This cannot be due to anything but the community that surrounded it and patronized it.

The architecture was special and spectacular. The graciousness of the lobby invited you in, and the warmth of the auditorium asked you to stay for a while. While waiting for the show to begin, you could be entertained by not just any organ, but one that shook the building. You could be warm in the winter and cool in the summer. You could be entertained by watching the magic mushrooms rise from the floor with cool air, and by looking at the elaborate decorations. When you walked across the Moravian tile floor, through the grand doors opening onto the specially designed rugs covering terrazzo floors, and you were ushered to your elaborate seats, you had arrived.

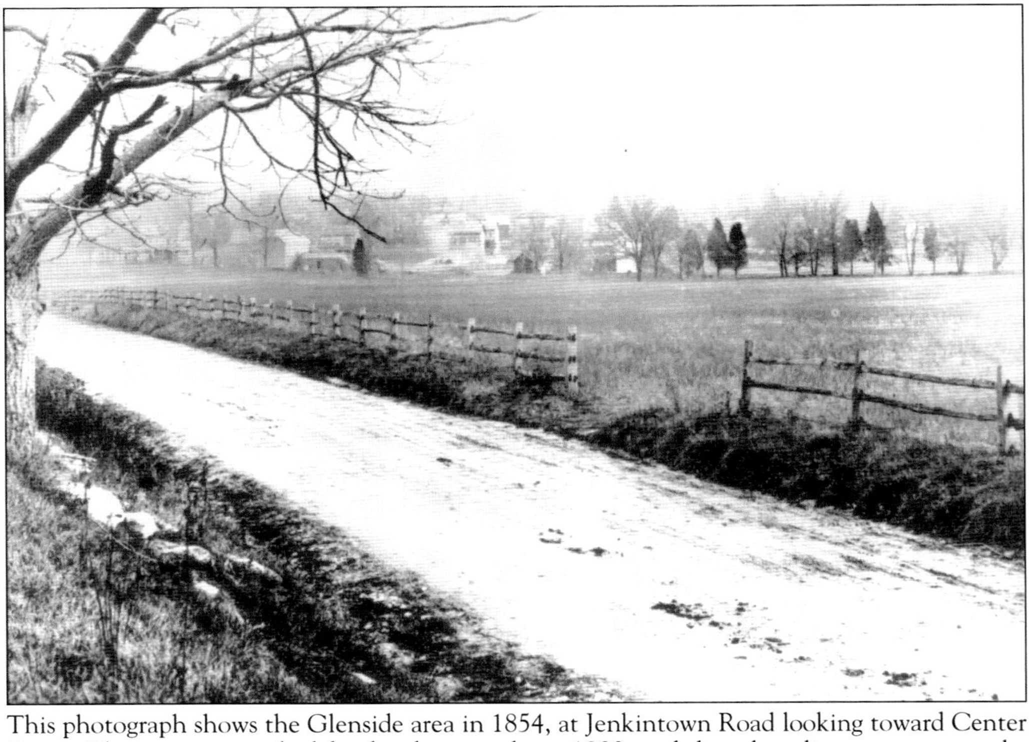

This photograph shows the Glenside area in 1854, at Jenkintown Road looking toward Center Street. The area was marked for development by *c.* 1900, and these bucolic scenes were to be just memory by the 1930s.

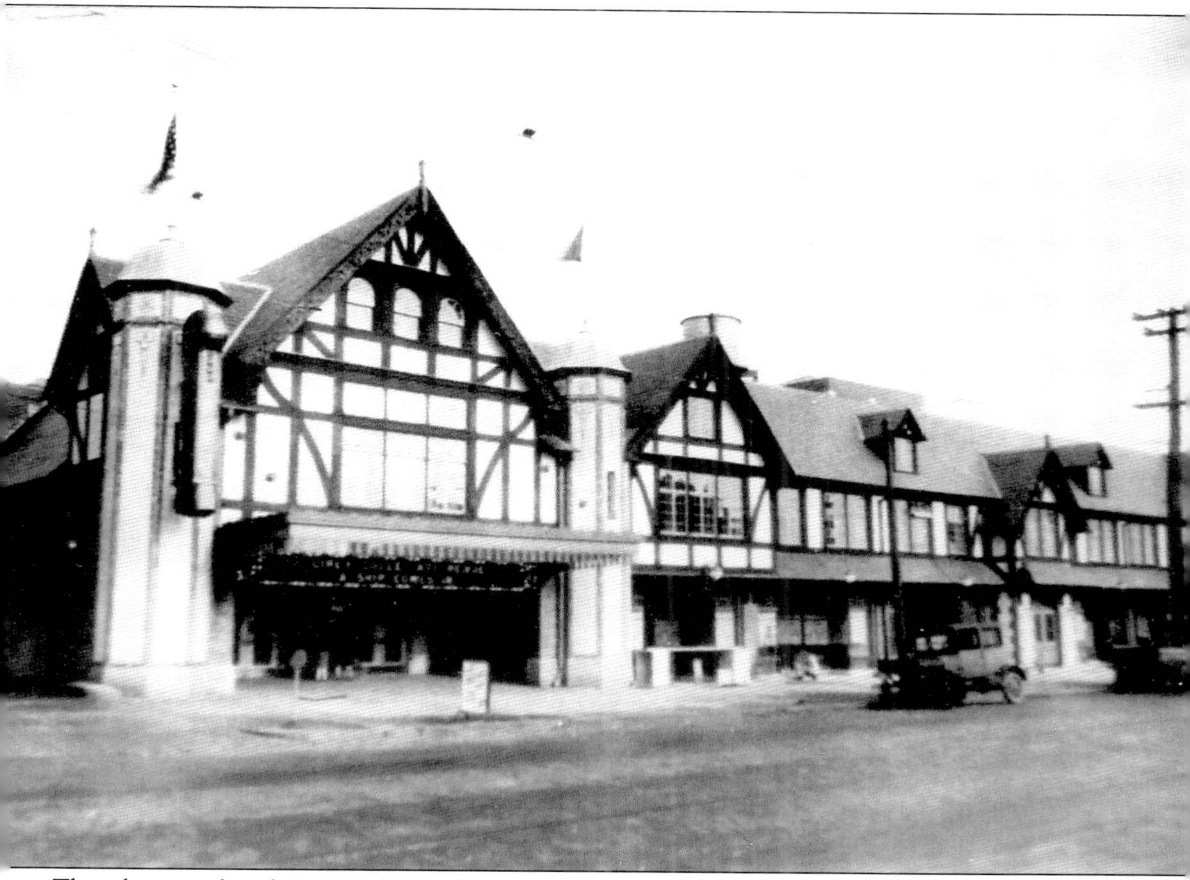

This photograph, taken a week after the opening of the theater, shows shops and the theater façade as they appeared in January 1929. The film of the week, *King of Kings*, was not as important a marquee draw as was the vaudeville act, *The Collegiate Girls Revue*. An example of the shift in perception of entertainment value, the opening of the Keswick Theatre coincided with the demise of vaudeville and the rise in popularity of the film industry.

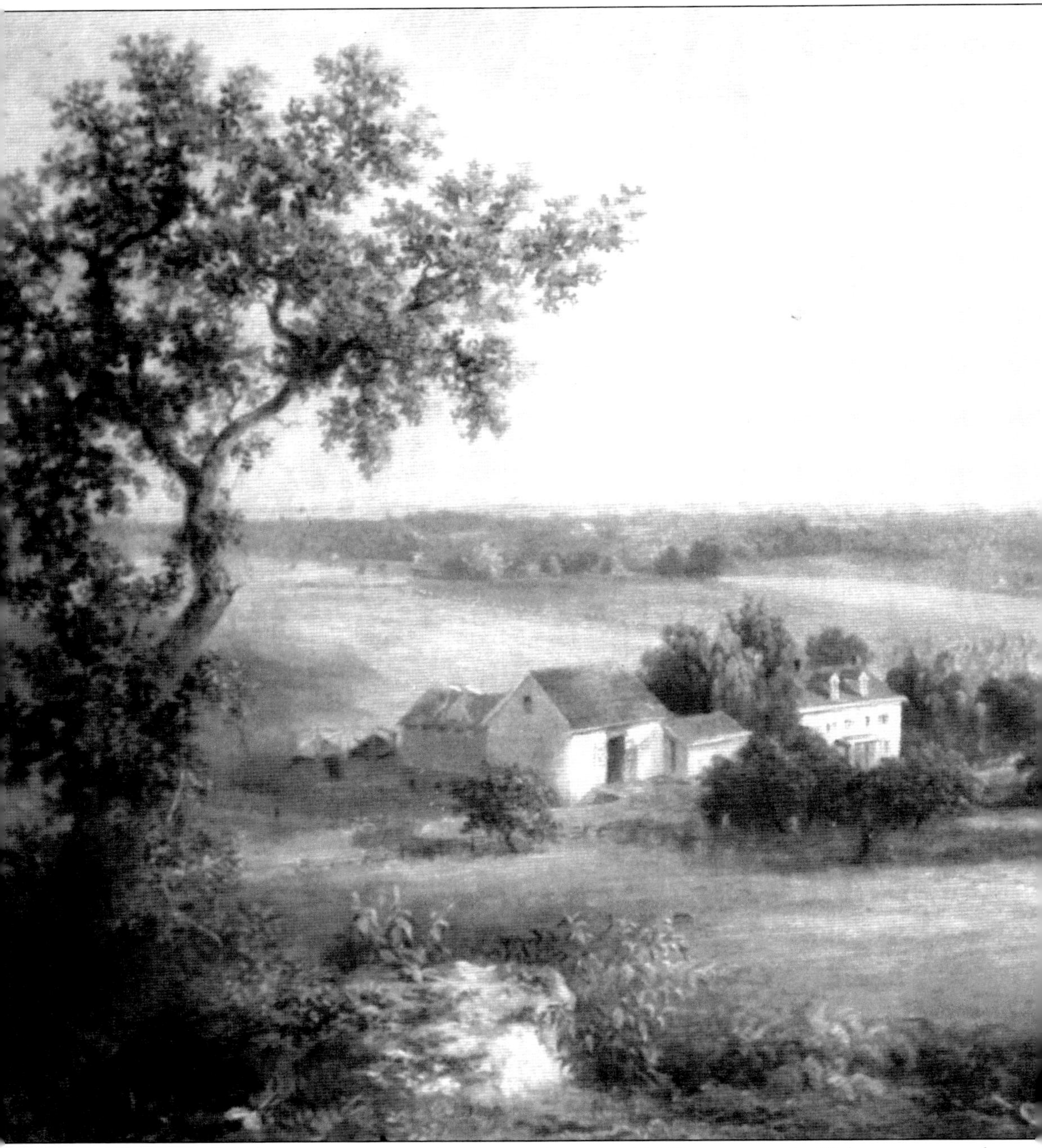

"Not very sightly, not very desirable" was what the *Exhibitor*, an early-20th-century trade journal, wrote about the location of the Keswick Theatre on December 15, 1928. Edwin Johnson not only believed that "if you get a notion, put it in motion" but also was a developer who saw the value of possibilities. He had chosen an area just beyond his real-estate offices at the corner of Easton and Wharton Road (later, Keswick Avenue). Johnson purchased 105 acres of this farmland from the Joseph Wharton estate. The area could be described as bucolic at the beginning of the 20th century. This photograph of a painting of the Wharton Estate,

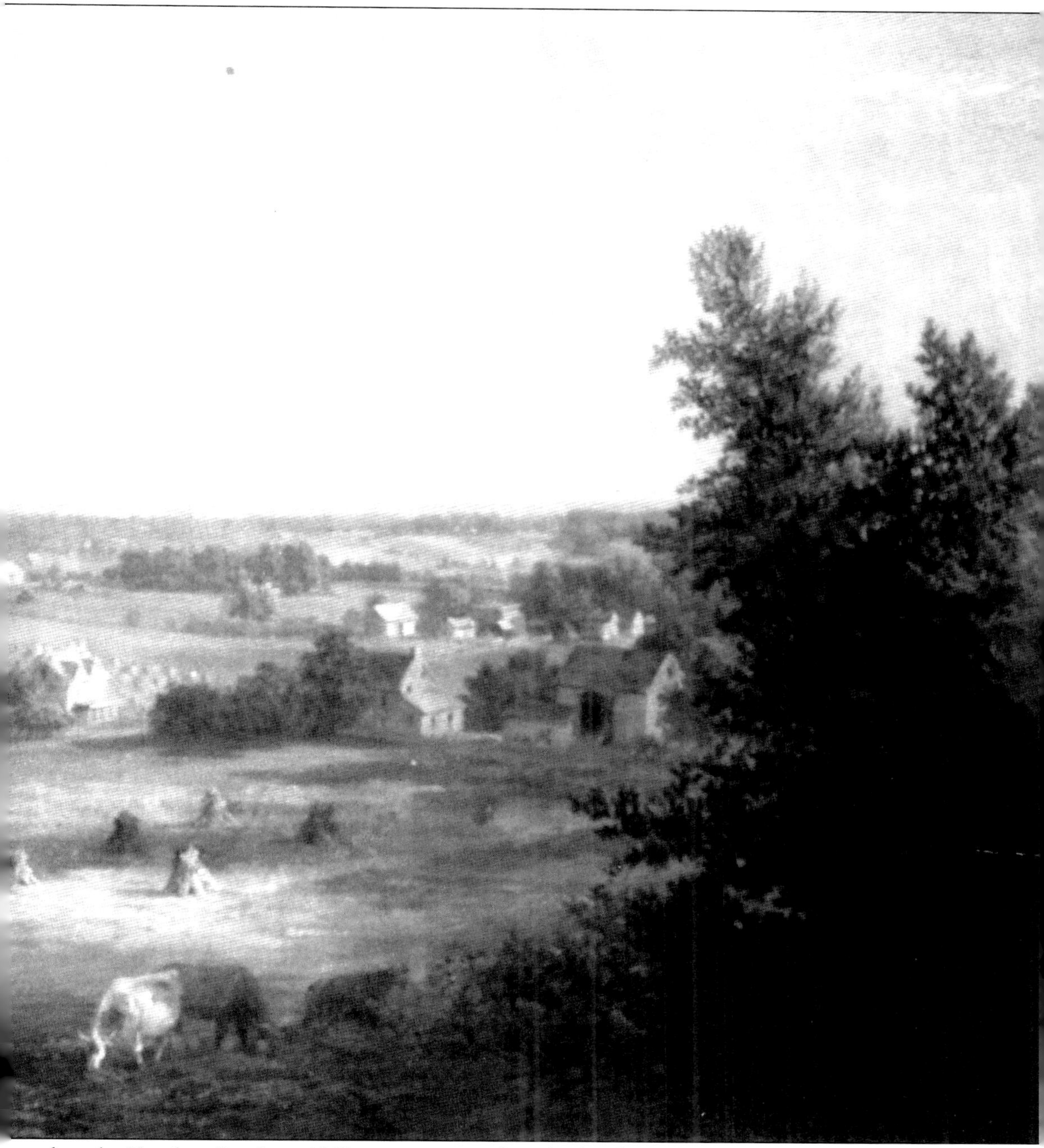

done by Xanthus Smith in 1860, was uncovered at the local Weldon Fire Company. It shows the acreage that was later developed by Johnson. By the early 1920s, the expanse once known as the Wharton Estate was becoming a neighborhood of well-to-do families, surrounded by several small towns (Jenkintown, Glenside, and Weldon). Almost a suburb of the suburb, the neighborhood included a hotel. It was common for relatives and friends to "come out to the country" and stay overnight either at the home of acquaintances or at nearby hotels or inns.

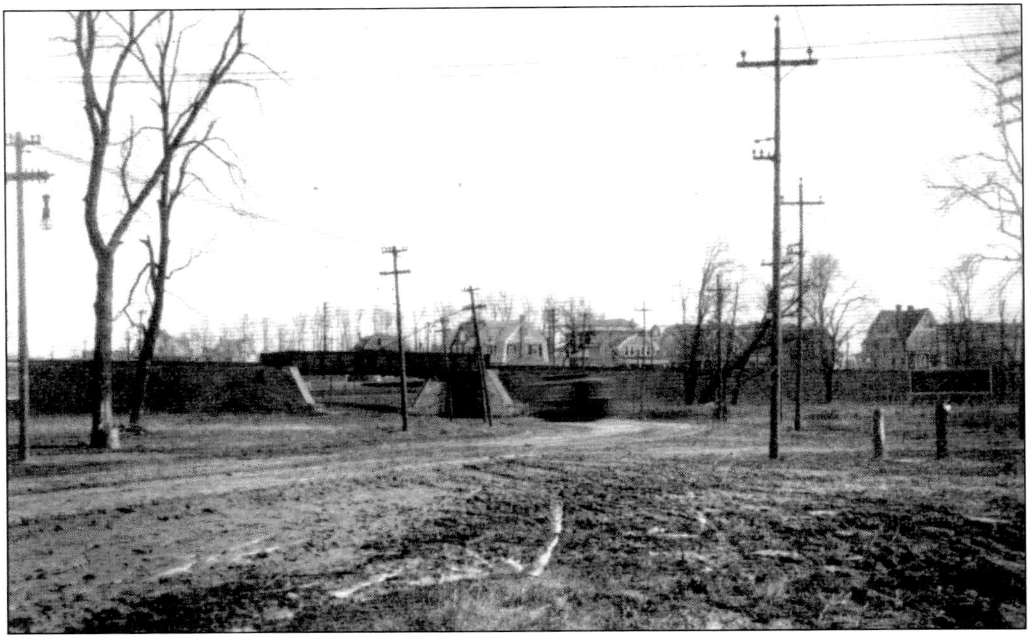

The trolley line was already running through Glenside on its way to the famous Willow Grove Park when Edwin Johnson began his real-estate development business in Glenside in 1925. The Reading Railroad also had a stop in Glenside. The blur in the center of the photograph is a trolley in motion.

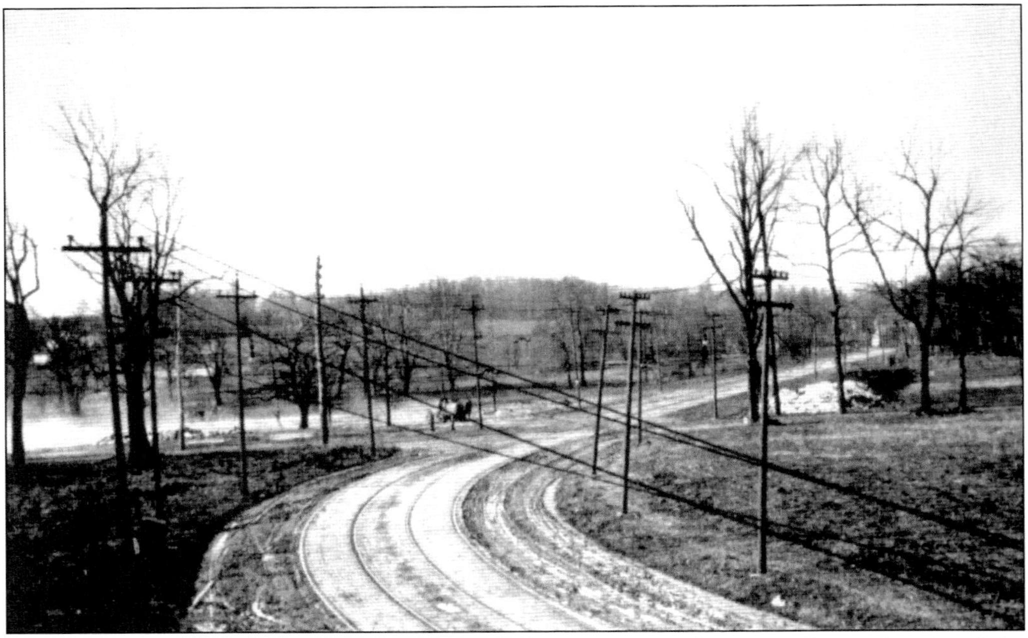

Area real-estate developers already advertised electric, gas, and sewer utilities. People of the middle class sought the good air for their children and idyllic but not rural areas away from industry. Thus, the suburbs were born. Glenside was an established town. This made relocation easier. Industry was soon to follow.

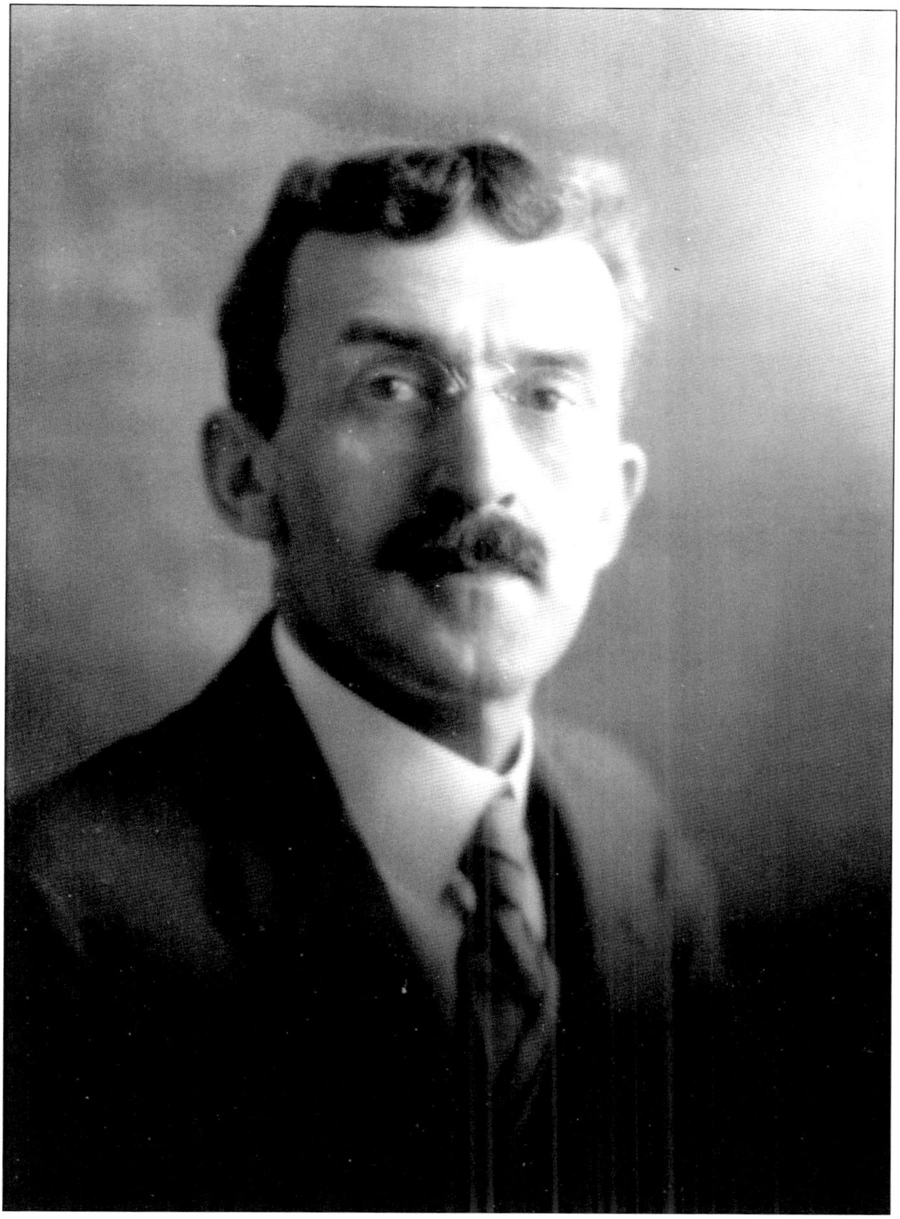

The goal was to sell the land and housing to individuals desiring to leave Philadelphia. In the 1920s, when money was to be had, Edwin Johnson came to Glenside from the Willow Grove and Roslyn areas, literally building his way back toward the city. The *Exhibitor* wrote that this undertaking was an "indication of his faith in the future of the territory." In 1925, Johnson contracted Horace Trumbauer, who had designed a family home a few blocks from the theater, to design an office building and shops on the corner of Keswick Avenue. This office served as Johnson's headquarters during his real-estate development days. Moving companies, businesses relating to the construction trades, and commercial ventures such as photography, food industries, and other businesses began to experience a boom in the Glenside area. Soon to follow were industries like Standard Press Steel, Bell Telephone, and Asplundh Tree Service.

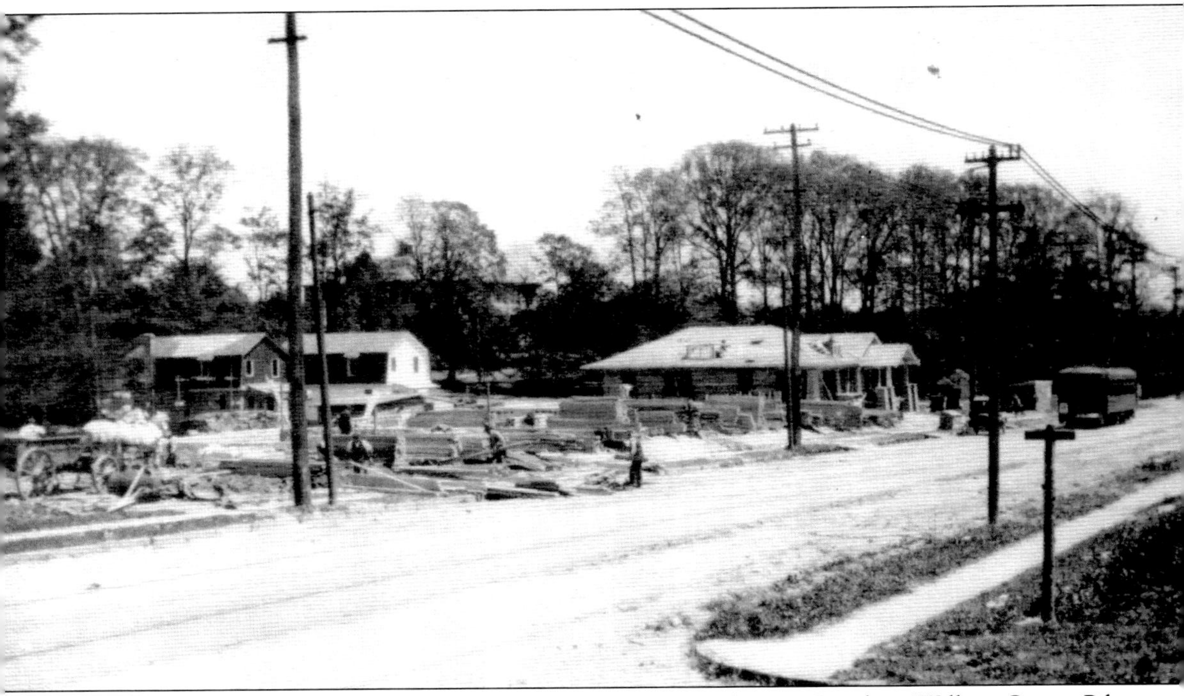

This is a view looking from Sylvania Avenue down Wharton Road to Willow Grove Pike (now Easton Road). Glenside was split between two townships, Abington and Cheltenham. On the Abington Township side, Glenside was originally called Weldon for the construction of the Weldon Hotel, which had been "well done." The hamlet was a tourist attraction, with the hotel as a place to stop for a meal on the way to or from Willow Grove Park. Low-lying streams feeding a pond (since filled in for housing by the Roberts developers) attracted summer dwellers, and cottages were built for "summer in the country." Abington Township had a fine high school, and Weldon had a new elementary school. There were libraries, a number of stores and grocers, and available work for those who did not want to commute to the city. As early as the late 19th century, influential individuals had purchased and set up opulent residences in the outlying areas. These families included the Wanamaker's Department Store family and the soon-to-be aircraft pioneers, the Pitcairns. There was a well-established firehouse. Telephone lines and a turnpike ran along what is now Easton Road.

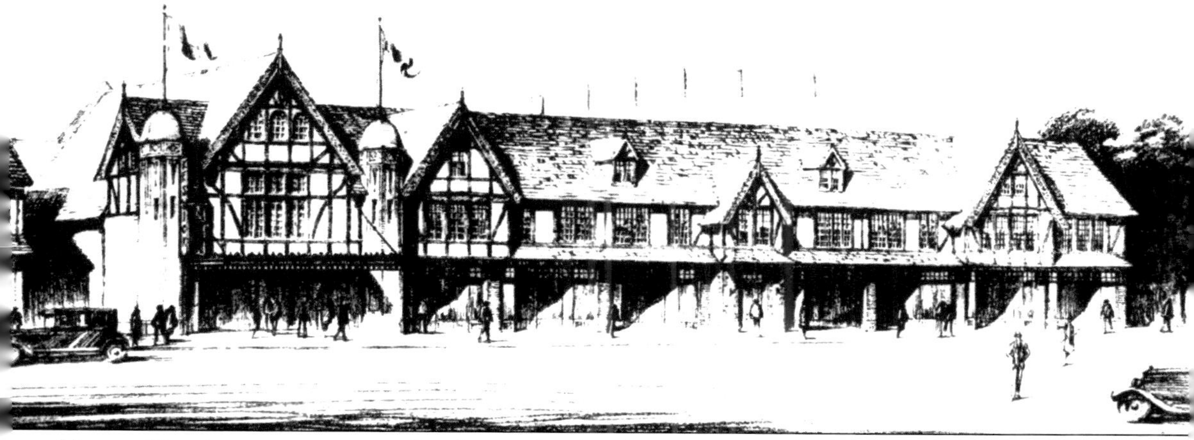

Horace Trumbauer was eventually chosen for the theater project. It is believed that he was assisted by associate architects Clarence Thalheimer and David Weitz. Trumbauer was the master architect, controlling the drawings throughout the process. He was also involved at that time with the Philadelphia Museum of Art—a massive project. Unknown is the influence of Justin Abele, a noted African American architect, who had day-to-day responsibility for much of Trumbauer's design studio. Although the façade of the building is Medieval Elizabethan or Tudor in design, most likely to match the office buildings and stores built adjacent to the venue, the theater itself can best be described as eclectic. It reflects the many influences of Trumbauer's architectural designs over the span of his career.

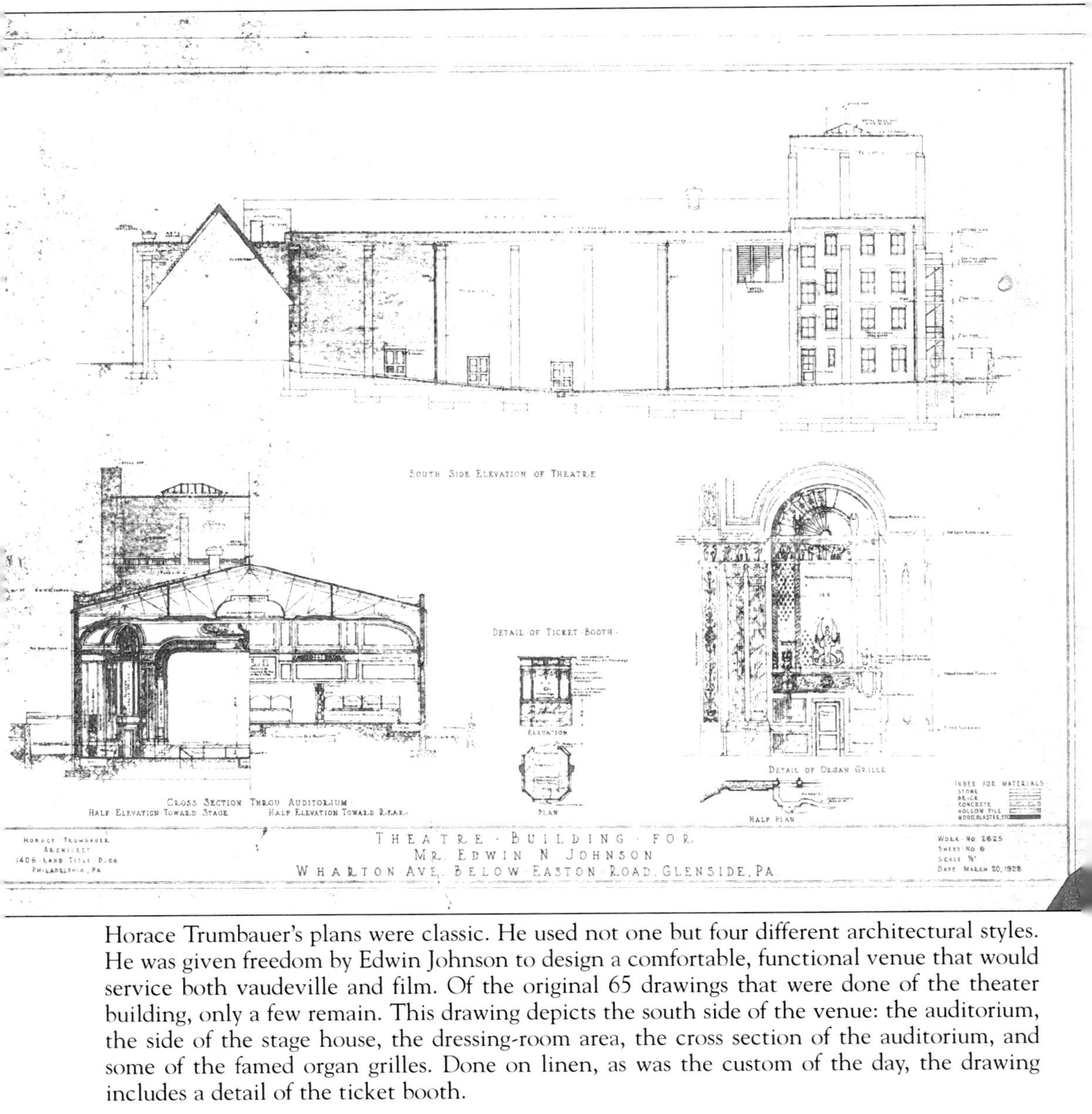

Horace Trumbauer's plans were classic. He used not one but four different architectural styles. He was given freedom by Edwin Johnson to design a comfortable, functional venue that would service both vaudeville and film. Of the original 65 drawings that were done of the theater building, only a few remain. This drawing depicts the south side of the venue: the auditorium, the side of the stage house, the dressing-room area, the cross section of the auditorium, and some of the famed organ grilles. Done on linen, as was the custom of the day, the drawing includes a detail of the ticket booth.

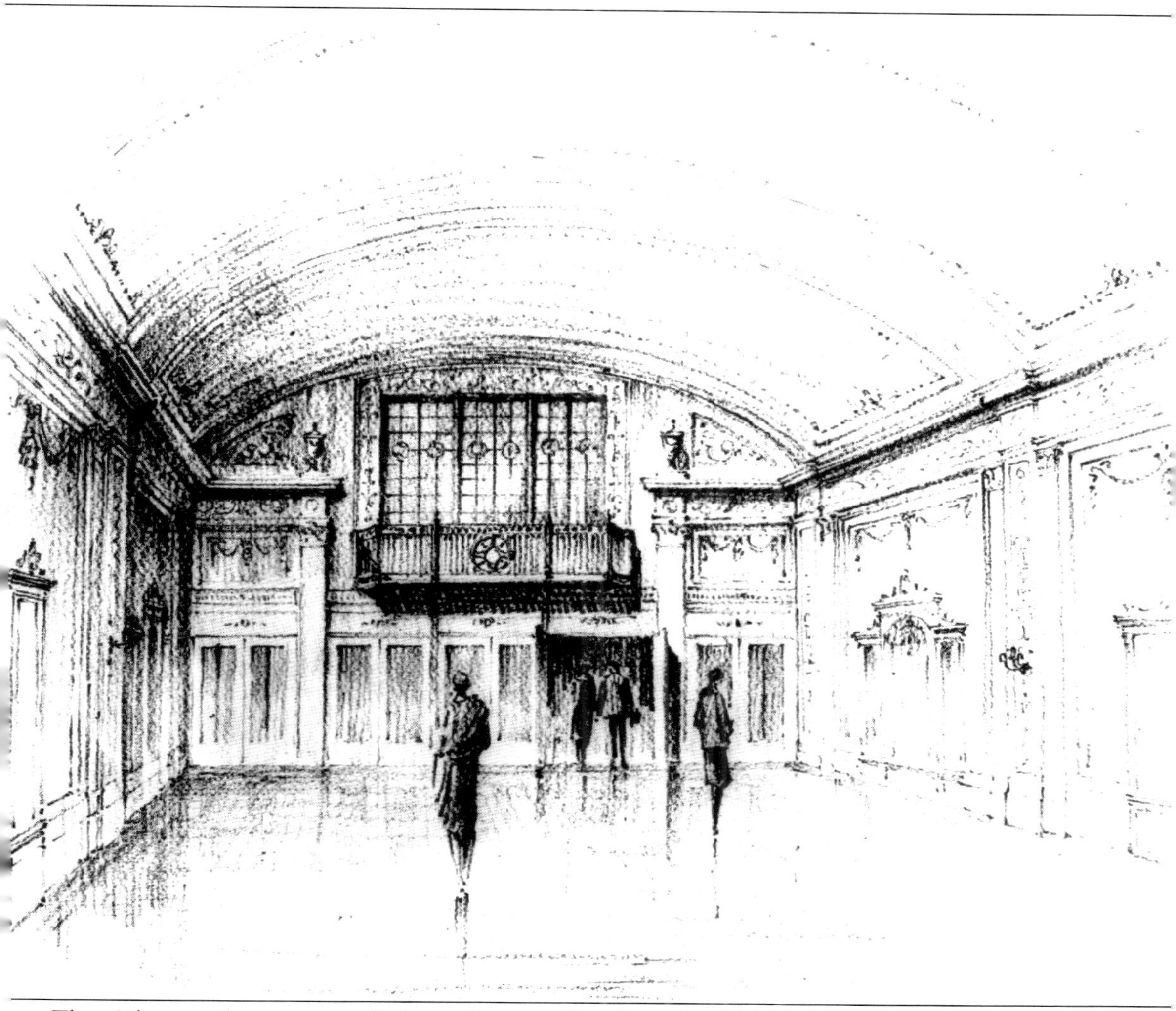

The Adams style was one of the architectural styles adapted by Horace Trumbauer. The entrance lobby of the theater reflects this in the ornate but not effusive use of ornamental plaster, mirrors, and flooring. The flooring shown is Moravian tile, which is believed to have come from the historic Mercer Tile Works of Bucks County. Intact to this day, the flooring is one of the few examples of this tile still in use. The Keswick Theatre is the last remaining Adams-style theater in the Philadelphia region. This drawing was used by the flooring company in advertisements. Turner Construction drew up estimates on April 28, 1928. Ground was broken in May 1928, just two months later. Edwin Johnson, Horace Trumbauer, and Turner Construction's commitment to quality had just begun.

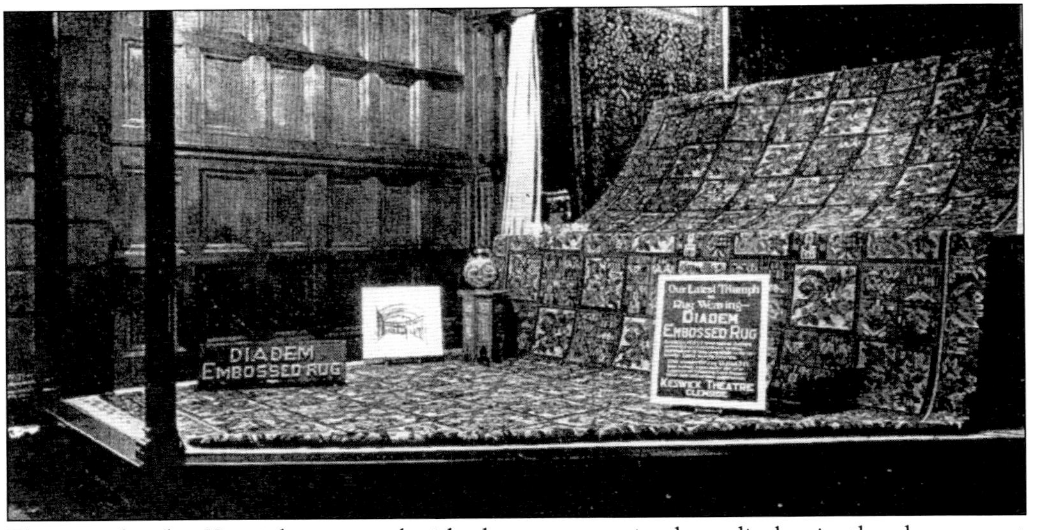

The rugs for the Keswick were so lavish that one remained on display in the showcase at Hardwick and Magee's showrooms for weeks before its installation. The diadem-embossed rug was manufactured specifically for the Keswick Theatre. The *Exhibitor* featured it in its magazine on December 15, 1928.

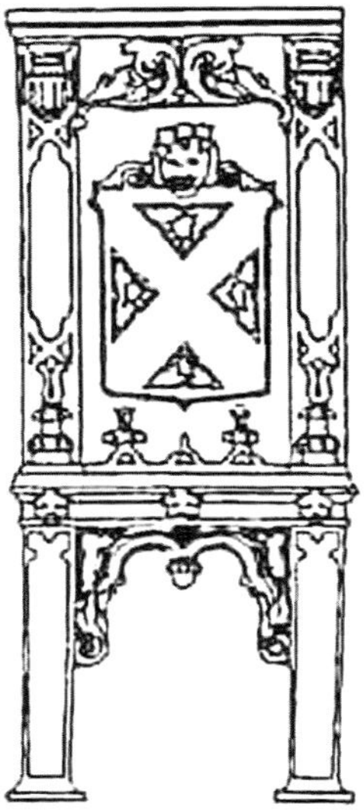

782

American Seating Company manufactured the first seats, which were covered in tapestry woven by the LaFrance Textile Industries of the Frankford section of Philadelphia. Even so, the Keswick was not considered to be as ornate as some of the other Philadelphia-area "vaude-film" palaces.

Voigt & Company provided the ornamental plaster for the theater. Although it was a Philadelphia Company, the owner, Max Voigt, lived in Glenside. A 1928 catalog (located at the Historical Society of Pennsylvania) announces the use of plastics in the company's mold-making work. The organ screen further exemplifies the Adams-style use of ornamentation based on classical Roman prototypes. For many years, curtains covered this example of plasterwork, which has survived fire, flood, and modernization.

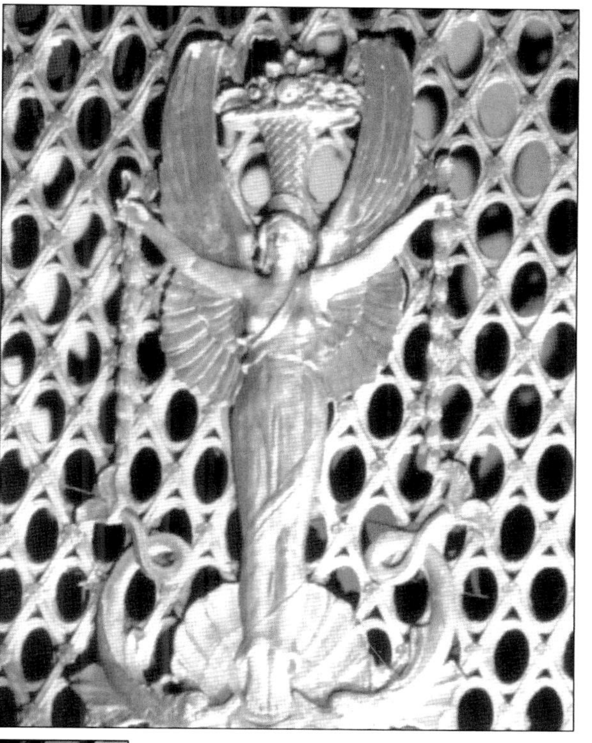

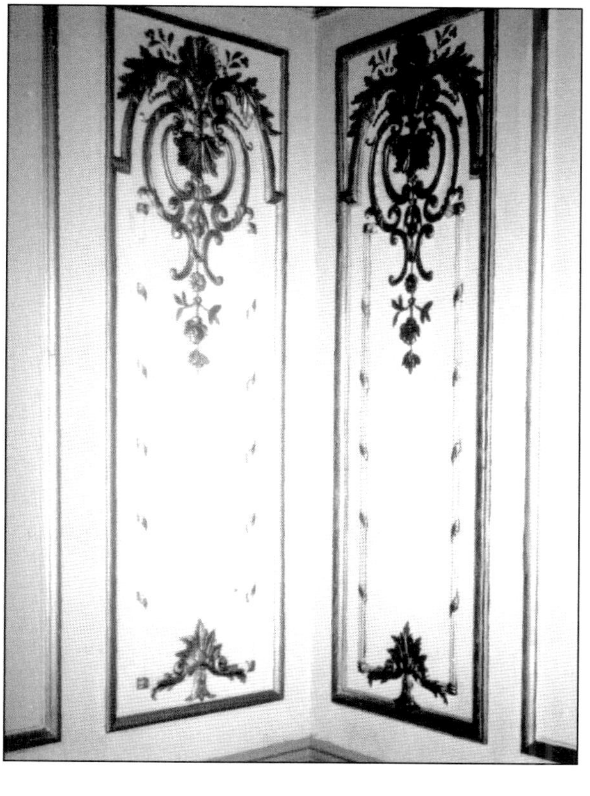

The less staid and more florid style of Louis XV was integrated into the design of the building. The ornamentation is more luxuriant and curvaceous, which may be why it was chosen as the style for the ladies' lounge. Horace Trumbauer had used this style in many of his private home applications (most notably Grey Towers, now Arcadia University). As the theater was a popular public assembly place, it might have been a strategy of Trumbauer's firm to incorporate as many of these styles as possible as on-site advertising of his talents.

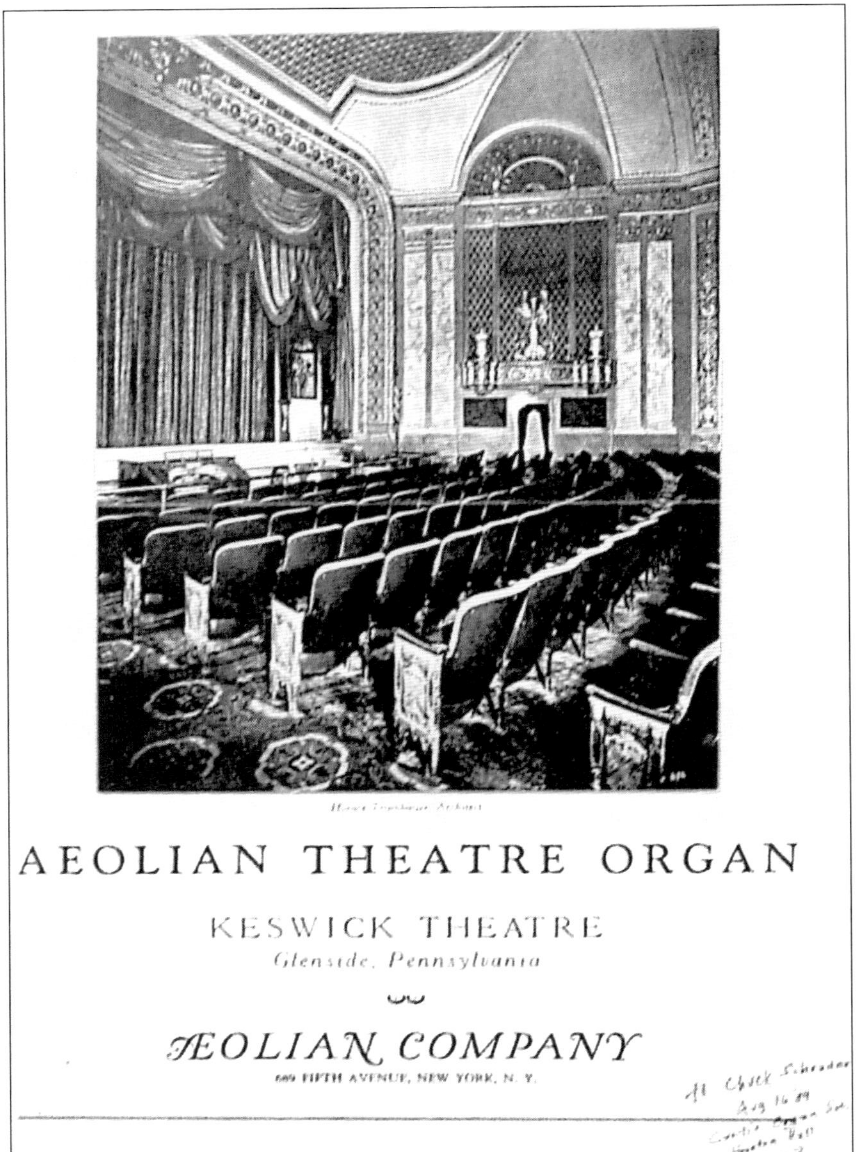

The Aeolian organ, visible in the pit area in this picture, was designed specifically for the Keswick Theatre and advertised as one of the first such instruments east of the Mississippi. Many of the movie palaces of the time had organs to compliment the silent films and vaudeville and as preshow entertainment. The *American Architect* featured the organ and its two chambers in the July 5, 1929, edition. The organ had a lift built in the pit so that it could be lifted up to stage level when necessary. The large ornate screens on either side of the auditorium hid the pipe work. The organ was considered a huge draw for the venue, even though talkies had arrived. Its presence further emphasized Edwin Johnson's desire to make the Keswick Theatre, and thus Glenside, the cultural hub of eastern Montgomery County. The $35,000 organ, removed sometime during the 1940s, as tastes in entertainment changed, shook the auditorium when it was played.

The walls of the foyer steps were originally graced with three wall panels designed for the Keswick Theatre and painted by Belgian-born Franz deMerlier (1878–1974), right, who had settled in the Philadelphia area by this time. The artist's work added elegance and sophistication to the venue. This photograph was taken by Richard C. Carter.

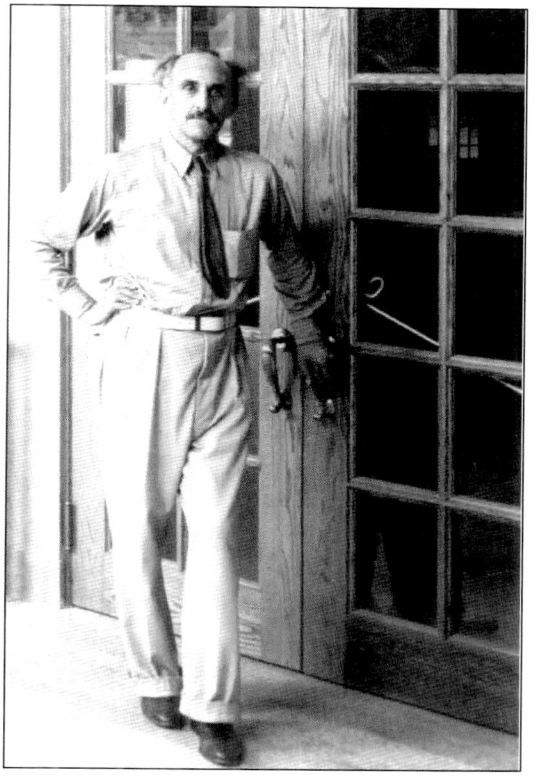

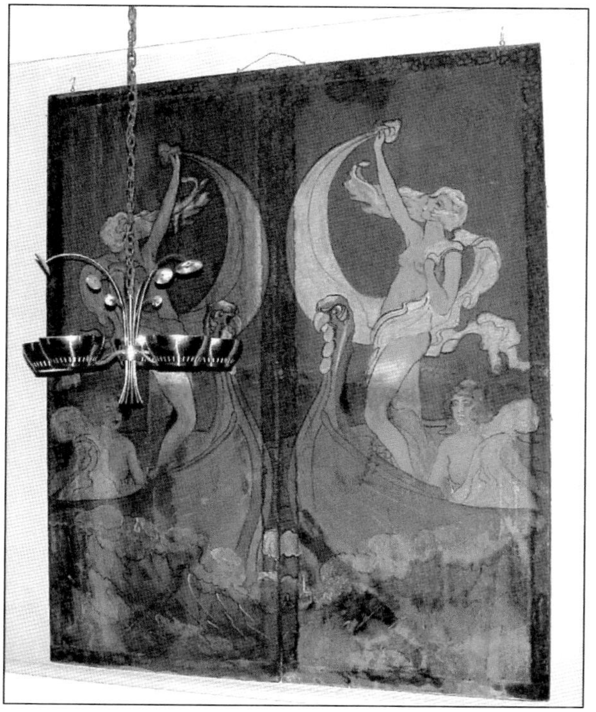

It is unknown whether deMerlier's works were originally paintings that were hung or murals painted directly on the wall, but it is suspected that they were removable panels. No trace of the panels has been uncovered, and today, the area is graced with an antique screen, origin also unknown, that is shown in photographs taken of the theater throughout most of the 1980s.

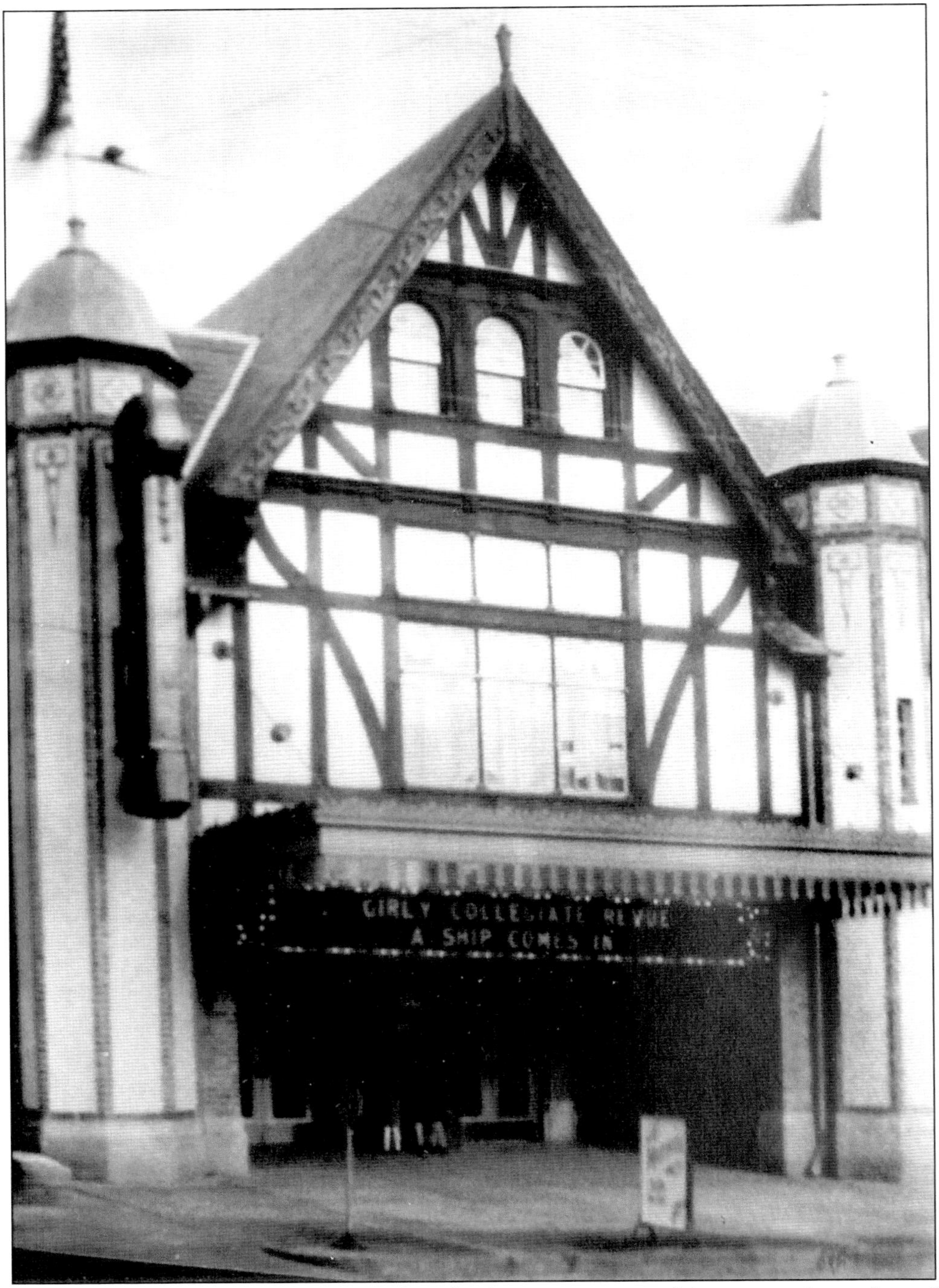

Turner Construction had been hired to handle the construction of the venue, shown here the week following its opening. Edwin Johnson premiered the Keswick Theatre on December 27, 1928, to 1700 people. In less than nine months, the venue was open to the public, although it is said that the tradespeople were still finishing up their work on the day the building opened. This photograph of the exterior of the venue shows people at the ticket booth

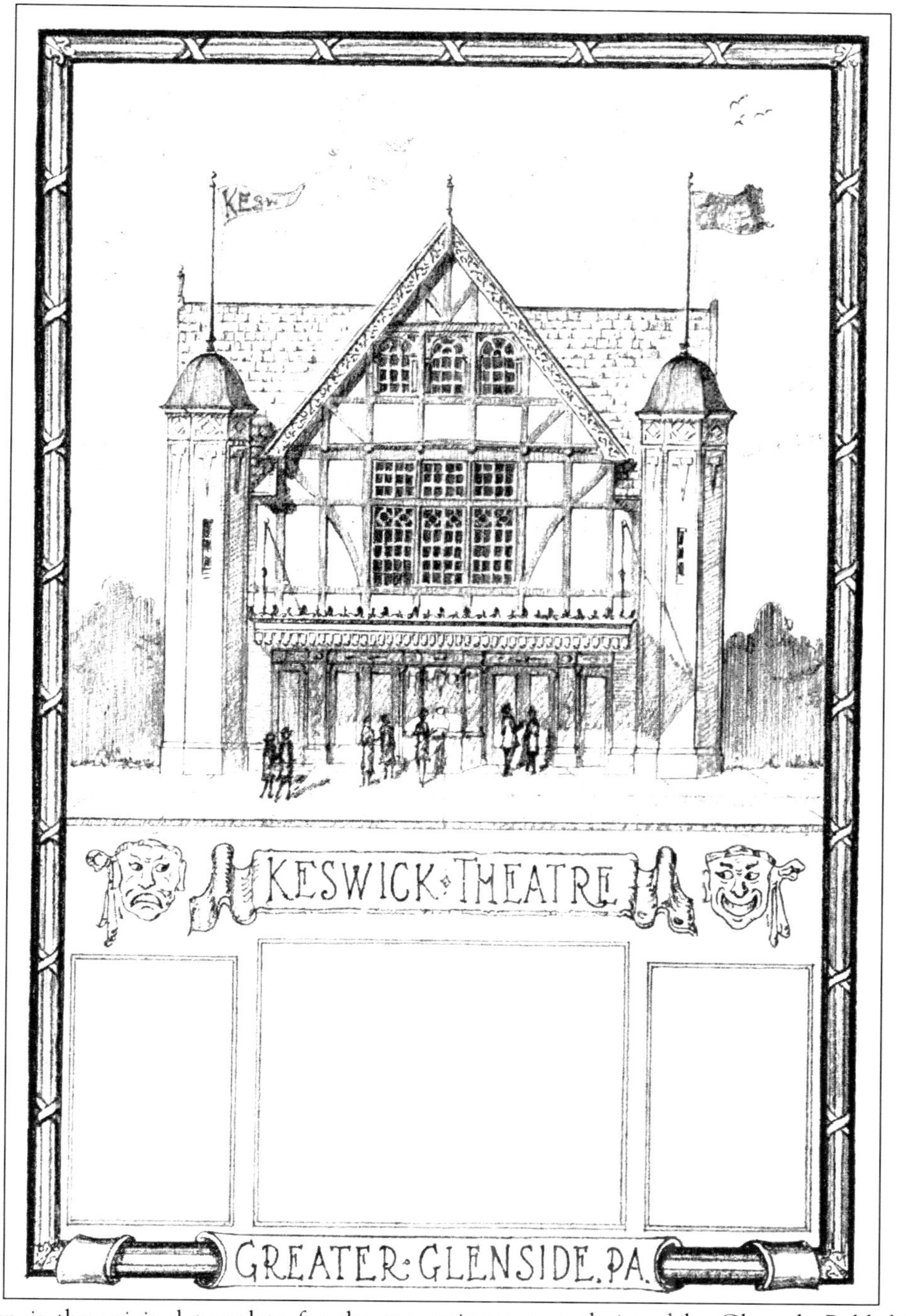

Shown is the original template for the souvenir program designed by Glenside Publishing. Several copies are known to still exist. By the 1930s, a very small program without advertising had replaced it. The program produced revenue opportunities for the venue as well as business for Glenside Publishing. Approximately 30 pages in length, bound, and on semigloss paper stock, the program advertised upcoming events, the neighboring businesses, and the companies that contributed to the Keswick Theatre's construction.

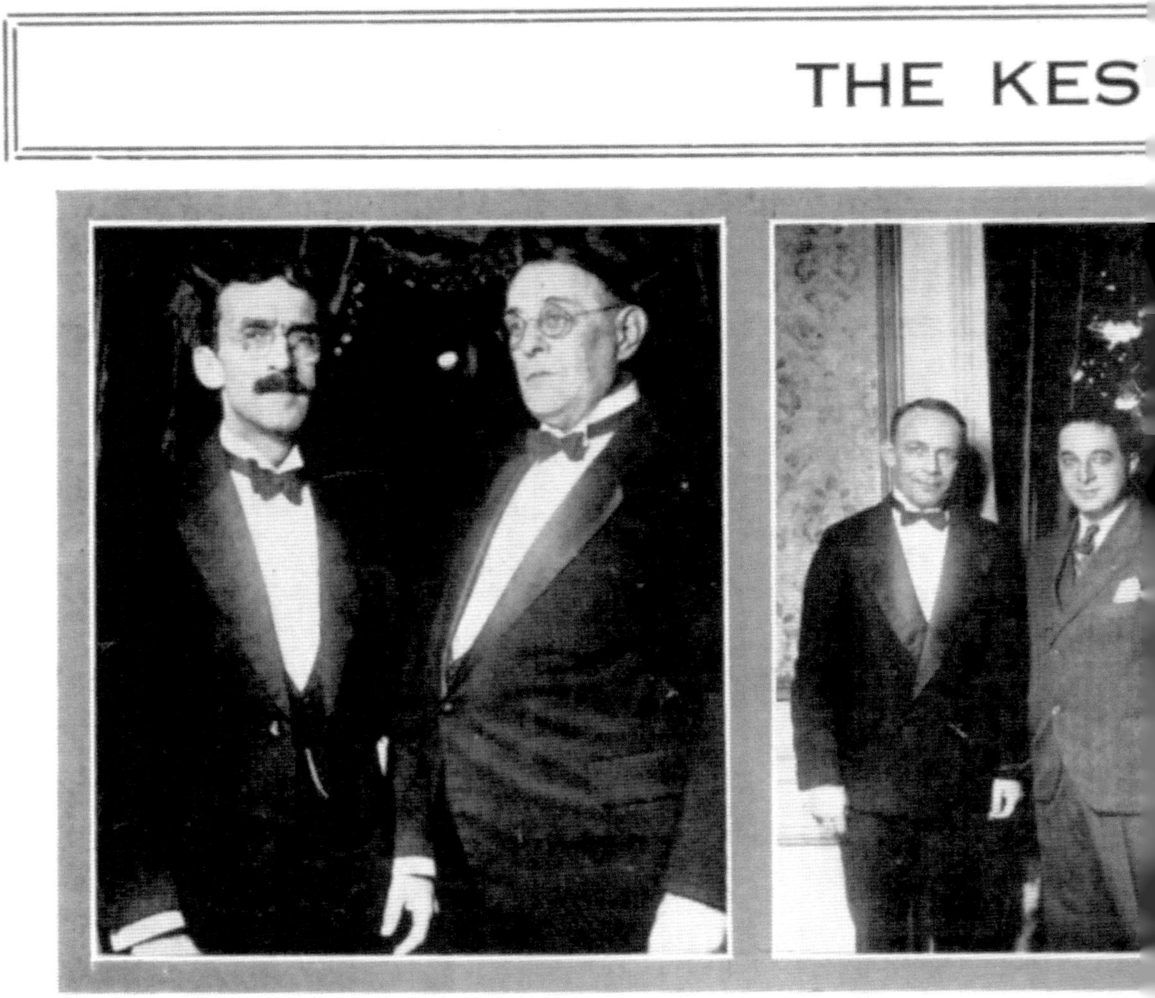

A few of the celebrities present at the opening of Edwin N. Johnson's r
of the house. Center: Jay Raymond, the well-known vaudeville bookin
of First National Exchange, and Harry Lavine, of United Artists. Right:
Rosenbe

Opening night included notables in the industry such as Harry Lavine of United Artists, Bill Mansell of the First National Exchange, and Jay Raymond, a vaudeville booking agent. Edwin Johnson, on the far left with the moustache, stands next to Harry Katzes, who was hired for his connections with Keith's and William Morris, the largest-growing force in talent booking at the time. The booking agencies usually ran circuits, and it was critical that the Keswick, as an independent house, had the correct connections to have acts to present. The film industry was growing a network of distributors, with the Film Exchange already mentioned in trade journals. It is unknown whether "First National Exchange" here refers to a movie distribution

CK OPENS

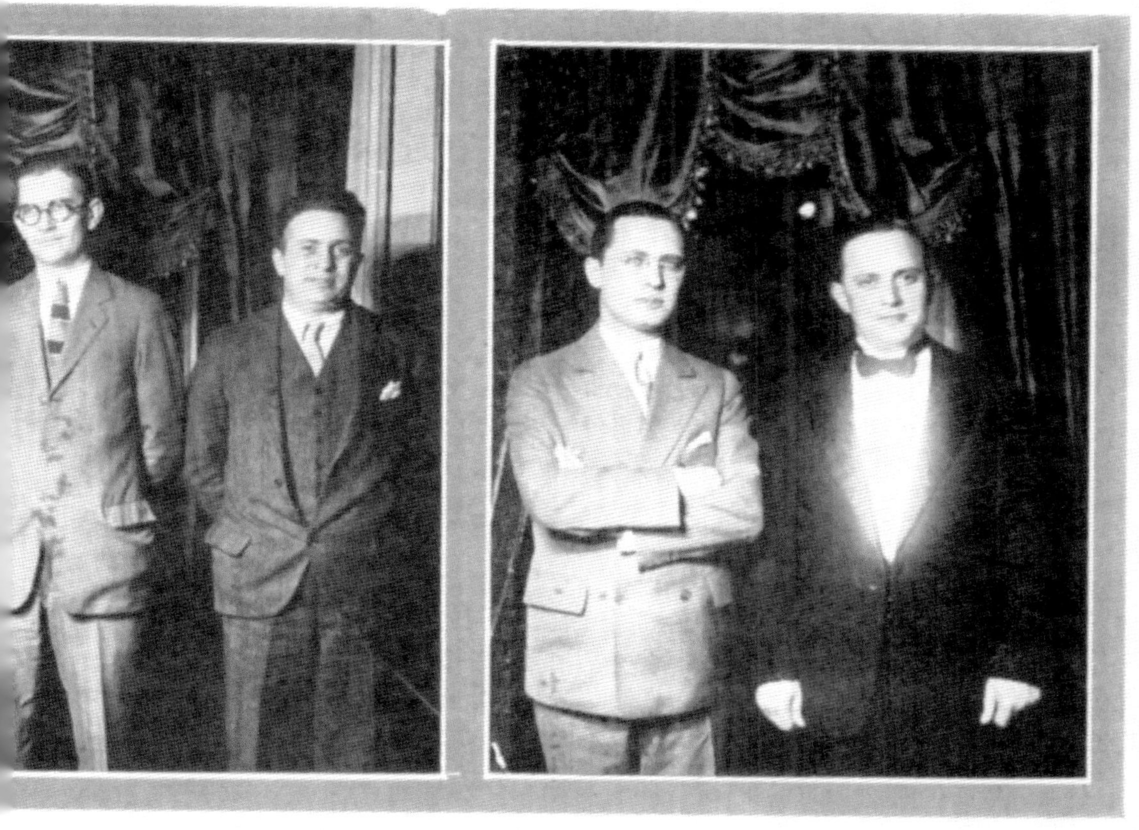

ick Theatre, Glenside. Left: Edwin N. Johnson and Harry Katzes. manager Ben Blumberg, of National Theatre Supply; Bill Mansell, assistant manager Thalheimer, of Thalheimer & Weitz, architects of the Keswick, and Al sh Studios.

organization or a financial organization. Attracting the newly formed United Artists representative to the opening (United Artists had just recently grown from the Pickford-Fairbanks studio) was also a critical step in securing films. However, advertisements tend to show that there was no one-studio alliance. Oral history has related that Johnson did run into problems with the film distributors at one time. The reference here to Clarence Thalheimer led to further investigation wherein it was discovered that Horace Trumbauer had sought help on the building during this time.

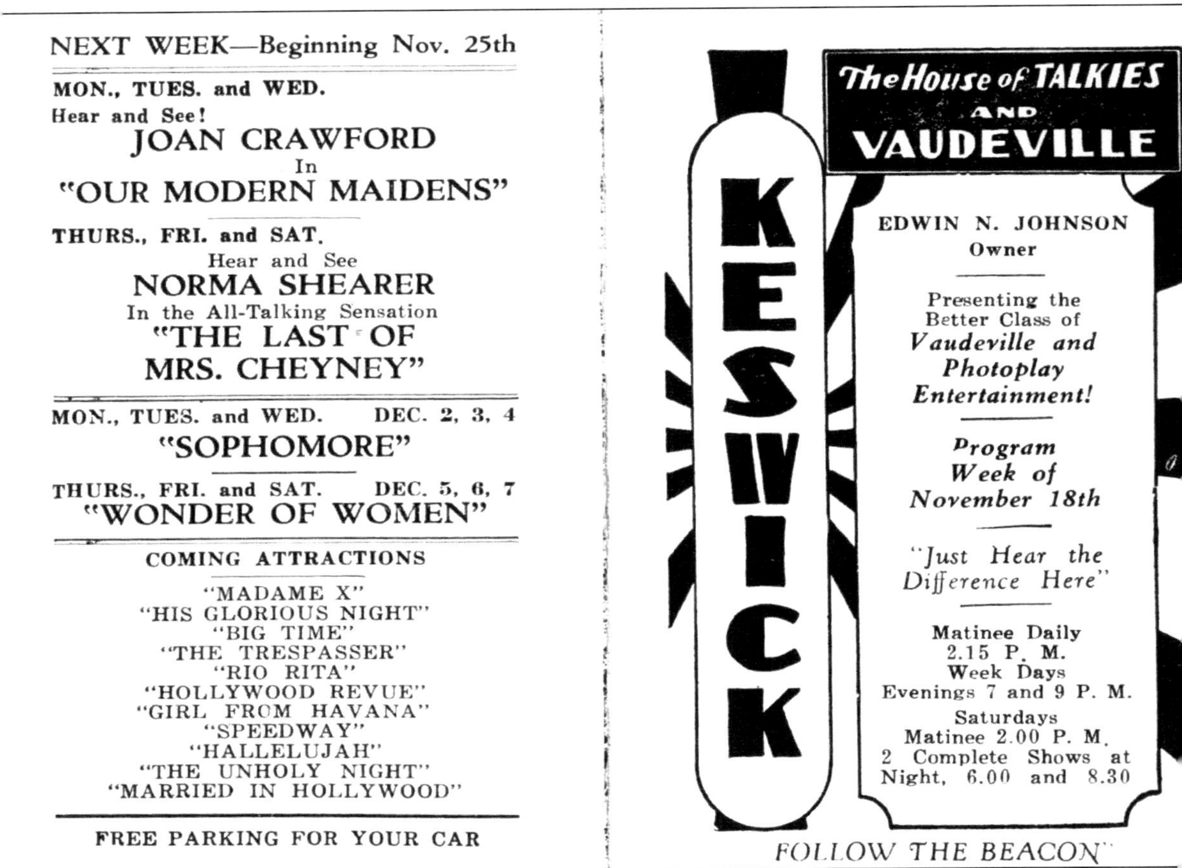

NEXT WEEK—Beginning Nov. 25th

MON., TUES. and WED.
Hear and See!
JOAN CRAWFORD
In
"OUR MODERN MAIDENS"

THURS., FRI. and SAT.
Hear and See
NORMA SHEARER
In the All-Talking Sensation
"THE LAST OF MRS. CHEYNEY"

MON., TUES. and WED. DEC. 2, 3, 4
"SOPHOMORE"

THURS., FRI. and SAT. DEC. 5, 6, 7
"WONDER OF WOMEN"

COMING ATTRACTIONS

"MADAME X"
"HIS GLORIOUS NIGHT"
"BIG TIME"
"THE TRESPASSER"
"RIO RITA"
"HOLLYWOOD REVUE"
"GIRL FROM HAVANA"
"SPEEDWAY"
"HALLELUJAH"
"THE UNHOLY NIGHT"
"MARRIED IN HOLLYWOOD"

FREE PARKING FOR YOUR CAR

The House of TALKIES AND VAUDEVILLE

KESWICK

EDWIN N. JOHNSON
Owner

Presenting the Better Class of *Vaudeville and Photoplay Entertainment!*

Program Week of November 18th

"Just Hear the Difference Here"

Matinee Daily
2.15 P. M.
Week Days
Evenings 7 and 9 P. M.
Saturdays
Matinee 2.00 P. M.
2 Complete Shows at Night, 6.00 and 8.30

FOLLOW THE BEACON"

By the early 1930s, most likely as economic times grew increasingly worse, the large program books were gone. Note in this advertisement that "Free Parking for Your Car," "Follow the Beacon," and "the Better Class of Vaudeville and Photoplay Entertainment" are all buzzwords to attract a certain clientele. Newspaper advertisements in the local paper indicate that acts such as Paul Specht, a Roaring Twenties big band leader turned artist manager, played the venue in 1929. Specht's band may have included artists such as Artie Shaw, Charlie Spivak, Roy Smeck, and others who went on to talented careers on their own or in other bands. Similar advertisements highlight Fannie Brice and "Broadway's Famous Funster" Lester Allen.

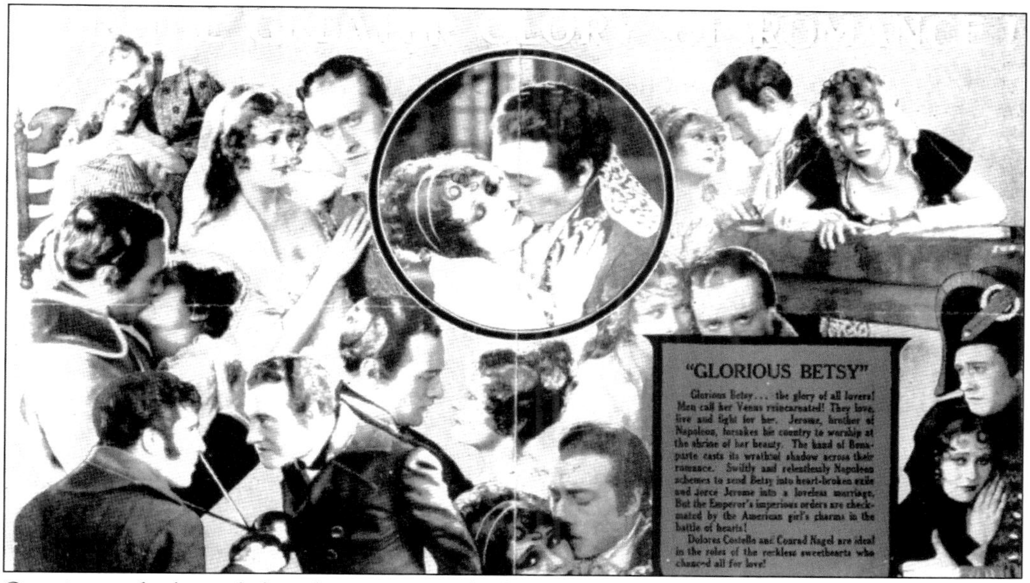

Opening night hosted the silent version of *Glorious Betsy*, which ran for the following week. The building was wired for talkies, but the sound system was not quite in place. The Warner Brothers picture being shown further emphasized the independence of the venue when an executive from United Artists was present in the building. Most theaters of the time ran one vaudeville circuit. Many movie theaters were actually owned by one production studio (Loews, Warner, and Fox).

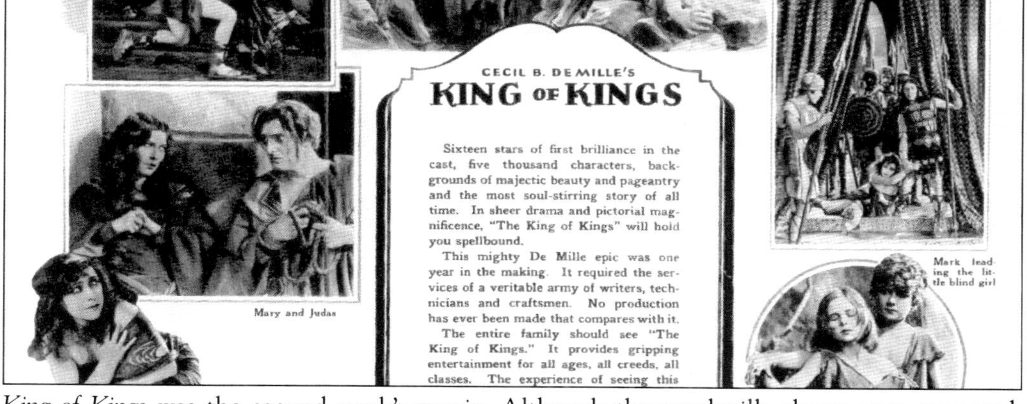

King of Kings was the second week's movie. Although the vaudeville shows were expected, movies were the new, exciting, and innovative item. From late 1931 into early 1932, the venue was not placing ads in the local newspaper for upcoming events, although neighboring movie houses such as the Embassy and the Grove were running ads consistently. They begin running again in late 1932.

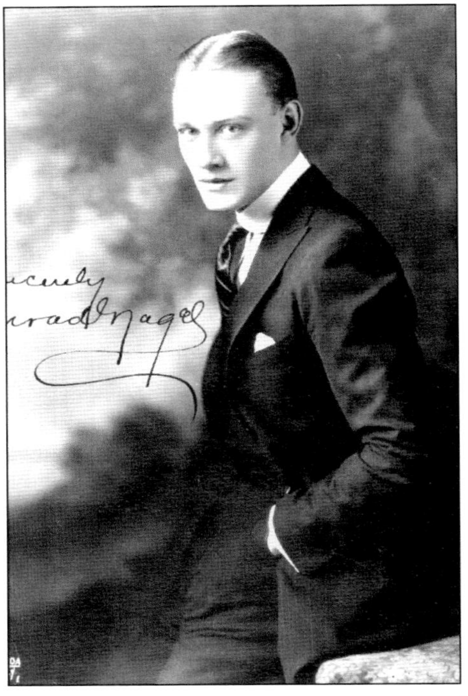

Conrad Nagel and Delores Costello are shown in two autographed photographs from the Harper Collection. Movie stars were becoming big promotional items, and the local newspaper, the *Times Chronicle*, as well as the Philadelphia newspapers, began to have pages reserved for the movies, stars, and stories. The advent of these movie houses in the suburban area increased circulation of the paper, as these items appealed to a broader group of readers. Such promotional tools became fond memorabilia for the subscribers. Patrons had an emotional response to the movies and shows they saw at the Keswick, which often marked a special event, date, or time in their lives. Readers would collect the articles, photographs, and reviews. As a consequence, this memorabilia has been collectible from a variety of patrons and their families to supplement what is known about the Keswick and the effect of the movie industry on the community. This effect was especially strong on children and young adults, who later helped save the venue, or whose children now attend events at the theater.

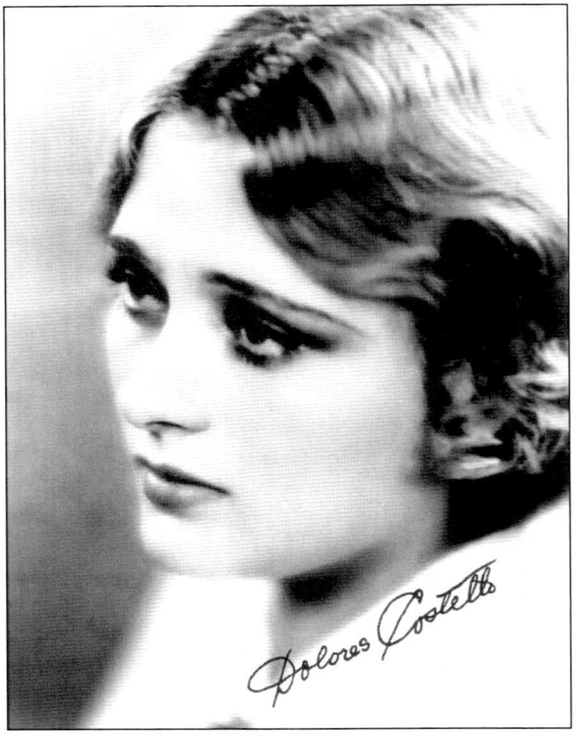

In order to acquaint you with the most beautiful and comfortable theatre in the Northern District of Philadelphia, and to have you enjoy an evening of high class Vitaphone and Vaudeville entertainment, we are pleased to enclose a free pass that will admit two persons. We trust that you will accept our invitation.

The Keswick Theatre, in Greater Glenside, is but a short distance from your home, and you will find a commodious and well lighted parking space for your car, free of charge.

Will you be our guest some afternoon or evening, during February or March?

E. N. Johnson

P. S. *Our Daily Matinee begins at 2:15 P. M. The Evening performance begins at 7 P. M. with the Vaudeville starting at 9 P. M.*

Shown is a personal invitation from Edwin Johnson, with a complimentary offer. He also dropped thousands of flyers from an airplane over the areas from Oak Lane to Hatboro to announce the opening of the venue. This is reflective of an era when "all that was new" was used to advertise. The eastern Montgomery County region also now had an airfield in Willow Grove, belonging to the established Pitcairn family of Huntingdon Valley. In one more unique way, word was out that the venue was open for business.

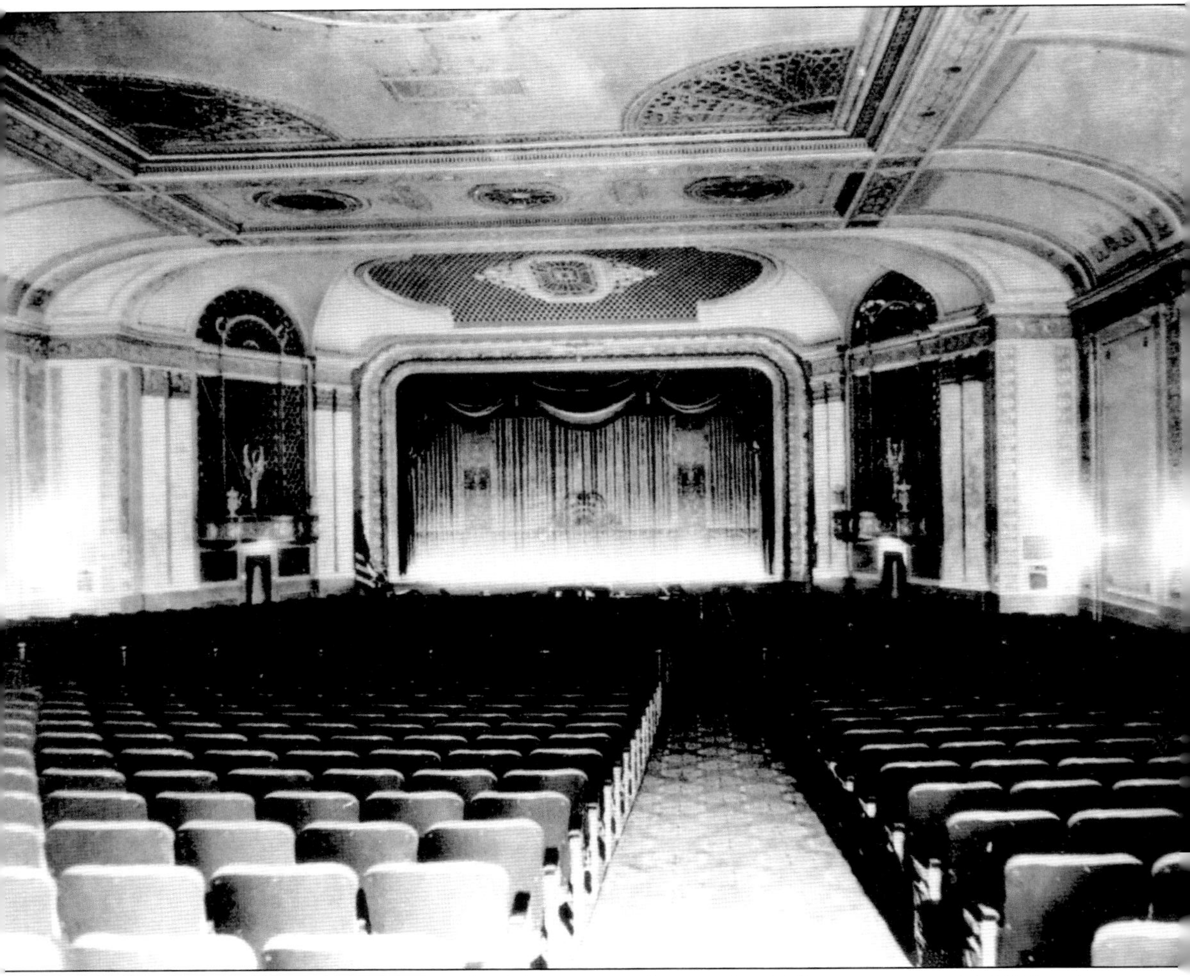

The auditorium, as shown in early 1929, was opulent indeed. The venue was highlighted in a January 10, 1929, advertisement in the *Times Chronicle* as having air that was "healthful being replenished every 90 seconds." The fresh air came in via tunnels underneath the aisles and up through what became known as "magic mushrooms" into the auditorium. For air conditioning, the tunnels were packed with ice. The building had been built on top of a creek bed; water ran through the tunnels, which aided the cooling process. The melted ice water returned to the streams. Fans above the organ grilles kept the air circulating. Although it appears here as if much of the ornamentation was plaster, a unique mixture aided the acoustics of the room. The grille above the stage was embellished with glass, as were other areas of the ceiling. The side panels of the room were fabric. The auditorium was sloped from the middle of the first section, which allowed the back half of the house to sit higher than the front. The long, narrow, raised configuration afforded a good sightline from every seat.

A MIRROR REFLECTING THE PASSING SHOW

GREATER GLENSIDE GAZETTE

A JOURNAL OF USEFUL INFORMATION

OUR FIELD PHILADELPHIA'S SUBURBS, THE CITY, THE WORLD

I, No. 2 DECEMBER, 1928 $1 Per Ye

OMETHING TO THINK ABOUT

By F. W. N.

ristmas. A wonderful season. derful for the American mer- s, who are able to pay all and record a substantial pro- December 31, owing to this cn of giving". Considerably than a half billion dollars of tmas club money was with- n from the banks during the weeks of December, and used orgy of Christmas shopping. n explains our Christmas erity.

—

Christmas has a deeper, and beautiful, meaning than mere iving. Read the story by er Glenside Gazette's Holly- correspondent, telling how of the movie stars use Christ- o create happiness for others. and Doug in the children's als, with Doug clowning and ng around on his hands amid pplause of the little ones. is religion put into practice.

istmas is the season of good- of unselfishness, of a desire hearts of all true men and n to help those who are less ate than themselves.

es Dickens made his "Christ- Carol" immortal because he t a vision of the real spirit hristmas and clothed it in English. Will your Christ- amount to anything more a big dinner and a little gift- ?

—

KESWICK OPENING TO BE MEMORABLE EVENT

Kiwanis Benefit Will Be Followed by Dolores Costello Film

Beautiful Dolores Costello, newly-crowned Queen of the Screen, assisted by Conrad Nagel, will open the Keswick Theatre Greater Glenside, Friday evening, December 28, with her most popular film, "Glorious Betsy."

Holiday week, 1928, will be a notable one in th[illegible] of Lower Montgomery County. On Christmas night, Decembe[illegible] Glenside Kiwanis Club will present their Kiwanis Follies, rin[illegible] urtain for the first time in Edwin N. Johnson's half-millio[illegible] e. It will be a big social occasion with prominent men and wo[illegible] every community in Lower Montgomery County, and hundreds [illegible] s from distant points, including many parts of Philadelphia, in [illegible] audience. The Kiwanis Follies will be repeated on Wednesday nigh[illegible] December 26, —a grand two-night benefit, under the auspices of Glenside's progressive Kiwanians, to help the under-privileged children, the entire receipts being devoted to this worthy cause.

Numerous organizations will participate in this community program, one of the most remarkable of its kind ever planned for the opening of an American theatre. Brief dedicatory exercises, with remarks by prominent citizens and prayers by the clergy will precede the Kiwanis program.

On Thursday night, December 27, the first Keswick Theatre program of vaudeville and motion pictures will be presented, with Dolores Costello in "Glorious Betsy" and high-lass vaudeville features. Admission on Thursday night will be free and by invitation only, the entire 1700 seats being reserved for those who contributed to the success of the Kiwanis benefit, for theatre and motion picture house owners, film exchange executives and members of prominent organizations of Philadelphia and Montgomery County.

On Friday night and Saturday night, December 28 and 29, the Keswick will be open to the general public. Matinees will be held for the first time on these dates with "Glorious Betsy" and the vaudeville acts both afternoon and evening. Admission for adults at the evening performances and Saturday matinee will be 50 cents, with 30 cents for children. At all week-day matinees the admission for adults will be 30 cents, and 20 cents for children.

Then, for an entire week beginning Monday, December 31, Cecil B. DeMille's "King of Kings," the screen master-piece of the century,—an epochal film lauded by the clergy, educators and newspapers throughout the world as the greatest of films, and known in the industry as "the seventh wonder of motion pictures," will be shown,—an offering peculiarly appropriate to the season of "peace on earth, good-will toward men."

No vaudeville acts will be presented during "King of Kings" week

Meet "Miss KESWICK"

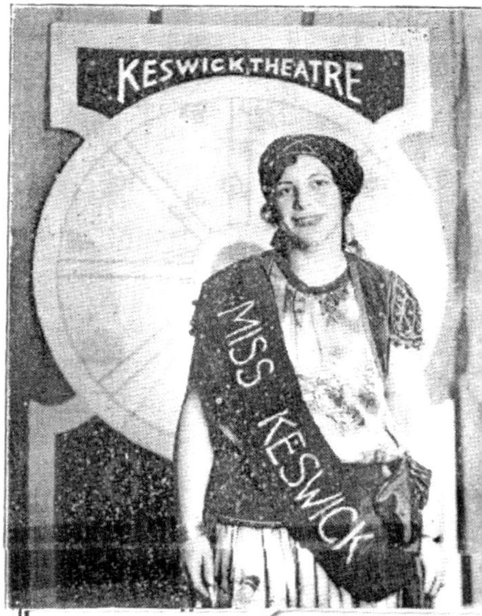

Another promotional venture was under way. Edwin Johnson paired up with longtime friend F.W. Norcross, previously of the *Public Ledger* and the *North American*. Together, they launched the *Glenside Gazette* as a promotional arm for the theater. The *Glenside Gazette* was distributed at the theater, as evidenced by the program listing. However, little else is known about its history in the area. The paper promoted the venue and eastern Montgomery County, with "Glenside at its hub." It became a marketing tool not only for Johnson but also for other real-estate developers in the area, such as Weir and Roberts.

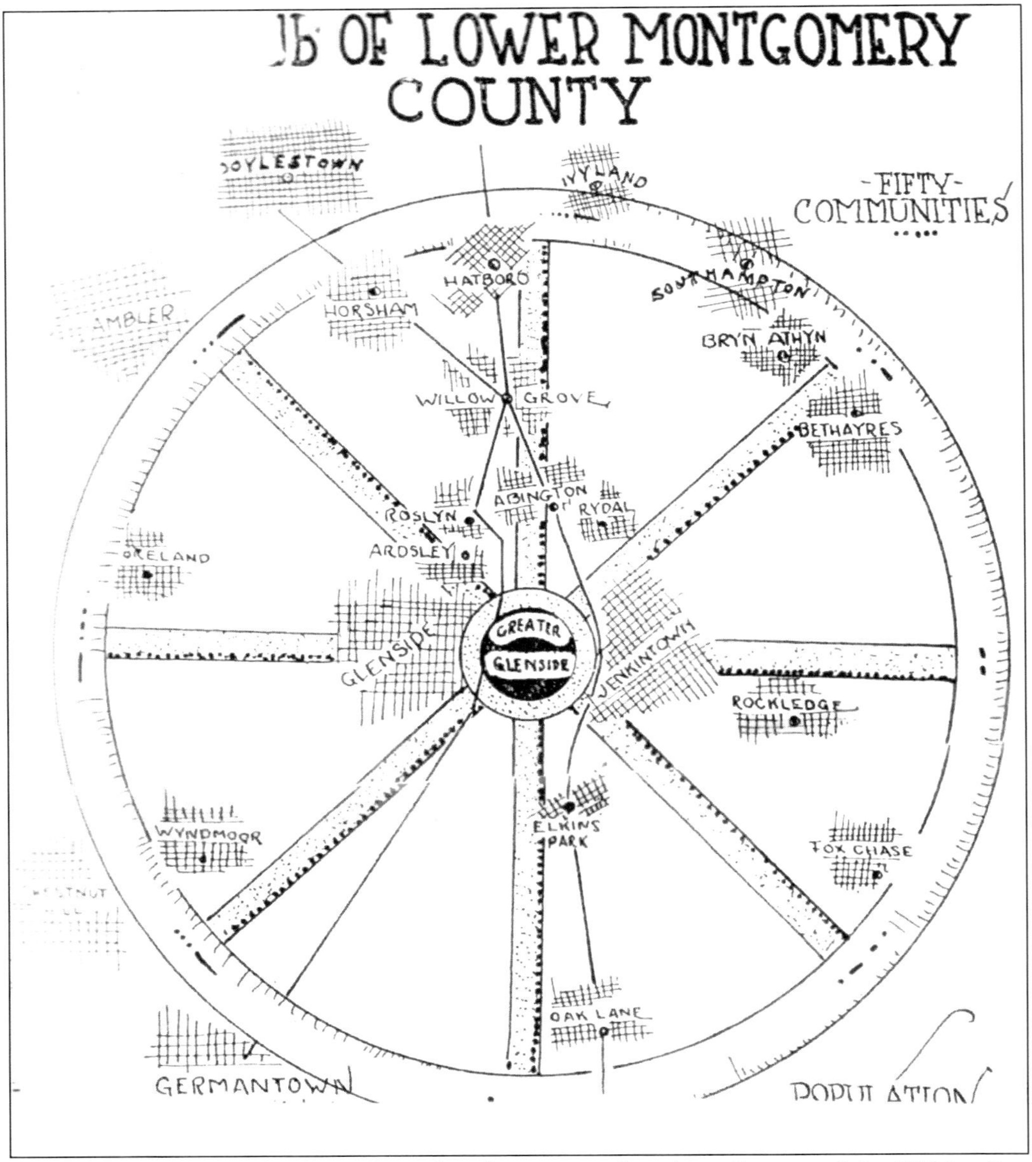

One copy of this publication has been found. Discovered in the collection of the Weldon Fire Company, it is the only one known to be in existence. It appears to have been produced locally. The hub, as displayed, highlights the two main transportation routes: Old York Road on the right, and Willow Grove Turnpike (later, Easton Road) on the left. These were the marketing areas that Edwin Johnson had chosen; they corresponded with his real-estate development business. Many of these communities had been in existence as early as the Revolutionary War in one form or another. With the suburban area reaching northwest from the city—Oak Lane, Germantown, and Fox Chase were all Philadelphia neighborhoods—this drawing emphasizes the convenience to the city and the amenities of the outlying areas.

The Keswick Theatre was built for commercial use, as were all of its sister theaters. A number of articles mention sponsorship. In addition to the advertisements in the program, as shown, Johnson had poster and ad frames installed. The advertising trend is repeated in the souvenir program, with ads for local companies, tradespeople, the *Glenside Gazette*, and building rentals. The latter reflects Johnson's real-estate background.

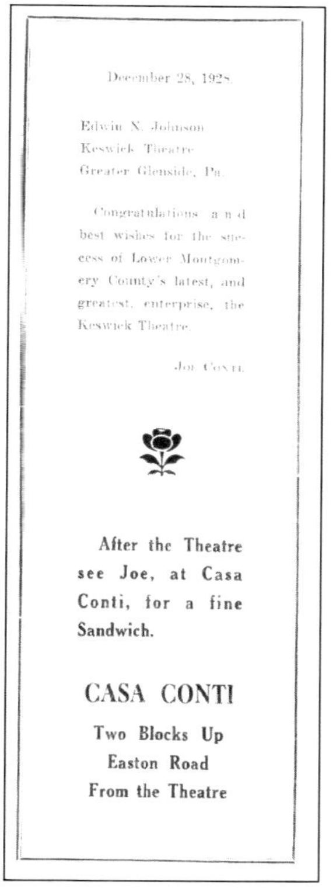

December 28, 1928.

Edwin N. Johnson
Keswick Theatre
Greater Glenside, Pa.

Congratulations and best wishes for the success of Lower Montgomery County's latest, and greatest, enterprise, the Keswick Theatre.

JOE CONTI.

After the Theatre see Joe, at Casa Conti, for a fine Sandwich.

CASA CONTI

Two Blocks Up
Easton Road
From the Theatre

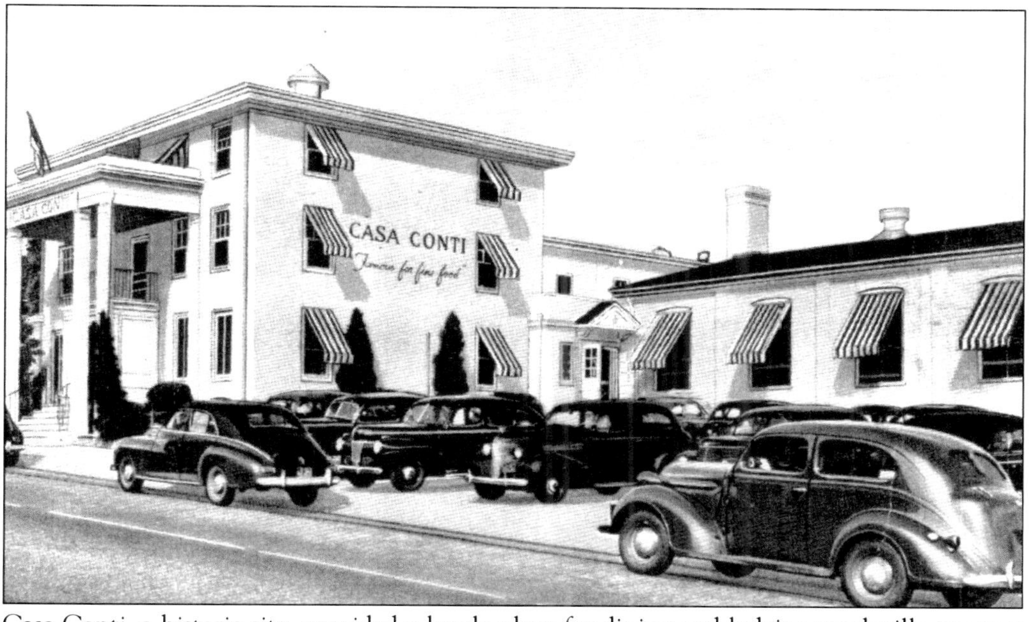

Casa Conti, a historic site, provided a lovely place for dining and lodging vaudeville troupers on the traveling circuit. The performers were used to traveling by public transportation from spot to spot, and the availability of this comfortable hotel two blocks from the venue was an added benefit.

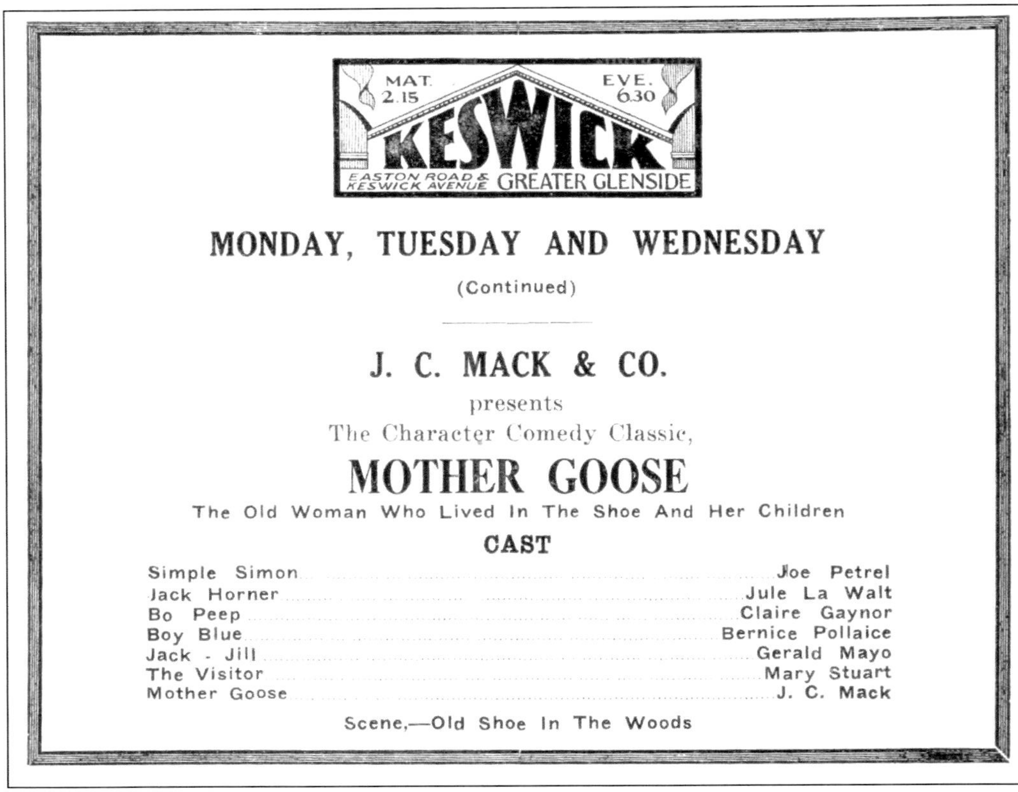
MAT. 2.15 EVE. 6.30
KESWICK
EASTON ROAD & KESWICK AVENUE GREATER GLENSIDE

MONDAY, TUESDAY AND WEDNESDAY

(Continued)

J. C. MACK & CO.

presents

The Character Comedy Classic,

MOTHER GOOSE

The Old Woman Who Lived In The Shoe And Her Children

CAST

Simple Simon	Joe Petrel
Jack Horner	Jule La Walt
Bo Peep	Claire Gaynor
Boy Blue	Bernice Pollaice
Jack - Jill	Gerald Mayo
The Visitor	Mary Stuart
Mother Goose	J. C. Mack

Scene,—Old Shoe In The Woods

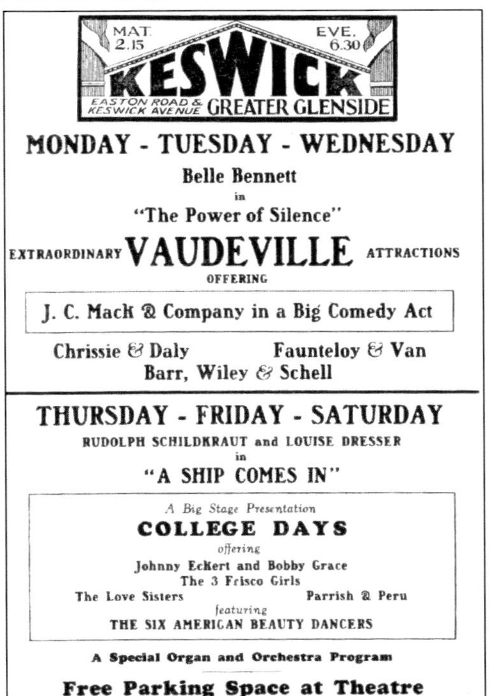
MAT. 2.15 EVE. 6.30
KESWICK
EASTON ROAD & KESWICK AVENUE GREATER GLENSIDE

MONDAY - TUESDAY - WEDNESDAY

Belle Bennett

in

"The Power of Silence"

EXTRAORDINARY VAUDEVILLE ATTRACTIONS

OFFERING

J. C. Mack & Company in a Big Comedy Act

Chrissie & Daly Faunteloy & Van

Barr, Wiley & Schell

THURSDAY - FRIDAY - SATURDAY

RUDOLPH SCHILDKRAUT and LOUISE DRESSER

in

"A SHIP COMES IN"

A Big Stage Presentation

COLLEGE DAYS

offering

Johnny Eckert and Bobby Grace

The 3 Frisco Girls

The Love Sisters Parrish & Peru

featuring

THE SIX AMERICAN BEAUTY DANCERS

A Special Organ and Orchestra Program

Free Parking Space at Theatre

Vaudeville acts including Paul Robeson, Fanny Brice, the Marx Brothers, and Step 'n Fetchit appeared at the Keswick. An extraordinary contortionist known as Punjab is said to have suspended himself from the marquee as part of the advertisement for his show. During the 1930s, the building also hosted the Little Rascals, who were on tour for their upcoming series of movies. Edwin Johnson's daughter enjoyed visiting with them, as did other neighborhood children.

Harry Brackinridge, stage manager for the Keswick Theatre, first recommended Casa Conti to performers who had been staying at city hotels and taking the train out to "the country." Brackinridge, whose father was also a stage manager, came to the Keswick from Keith's Theatre. He is pictured here shortly before taking the job at the Keswick in 1926.

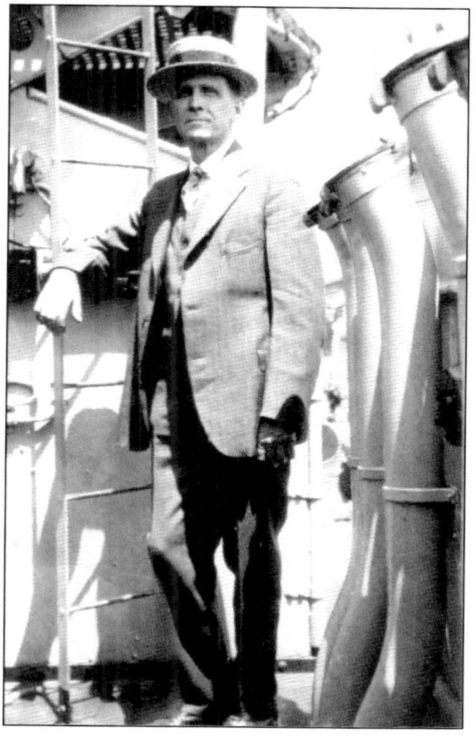

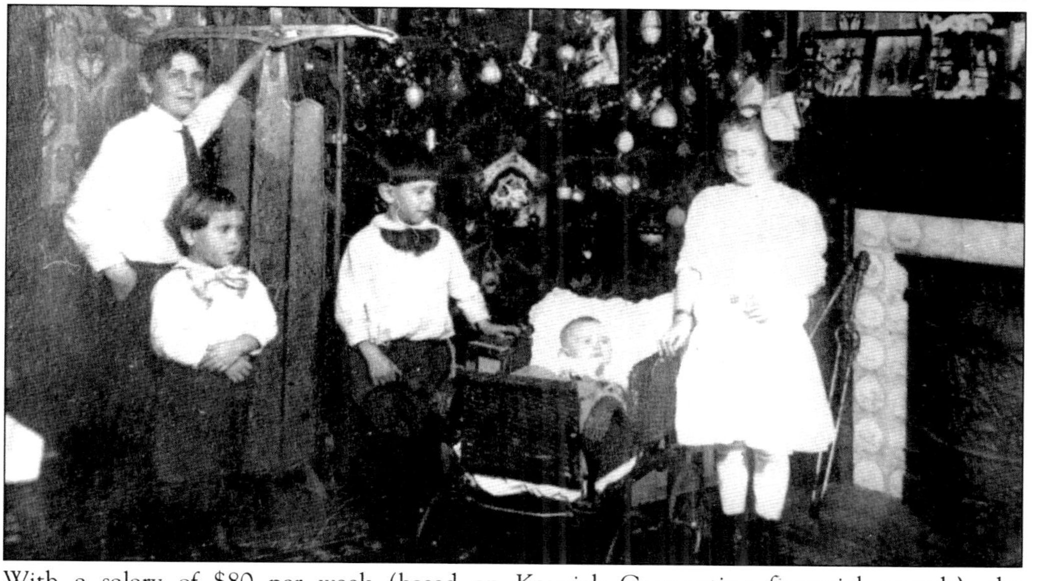

With a salary of $80 per week (based on Keswick Corporation financial records), the Brackinridges could afford to live well. They became residents of the Glenside area and lived in several local residences before moving to the countryside area of Ardsley, less than one mile from the theater. Much of the family remained in the area in years to come. Harry Brackinridge's duties at the theater, based on the recollections of his granddaughter Edith, included not only backstage work but also the construction in the alley of a 14-foot-long bench—rigged with a shock in it—on which the stars could "relax."

Isabella Dahlia Garden

ARDSLEY, PENNSYLVANIA

BELL PHONE:
OGONTZ 1279-W

POST OFFICE: GLENSIDE, PENNSYLVANIA
P. O. BOX 249

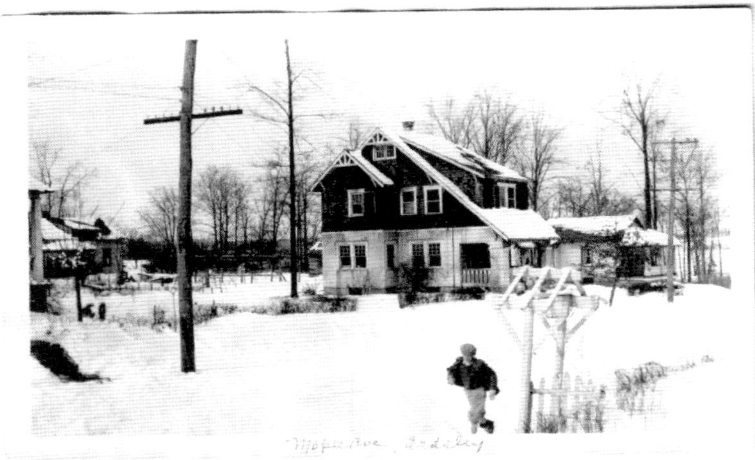

Traveling performers often were invited to the Brackinridge home in Ardsley, where Harry Brackinridge kept elaborate dahlia gardens. The house is pictured with the garden's letterhead. Brackinridge, who related theater stories to his family in later years, once told Roy Rogers that he "would do better if he spoke"—the actor's first shows were in mime.

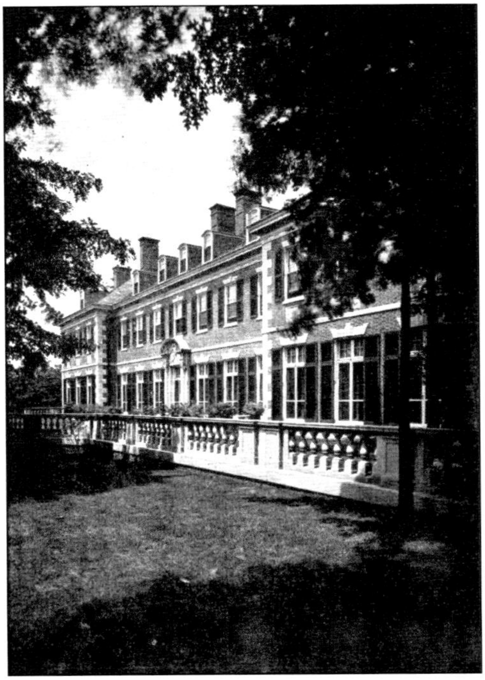

This image, taken from the inside cover of the souvenir program book, shows Horace Trumbauer advertised his services. One of Trumbauer's main sources of income was providing well-to-do families with "residential palaces." Trumbauer and Johnson desired to attract a patronage that would also be financially able to purchase services from the architect.

ALL BUSINESS MEN
OF MONTGOMERY COUNTY

will be regular patrons at The Keswick. If you have anything to sell to the 100,000 who live around "The Hub," advertise in the

KESWICK PROGRAM

GREATER GLENSIDE PUBLISHING CO.

KESWICK BUILDING

Phone, Ogontz 111 GREATER GLENSIDE, PA.

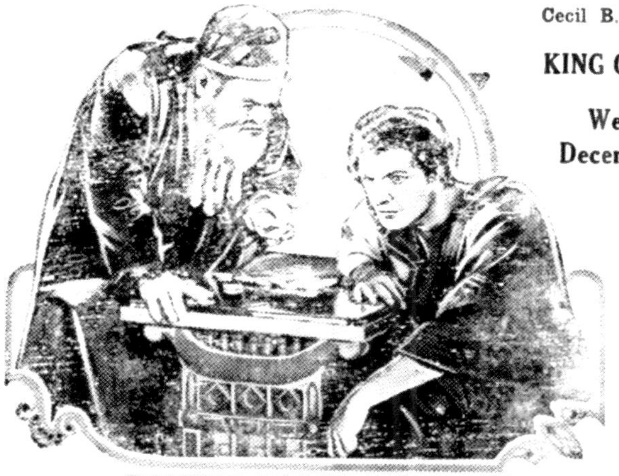

THE BETRAYAL FOR THIRTY PIECES OF SILVER

Cecil B. De Mille's

KING OF KINGS

Week of
December 31

Keswick's Synchronized and Talking Pictures

On or about January 17, the Keswick Theatre will begin its sound, and talking, pictures.

Owing to the tremendous demand for Vitaphone, Movietone and Photophone equipment, the above date is the earliest possible for its installation.

Some theatres, which have ordered this apparatus, will not be able to obtain it until next fall.

This program advertisement promoted the *Glenside Gazette*. The program regularly advertised the availability of the venue for rent for any type of an event. Johnson meant business. This page is also meaningful, as it indicates the backorder of sound equipment. After the equipment arrived at the Keswick Theatre, *The Hit of The Show* was one of the first talkies in the area, despite the fact that there were competing movie theaters nearby: the Embassy-Hiway in Jenkintown, the Grove in Willow Grove, and the Glenside-Nixon, just two blocks away. There were also venues in Germantown, Hatboro, and Ambler. With this much competition—most of it built before or around the same time of the Keswick Theatre—and a population that was just growing, marketing would have been a key component to ticket sales. Another component was giveaways such as dishes, glasses, and such. The Keswick was involved in these practices from the early days of its existence.

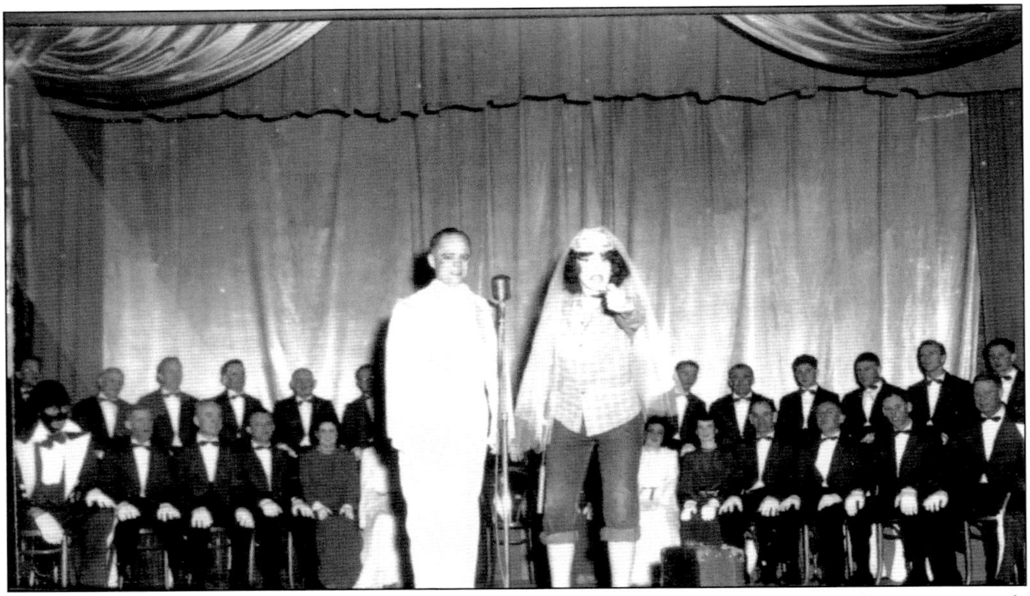

Reflected in advertisements is Edwin Johnson's commitment to the community. Beginning with the Kiwanis benefit for underprivileged children, held two days before the building opened to the public, many organizations became involved at the Keswick Theatre. The Everywoman's Club chaperoned the children's matinees, and the St Luke's Band of the local Roman Catholic Church provided entertainment. Boy Scouts served as ushers for the children's matinees. Johnson also allowed the library to use the top floors of the adjacent store buildings as a rent-free temporary home.

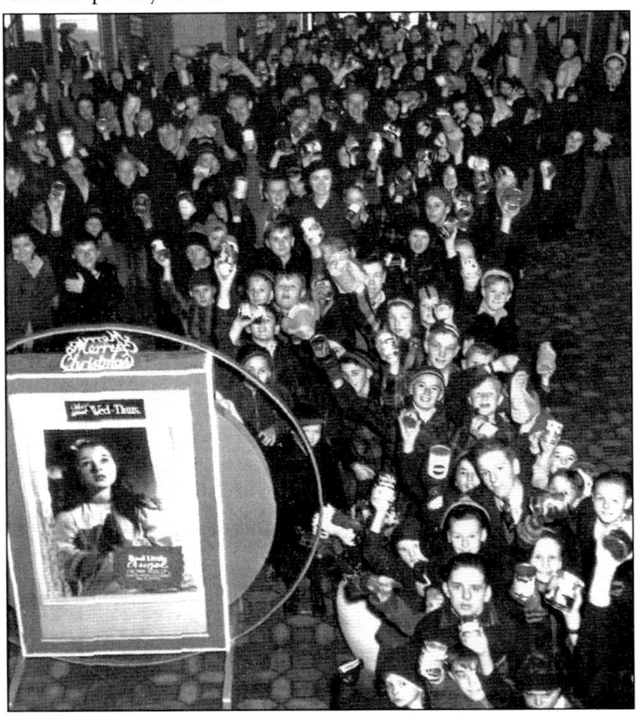

This photograph of a food drive held at the Keswick Theatre shows that community and entertainment do mix. Local entertainment proved important to the community then, and that tradition stayed with the Keswick Theatre. Ted Rouston, a later manager, held dance lessons at the venue every Saturday, and a "call" went out in the newspaper for auditions for a movie to be filmed in part at the Keswick in 1929 and 1930. Whether the film was ever completed is undocumented.

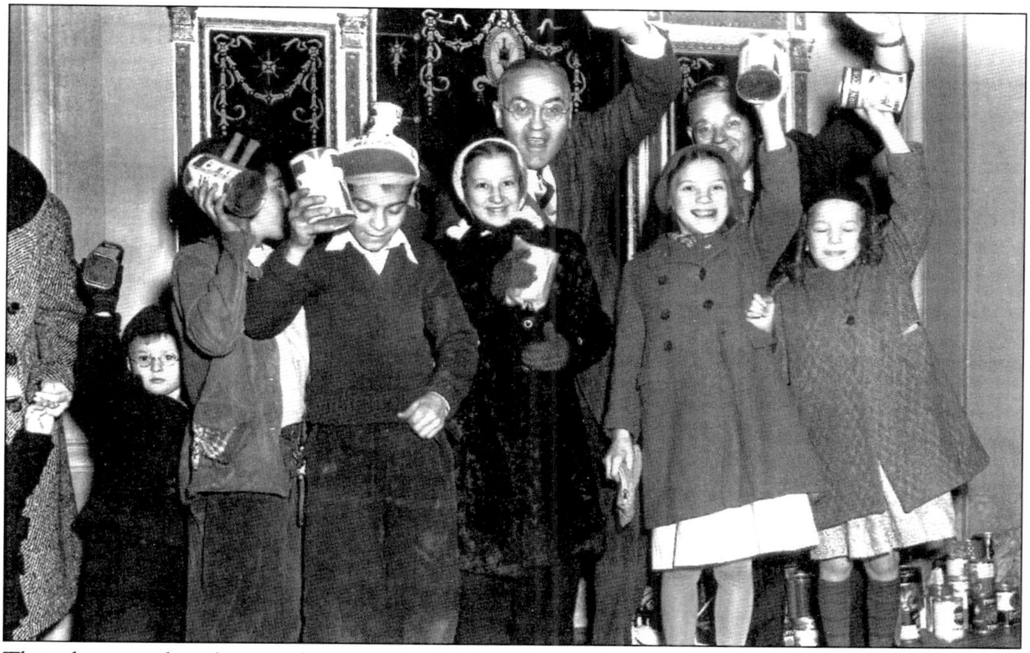

This photograph, taken at the same food drive, shows the original lobby frames and the ornate decorative work that was part of the theme. The adult pictured here may be the theater manager.

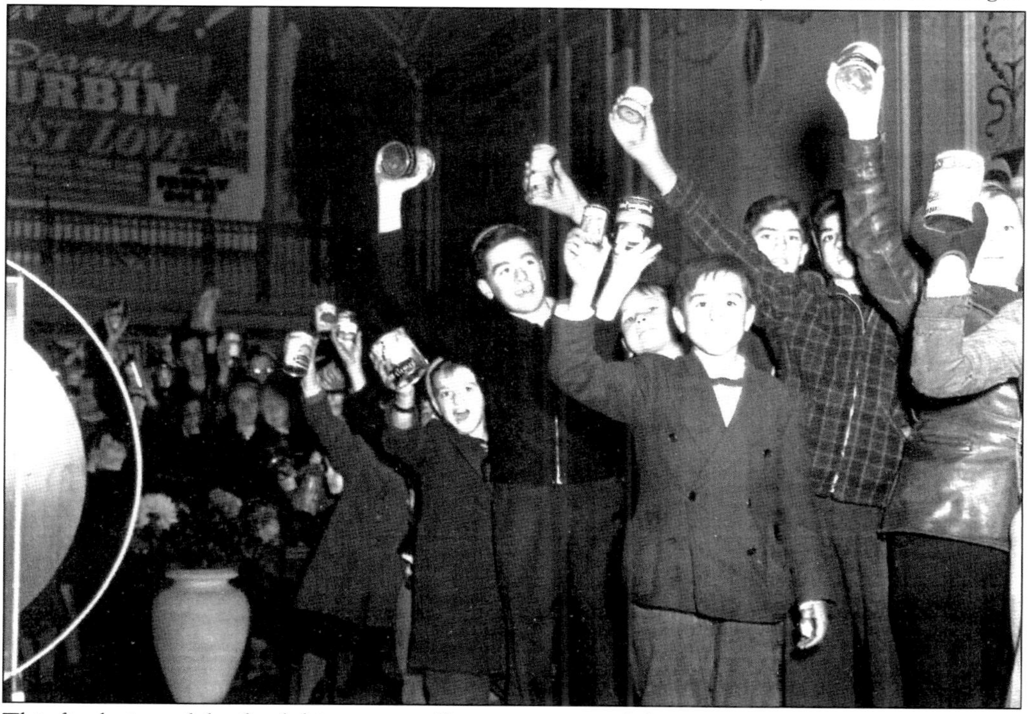

This final view of the food drive series offers a rare view of the interior of the theater. Visible is the inside marquee area where the exterior windows look out over Keswick Avenue. It is clear that advertising was placed in this area, and that balustrades were present.

THIRTY – FOURTH ANNUAL DANCE REVUE

PRESENTED BY THE PUPILS OF

THE HEGER ACADEMY OF DANCING

JENKINTOWN, PA.

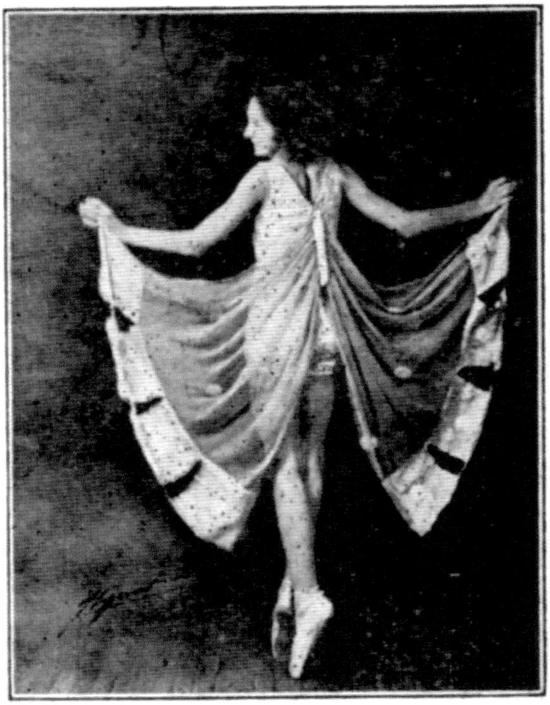

KATHRYN HEGER JOCKERS

The first record of dance recitals at the theater is from 1933. The front page of the *Times Chronicle* carried a list of all of the dancers, along with an article about the sudden death of Martha Blum, widow of department store founder Ralph Blum. Dance was an important part of the social accomplishments of young ladies. Teaching them grace and deportment, as well as exercise and aspects of teamwork, were part of education even in the 1930s, during the Depression. Dance recitals are still held at the Keswick Theatre throughout late May and during all of June. One of the current ushers remembers being on the stage with the Heger School and missing her steps completely. The lesson of discipline, the value of fellowship, and the opportunity to stand in front of an audience are experiences that parents are eager to provide for their children.

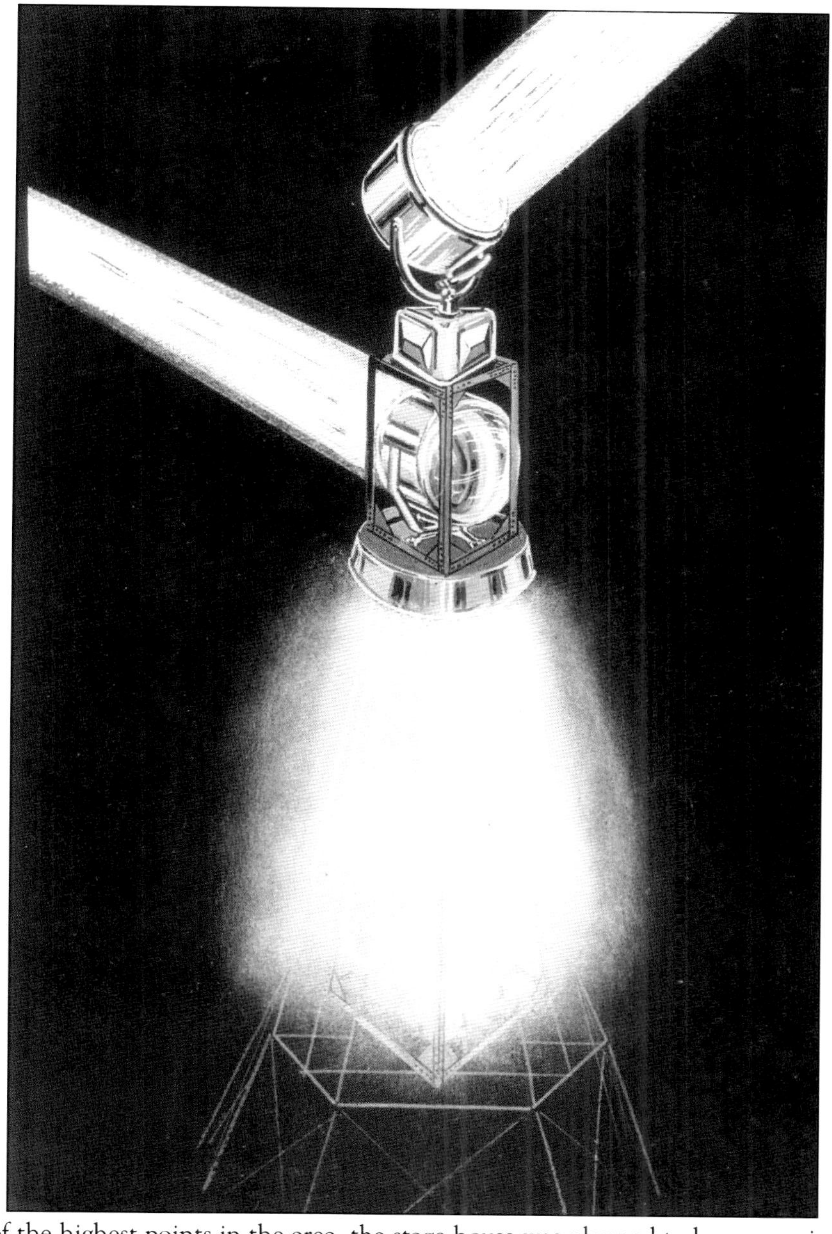

As one of the highest points in the area, the stage house was planned to house an airplane beacon with a 15,000-gallon water tank mounted below its structure. On February 14, 1929, the Keswick advertised the dedication of the $10,000 airplane beacon. The beacon was to point the way to the Pitcairn airfield. The well-to-do Pitcairn family had recently entered into the aircraft industry with the Mailwings (the predecessor to Eastern Airlines). The Pitcairns' contributions to aircraft history also include the designs that led to the modern-day helicopter. The airfield eventually became the Willow Grove Naval Air Station. The Pitcairns still live in the area and patronize the venue. The advertising ploy became "follow the beacon," and many did, coming up Olney Ave and Broad Street or via the trolley lines. Advertisements used from this time forward clearly feature the beacon as a marketing tool.

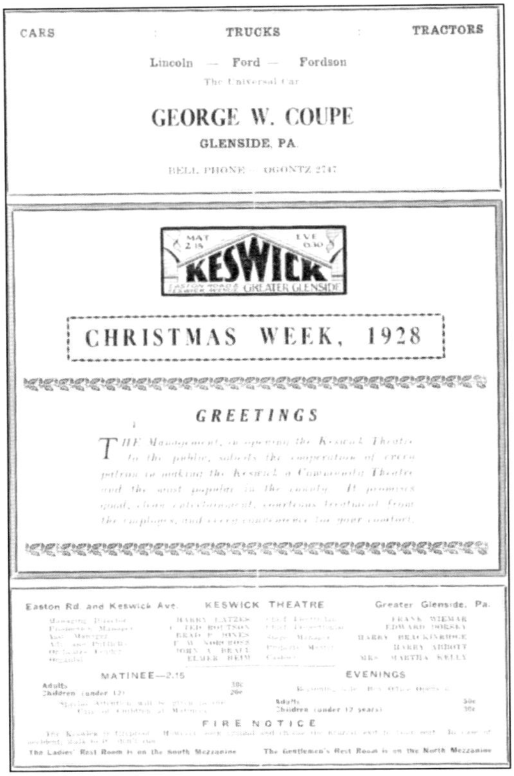

Shown in the first program is a mix of strategic items representing that which came to identify the Keswick Theatre throughout its history: support of local business, hospitality, concern for safety, and competent staff. Note that by the early 1930s, Ted Rouston had replaced Harry Katzes as building manager.

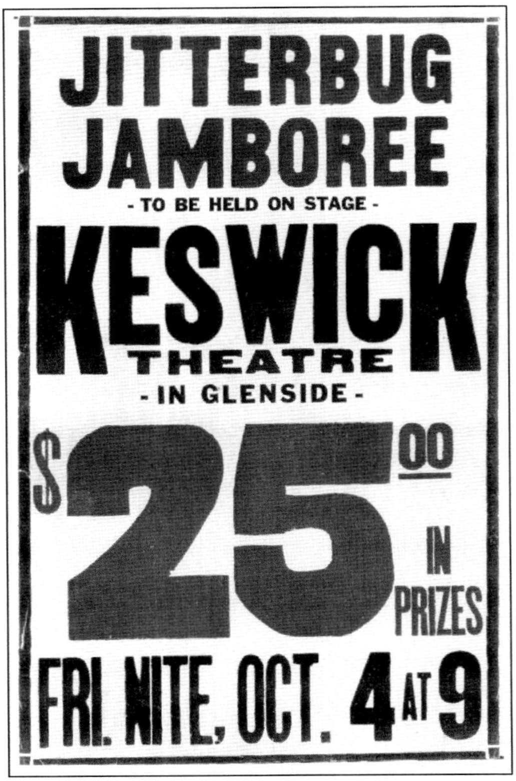

By 1930, new methods of attracting patrons were under way, including jitterbug competitions, jai alai games, and Saturday morning matinees. The theater played *Amos and Andy* radio broadcasts from the stage before shows. The Keswick was ready to give patrons whatever it took to get them into the venue. Radio Station WIBG (the IGB stands for "I Believe in God") had its offices here and broadcast from the venue.

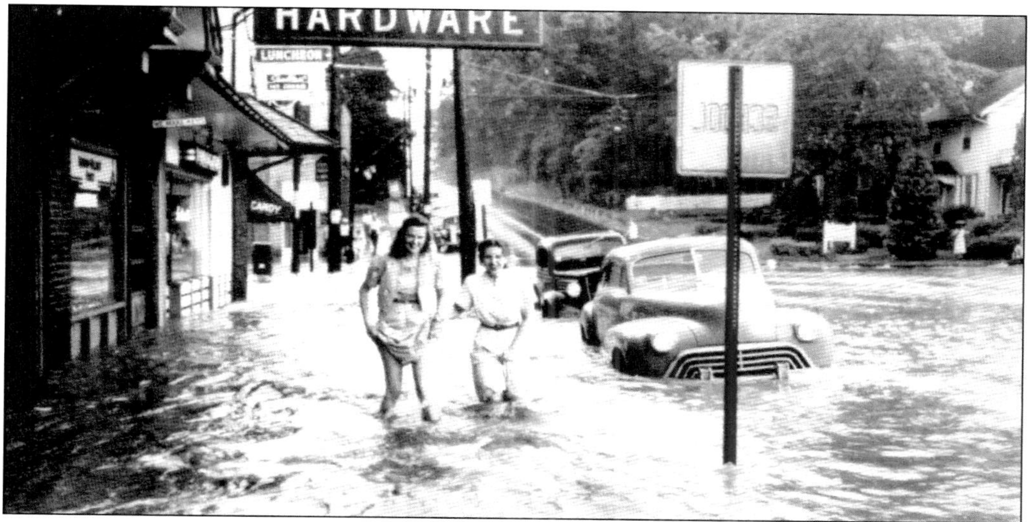

By 1936, the Depression was in full swing and times were tough, even without major floods. It is evident from the scarce financial records left that Edwin Johnson had lost day-to-day control of the Keswick Theatre. One local source attributed this to the theater's independent status and the inability to get films. This idea is substantiated by the fact that advertisements for the venue had dwindled to practically nothing by the late 1930s. The hardware store shown was where Penny's Flowers got its start.

"A HOME-LIKE PLACE"

TOM LANCASTER
Managing Director

KESWICK THEATRE

H. TED ROUTSON
Asst. Mgr. & Publicity

Glenside, Pa. Phone, Ogontz 4141

WEEK OF NOVEMBER 18th

MONDAY, TUESDAY and WEDNESDAY

RADIO PICTURES, INC., DAZZLING SCREEN TRIUMPH!
See and Hear The Sensation of Sensations! See and Hear
THE "100%" ALL-TALKING, ALL-SINGING MASTERPIECE

"STREET GIRL"
With
BETTY COMPSON
JACK OAKIE - NED SPARKS - DORIS EATON - JOSEPH CAWTHORN
And 100 Other Musical Comedy Artists
In a Gorgeous Revel of Joy-Fired Drama and Soaring Melody
Vitaphone Act—Frances Shelley and the 4 Eaton Boys
PATHE NEWS COLOR CLASSIC—"FESTIVAL OF BAGDAD"
ALSO A BIG STAGE SHOW

THURSDAY, FRIDAY and SATURDAY

METRO-GOLDWYN-MAYER'S "ALL TALKING" FEATURE
See and Hear The Epic of Everyday Life See and Hear

"THE IDLE RICH"
With
CONRAD NAGEL - BESSIE LOVE - LEILA HYAMS
VITAPHONE ACT—MURRY & OAKLAND IN "SATIRES"
An RKO All-Talking Comedy, "Head Work"
PATHE NEWS PATHE FABLE, "JUNGLE FOOL"
ALSO A BIG STAGE SHOW

The programs of the time still list Edwin Johnson as the owner, and the financial records show Johnson receiving regular payments from the Keswick Theatre Corporation through some type of escrow arrangement. Research shows that Johnson or his company became insolvent in 1936. By the late 1930s, several area movie houses were showing the same films regularly, perhaps to provide competition for the Keswick.

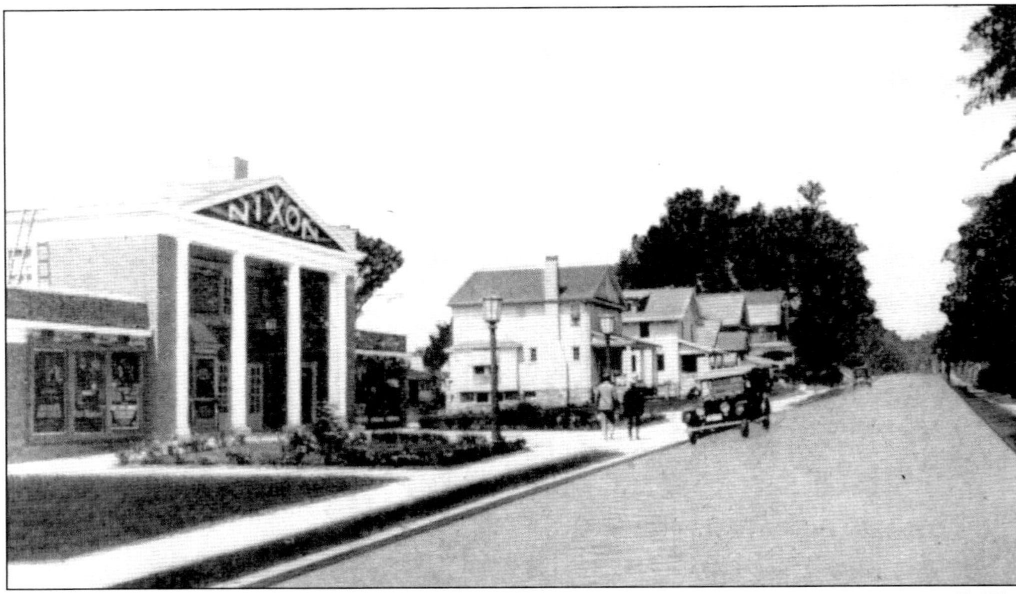

As the venue moved toward an all-film policy in the later years, competition was stiff. The Glenside-Nixon Theatre had been built first, in 1922, just five blocks away. The smaller Embassy-Hiway Theatre was in business about three miles away in Jenkintown; there were also venues in both Willow Grove and Hatboro. Edwin Johnson and his associates were said to have strict segregation policies. At the Keswick Theatre, this meant that African Americans had to sit on the far-left side of the theater, although no separate doors or balconies were built for them. The community also had a strong Americanization promotion being held at the Saturday morning matinees, perhaps aimed at the sons and daughters of local Italian and Irish immigrants who were settling in the area.

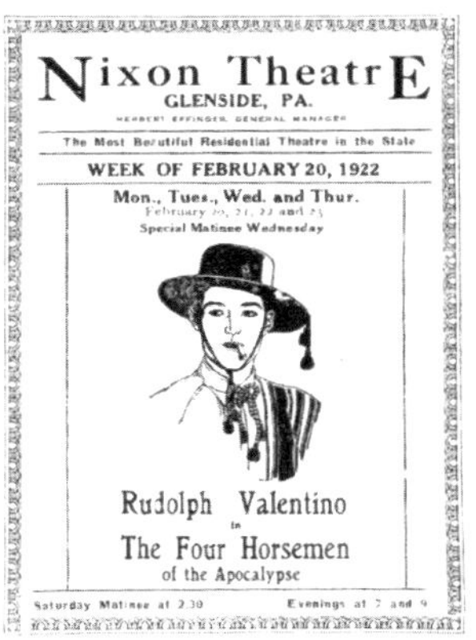

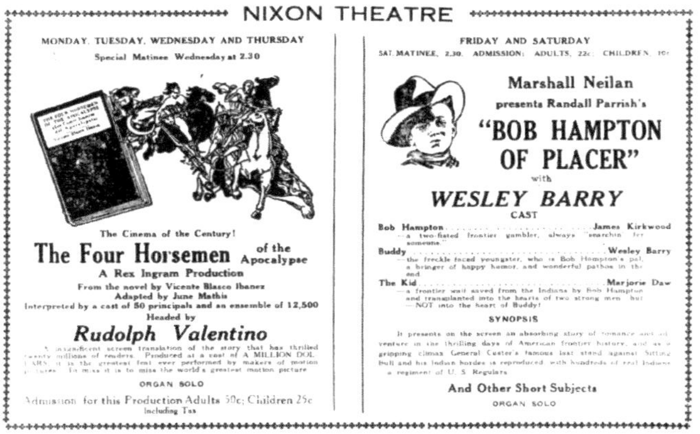

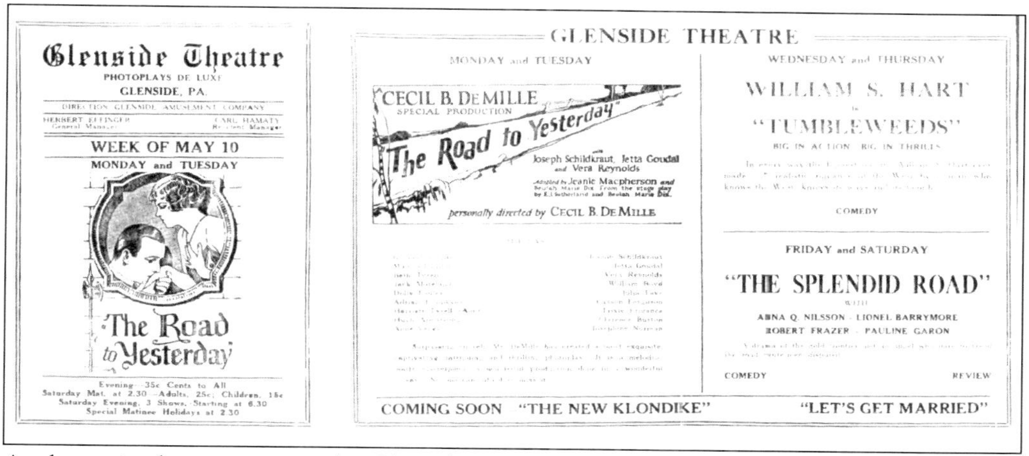

Glenside Theatre
PHOTOPLAYS DE LUXE
GLENSIDE, PA.

WEEK OF MAY 10
MONDAY and TUESDAY

The Road to Yesterday

Evening 35c Cents to All
Saturday Mat. at 2.30 Adults, 25c; Children, 15c
Saturday Evening, 3 Shows, Starting at 6.30
Special Matinee Holidays at 2.30

GLENSIDE THEATRE

MONDAY and TUESDAY

CECIL B. DE MILLE
SPECIAL PRODUCTION
The Road to Yesterday
with Joseph Schildkraut, Jetta Goudal and Vera Reynolds
Adapted by Jeanie Macpherson and Beulah Marie Dix
personally directed by CECIL B. DE MILLE

WEDNESDAY and THURSDAY

WILLIAM S. HART
in
"TUMBLEWEEDS"
BIG IN ACTION BIG IN THRILLS

COMEDY

FRIDAY and SATURDAY

"THE SPLENDID ROAD"
with
ANNA Q. NILSSON LIONEL BARRYMORE
ROBERT FRAZER PAULINE GARON

COMEDY REVIEW

COMING SOON "THE NEW KLONDIKE" "LET'S GET MARRIED"

As shown in these programs, the Glenside-Nixon Theatre had an active schedule, indicating that competition must have been fierce. The Keswick Theatre shops, seen below in 1938, had become a bustling commercial area, as Edwin Johnson had hoped. The unique combination of stores, restaurants, and entertainment helped to make the area a busy neighborhood. The establishments that survived adapted to change. One example is a candy and ice-cream store on the corner of Easton and Keswick that later became a tavern.

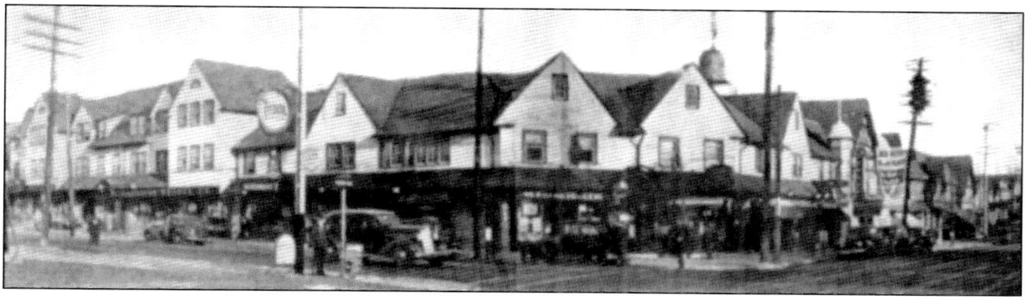

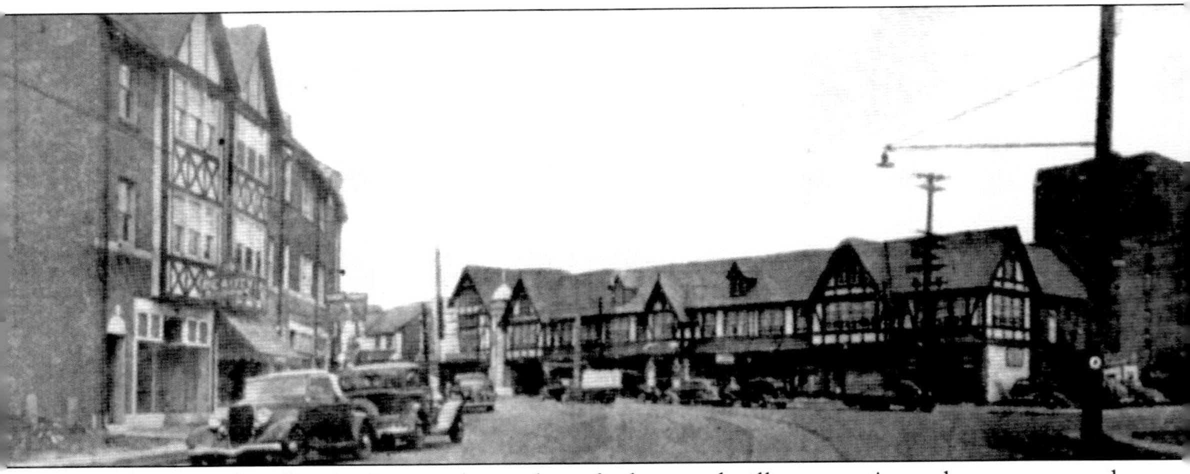

The Keswick suffered a fate similar to that of other vaudeville stages. A tough economy made movies a more attractive purchase than live entertainment. Although oral history relates that the stage was still used regularly into the 1940s (one local resident recalls seeing Duke Ellington there), the number of live shows dwindled. The golden age of the Keswick stage was virtually over. The recollections of Glenside natives of the 1940s are of a new manager, Albert Fischer, known as "Mr. Hollywood." The Keswick Theatre was still regarded as the place to go for dates, Saturday afternoons, and special events. Benjamin Blumenthal was involved in the stores and apartments not related to the theater itself. Real-estate records show the building being mortgaged to Land Title Bank and Trust for a group of investors in 1949. One of these investors was Roasalean Betz Ottman, a descendant of John Betz, owner of a brewing company. (Early film pioneer Siegmund Lubin purchased Betz's estate, Betzwood, located near Valley Forge.) The venue remained a local gathering place until 1952. Local entrepreneur Vincent Pennypacker Sr. mentioned the continued existence of the venue in later years, as his business, Penny's Flowers, grew up nearby. As the theater declined, the neighboring businesses felt the effect.

Two

THE MOVIE PALACE 1952–1979

The Keswick Theatre entered the Hollywood era with trepidation. The building was in shambles and needed a true entrepreneur to make it a viable business once again. In order to save the building from destruction, local businessmen stepped in and purchased the property until decisions could be made as to its future. Again, someone believed in its viability.

When Melvin Koff rose to the challenge in 1954, he employed creativity in his business dealings that helped save the venue. Attracted to the theater's architecture and elegance, Koff literally traded the Glenside Theatre, a few blocks away, to purchase the Keswick. The caveat was that the Glenside would no longer present music, and that grand building became office space.

The Keswick was redesigned to meet the needs of movie-going audiences. The articles of the day indicate that the modernization was met with excitement and happiness. The orchestra pit was covered over, as it would no longer be needed. The grand lobby was hidden behind plastic panels, and the box office was replaced by modern "ticket spitters." Glass, chrome, leather, and vinyl came to represent the venue. Popcorn and licorice were sold at a new concession stand, as there was more profit in the concessions than in the film. The magic brass mushrooms disappeared. Modern seats replaced the elegant seats of the 1920s. The audience was happy.

Show times changed to meet the needs of the audience. A late show was added to accommodate people getting off work from Standard Press Steel's late shifts. Saturday matinees continued for the children. A new group of individuals, called teenagers or adolescents, had burst onto the scene. The growing community of Glenside and Abington Township needed places for these youths to gather, and the building was a good place for dates and post-prom "lock-ins." The venue was ready to service the community once again. The movie palace era was off to a hopeful start, despite the adversity that had befallen the building. On July 28, 1955, Koff unveiled his revamped Keswick, and for the next 25 years, the theater held a new place in the hearts of the community.

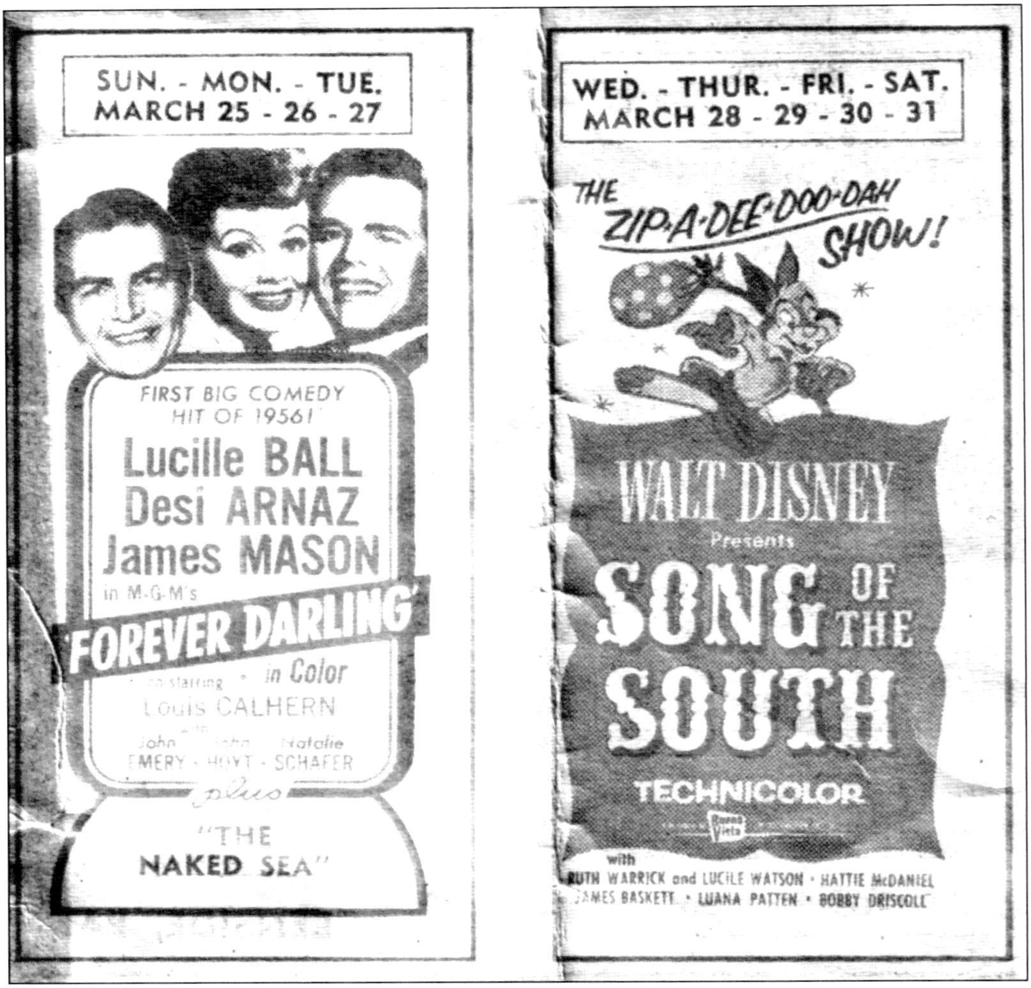

This small program from the 1950s was a keepsake handed out by theaters. The main purpose was to advertise upcoming events to the patrons. In a time long before Internet schedules, this marketing tool went home with patrons so that they would know what was playing the following week.

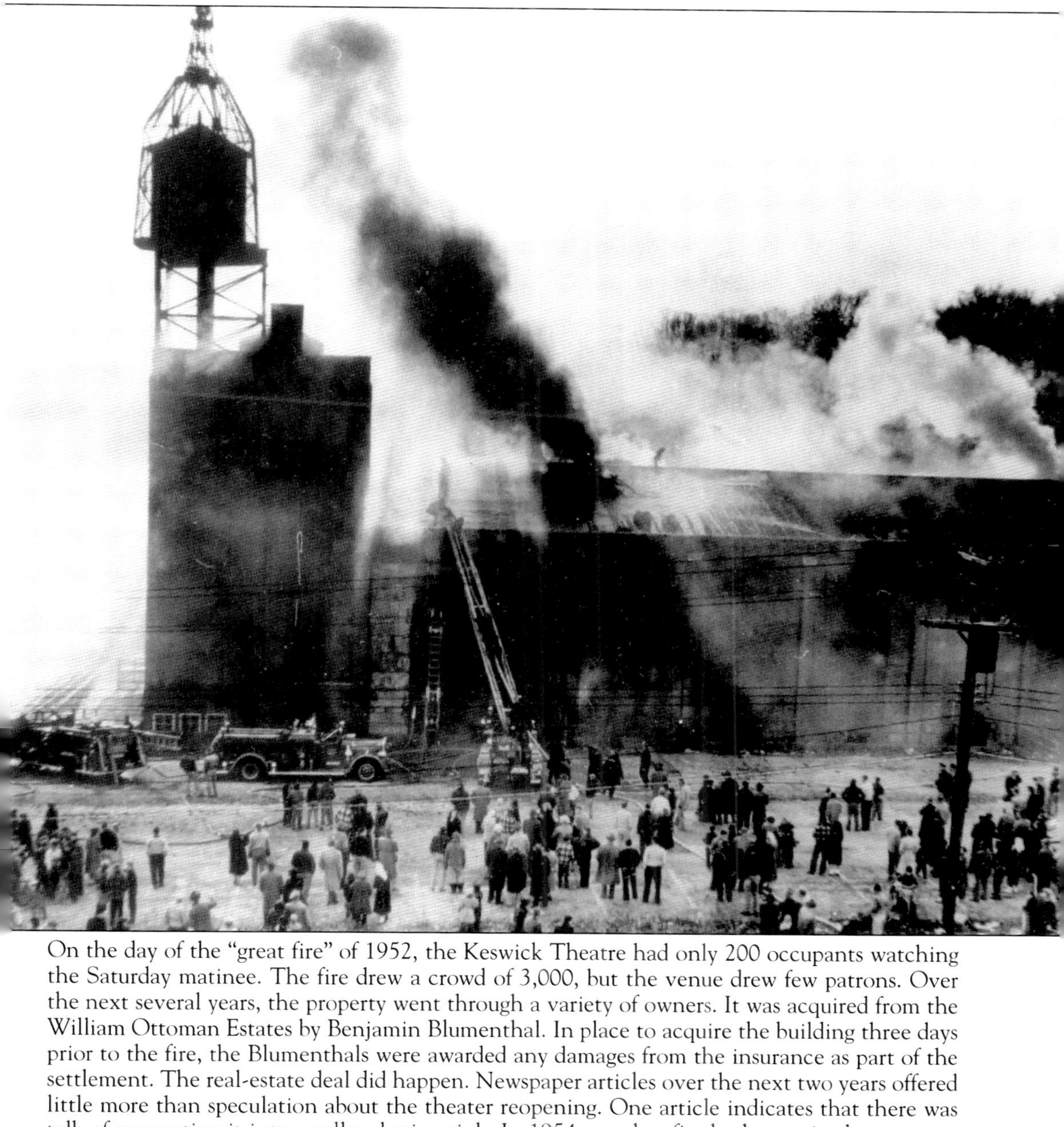

On the day of the "great fire" of 1952, the Keswick Theatre had only 200 occupants watching the Saturday matinee. The fire drew a crowd of 3,000, but the venue drew few patrons. Over the next several years, the property went through a variety of owners. It was acquired from the William Ottoman Estates by Benjamin Blumenthal. In place to acquire the building three days prior to the fire, the Blumenthals were awarded any damages from the insurance as part of the settlement. The real-estate deal did happen. Newspaper articles over the next two years offered little more than speculation about the theater reopening. One article indicates that there was talk of converting it into a roller-skating rink. In 1954, another fire broke out in the manager office. The neighboring Hiway and Glenside Theatres were still operating, and the advent of television was here. Thus, the Keswick, although sentimental to the neighbors, was not missed uniquely for its entertainment value. However, something about both the building and the area begged that the theater be reopened.

250 Children Escape Fire In Theater at Glenside as Girl Ushers Head Off Panic

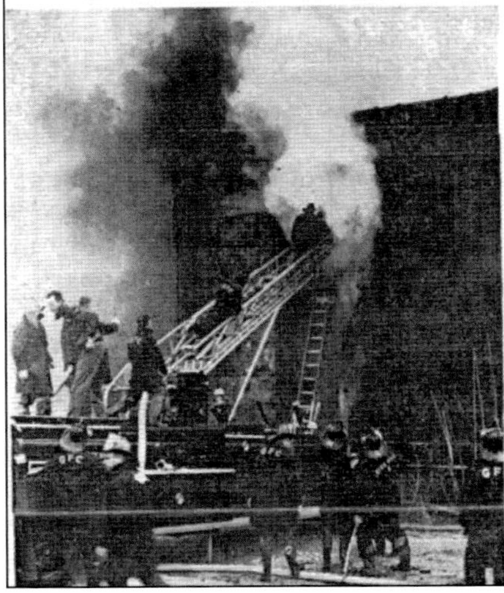

The fire made news in all of the Philadelphia papers. (The paper in which the first article was published is unknown, as only the actual article survived in the Weldon Fire Company scrapbook.) The Keswick was saved thanks to a quick response by the Weldon Fire Company. The two girl ushers, neighborhood residents, were given citations for their tremendous work in clearing the venue. Injuries were minimal injuries, and no deaths were associated with the fire. The roof was chopped open in several places, the ornamental ceiling in the auditorium was ruined, the ornate seating was soaked, and smoke damage was extensive. The chandelier disappeared. The residents all came out to see their beloved theater in smoke and flames. Then, the building sat empty for almost three years while the variety of owners decided what to do with it.

Firemen Battle Fire at Keswick Theatre

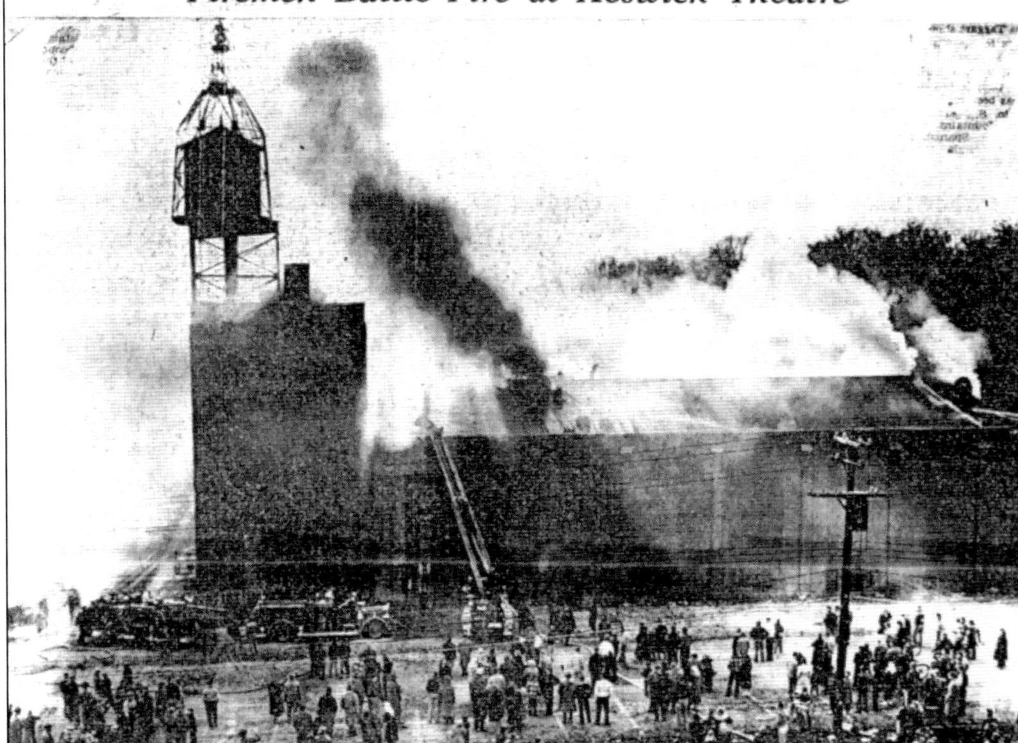

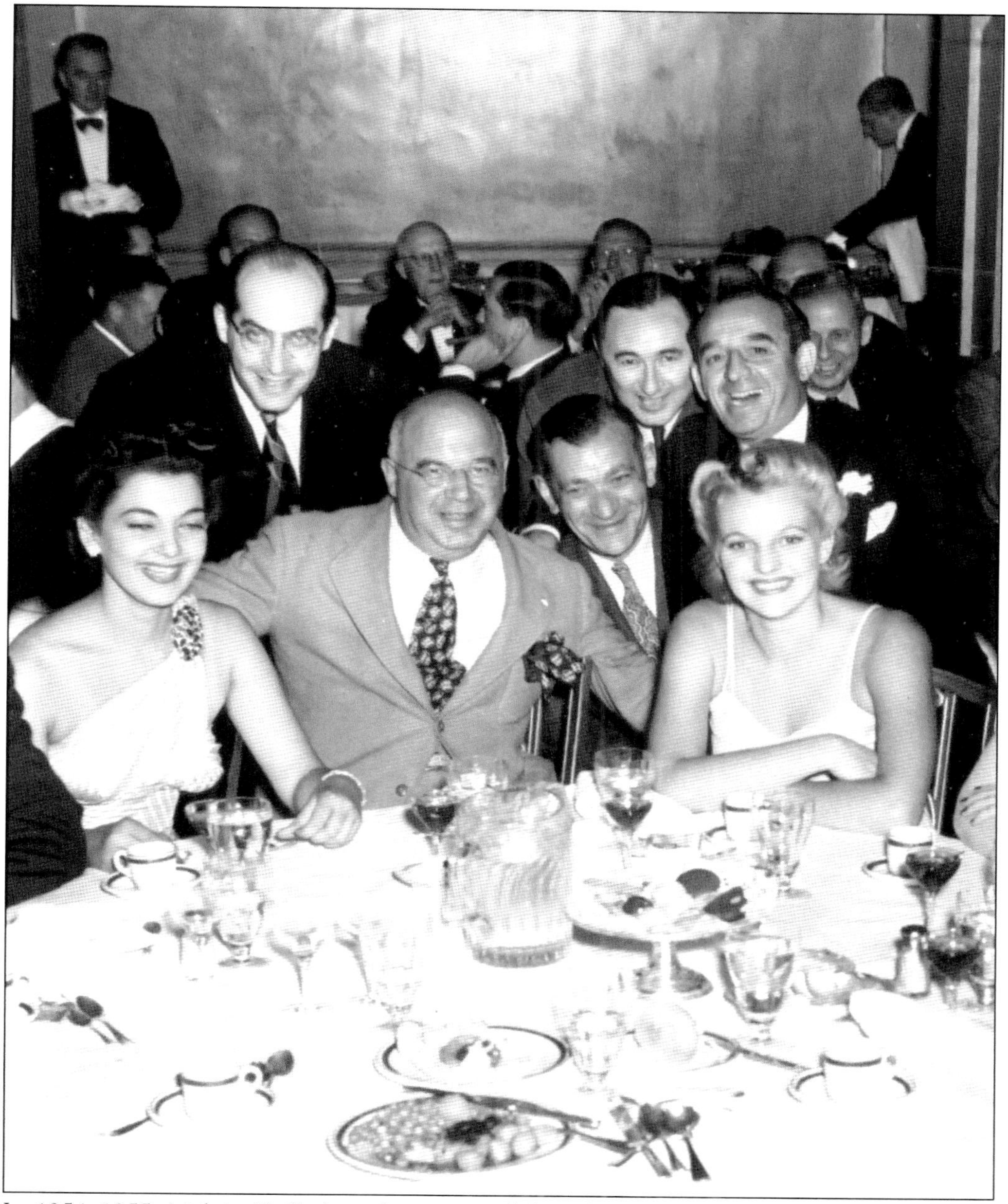

In 1954–1955, Melvin Koff, then the owner of the Glenside Theatre, stepped forward with a unique real-estate deal for the owner of the Keswick. The Keswick Theatre was to have life once again. Koff was a consummate film man, a visionary businessperson, and a truly community-spirited individual. Involved in movies from a young age, he began his career as a runner, taking films from one venue to another. Working for many years in film distribution, he traveled frequently to Hollywood, met the stars on a regular basis, and was a longtime member of the Variety Club. He ran one of the country's first drive-in theaters. He is shown here on the left in the second row, behind actress Ava Gardner, at a promotional event.

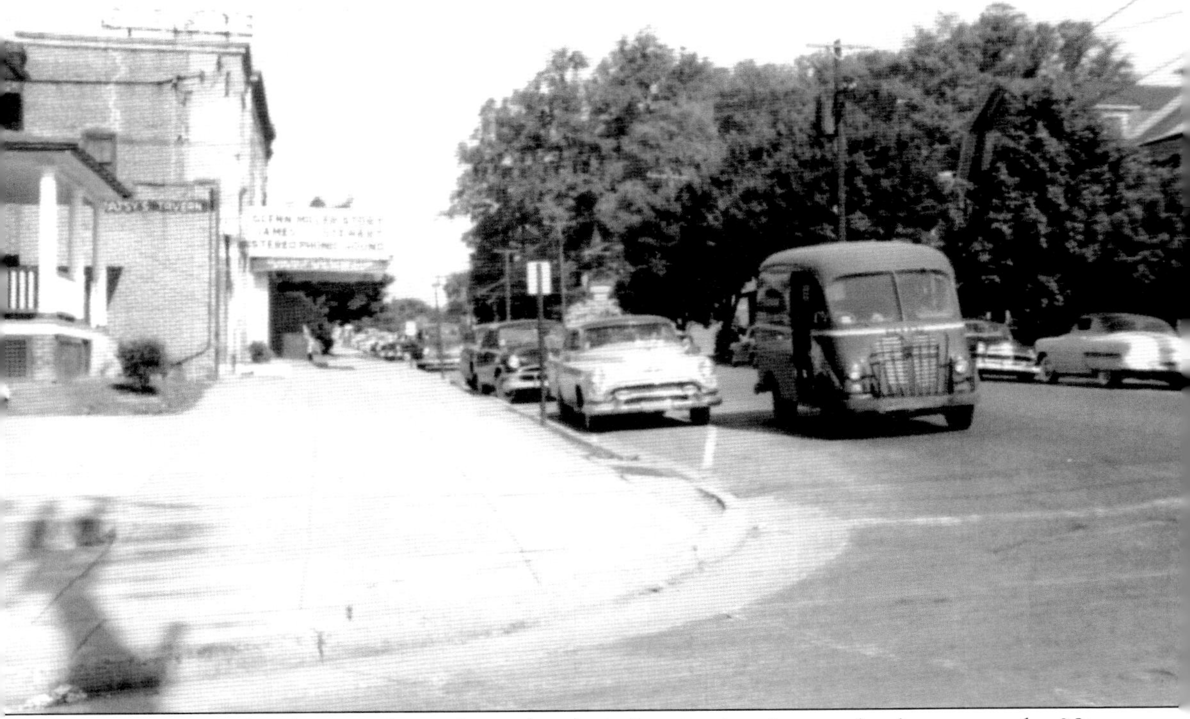

The Glenside Theatre, shown here shortly before it closed, was also known as the Nixon Theatre in the days when it belonged to the Nixon distribution circuit. It was built in 1922, six years before the Keswick Theatre. It was less than five blocks from the Keswick, but the neighborhood supported both venues during the height of the early movies. As part of the Melvin Koff's business deal to obtain the Keswick, the Glenside Theatre became offices. The building still stands today, although it has been altered somewhat. Koff also opened the 1812, in Philadelphia's posh Rittenhouse Square area, with the idea of giving the residents of the neighborhood a taste of elegance while they viewed the films.

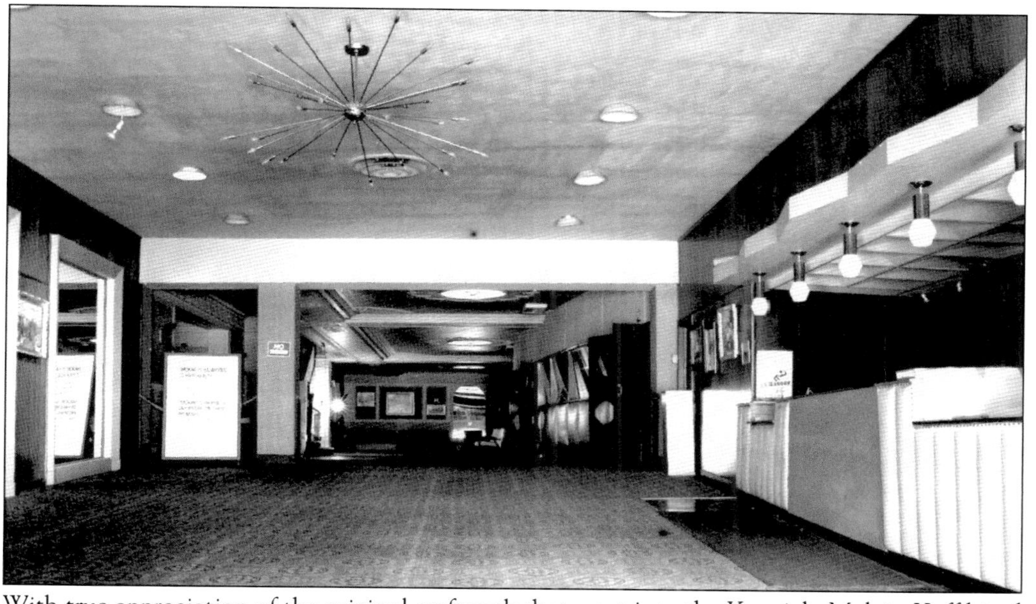

With true appreciation of the original craftwork that went into the Keswick, Melvin Koff hired architects David Supowitz and Shander Berger to modernize the Keswick. The architects set about carefully melding the old and the new. In an exercise that tucked away the exquisite beauty of the venue behind the modern, and that, in some cases, married the old and new, they recreated the Keswick once again as a hip place to be.

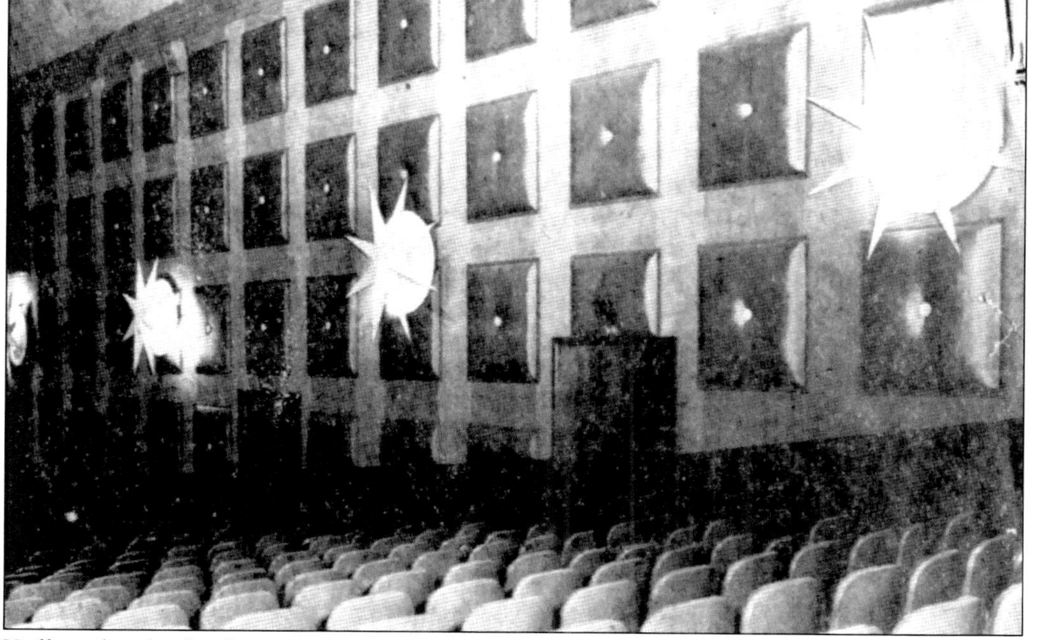

Koff used only the finest and most modern in seats, furnishings, fixtures, and cinemascope equipment. Within months, the building was turned from smoky remains into a place of beauty and modernity. The gilded walls may have not been visible, but they were carefully hidden behind the wall covering.

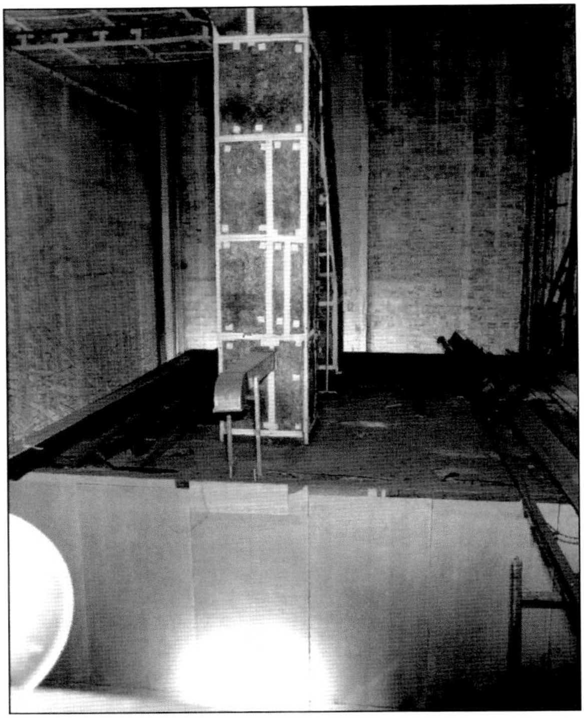

The building was also equipped with new ventilation equipment, conveniently placed on stage in order to keep folks warm but also safe. The great fire—believed to have started in the theater loft but definitely carried forward by the ventilation system—would not happen again.

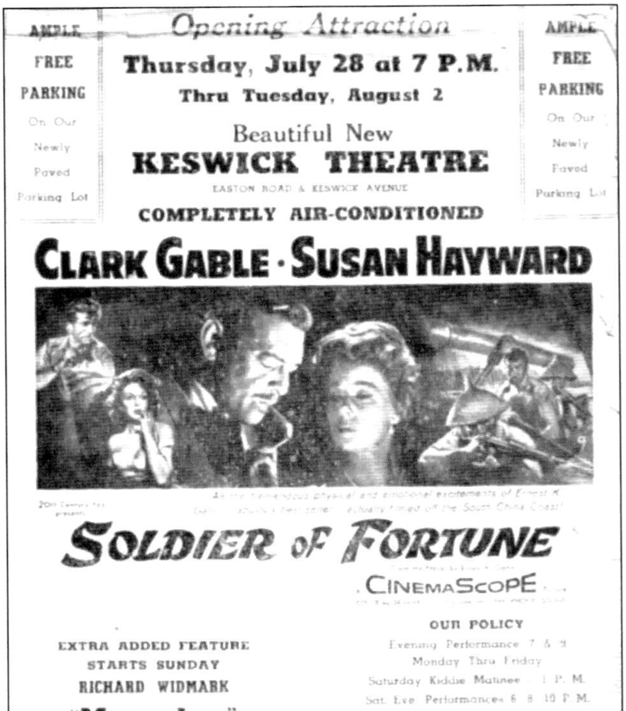

This advertisement from the *Times Chronicle* clearly accentuates the air conditioning. However, the free parking was also important at the time. Later photographs show parking lot signs specifying use for Keswick patrons. Also of interest are the hours and the mention of the Kiddie Corner, which became a Glenside happening. Many current patrons still mention which films they saw here, as well as the bike giveaway and other staples of Saturday mornings.

In addition to offering reasonable prices and good promotion, Melvin Koff was generous within the neighborhood and among his rental clients. He went years without raising rents for struggling businesses, always took care of any of his apartment dwellers who might be living on a fixed income, and continued to be a regular Variety Club member. He is shown here, in the back left, with friends.

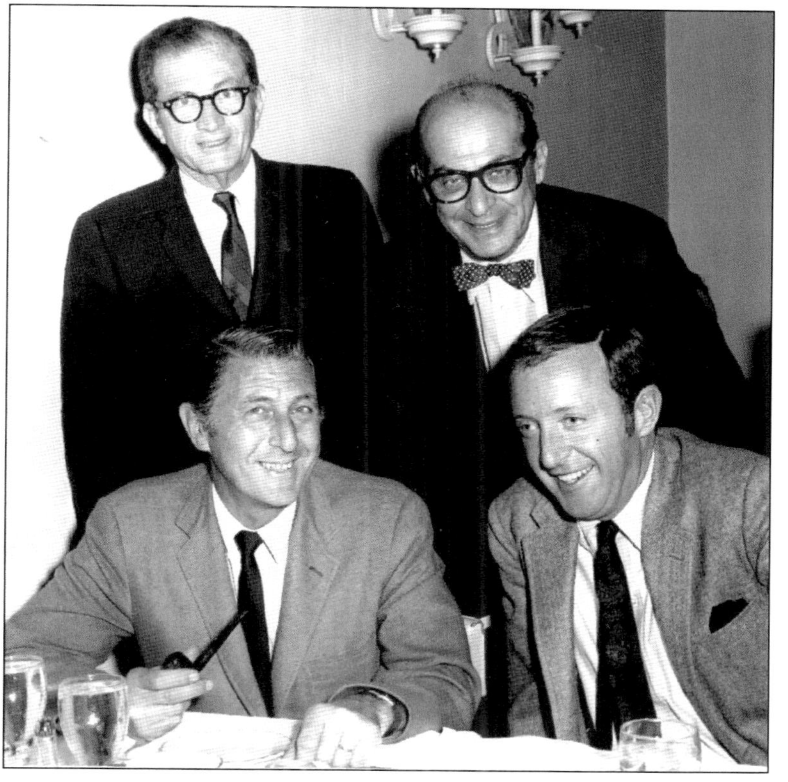

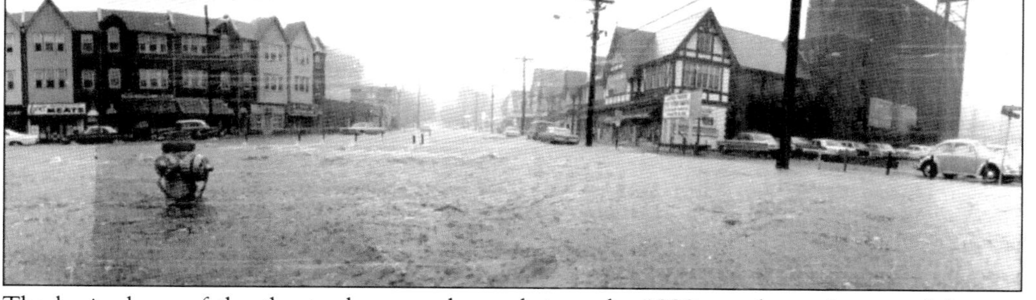

The basic shape of the theater has not changed since the 1920s, as shown in one of the rare photographs of this side of the building, taken in 1967. However, the front of the building has changed: a revamped marquee, done sometime between 1950 and 1955, makes the theater look more modern. Note that the venue still advertises free parking. By the 1980s, this scene was history, as this portion of the parking lot was gone and this end of the façade of the buildings was changed drastically.

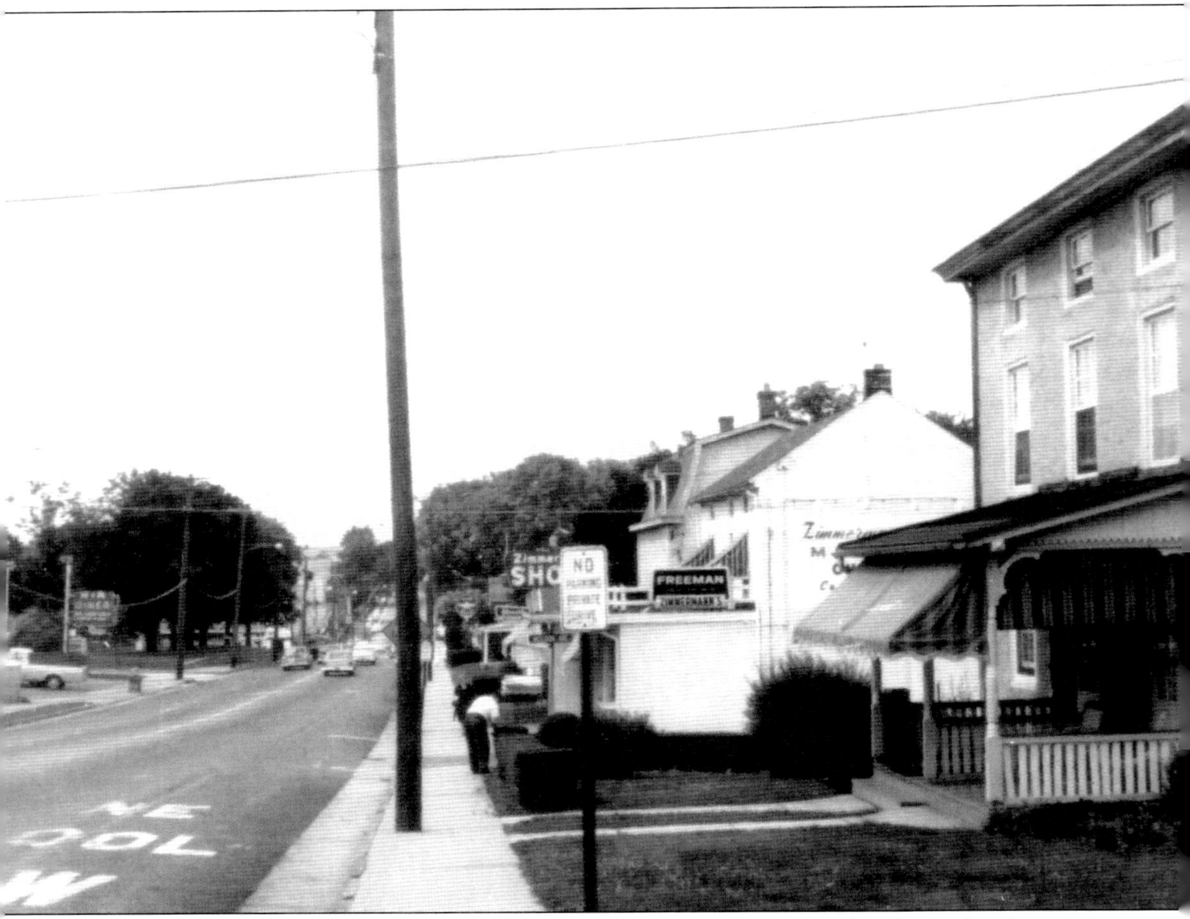

The commerce in the area was growing nicely. The Zimmermann Shoe Store family members were highly supportive of the Keswick efforts. Their daughter, Joan Mosler, has led the volunteer ushers for more than 10 years. Glenside was now well established with families, schools, and industry. Second and third generations had begun to live and work in the Glenside area. The newspaper article reporting the reopening of the theater in 1955 hailed the venue as an economic addition to the neighborhood. Dick Gerding recalls Melvin Koff allowing him to utilize the vacant backstage area as a darkroom after his photography needs began to outpace the space in his Keswick Avenue shop (where Gerding's father had also had his shop). Koff's daughters recall their father's remarkable sensitivity in marketing and promotions. Whether it was offering family discounts for local unions that were striking, senior citizen discounts, or the occasional free ticket to a youth as payment for performing a job, there was always plenty to be shared with the community. Koff was a family man, and he supported this in both word and practice. A newspaper article from the 1960s credits him for protecting children under 17 as R-rated films became popular. He was often known to send youngsters home if they had been dropped off at the venue.

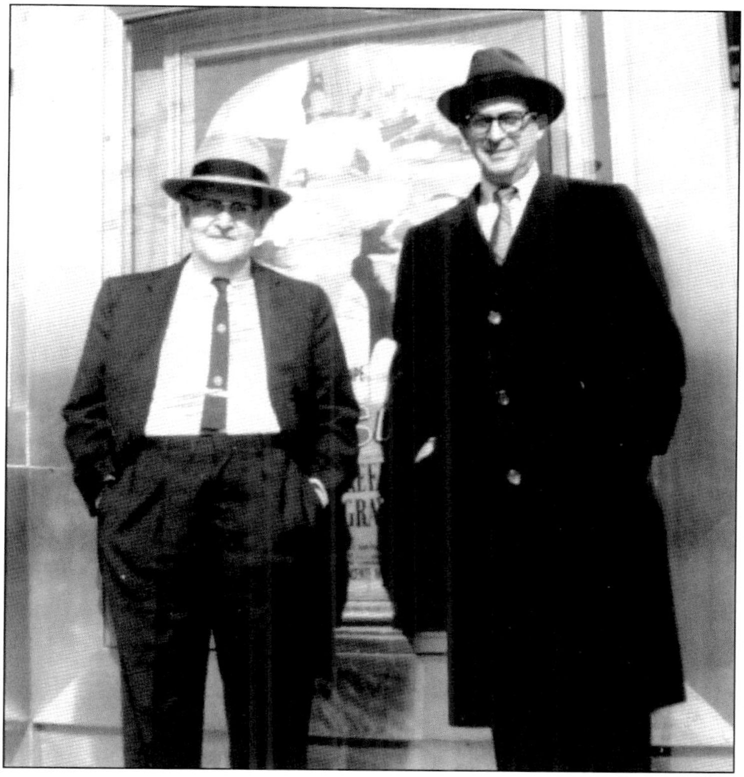

Melvin Koff's consideration of his employees was returned in kind. One instance involved Jimmy O'Connell, the longtime ticket taker at the theater. O'Connell, left, was believed to be well into his seventies when he posed with Koff for this 1956 photograph. O'Connell passed away at his station between shows.

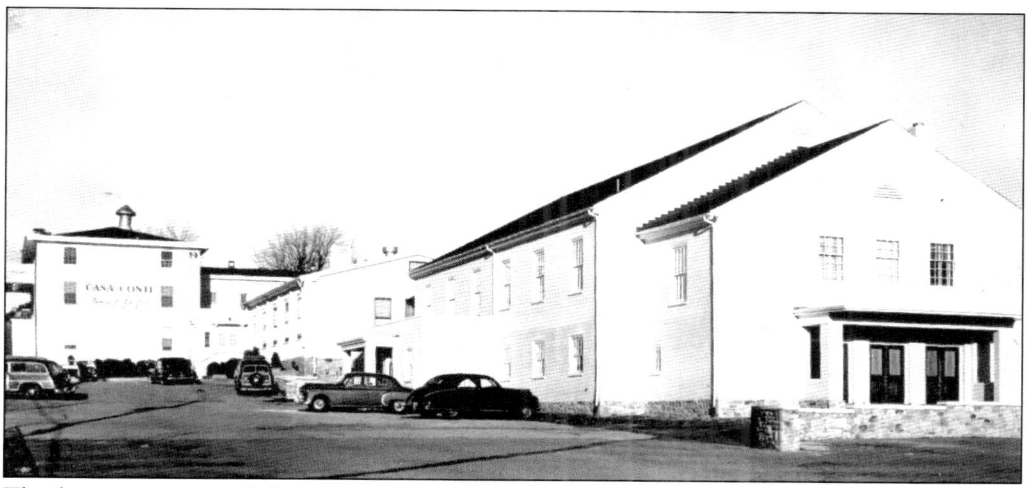

The businesses around the theater saw growth during this time, and those that were most successful also adapted to the changes taking place. As an example, Casa Conti, which originally housed vaudeville stars, expanded its space to include banquet rooms. This 1952 photograph reflects that growth and adaptation.

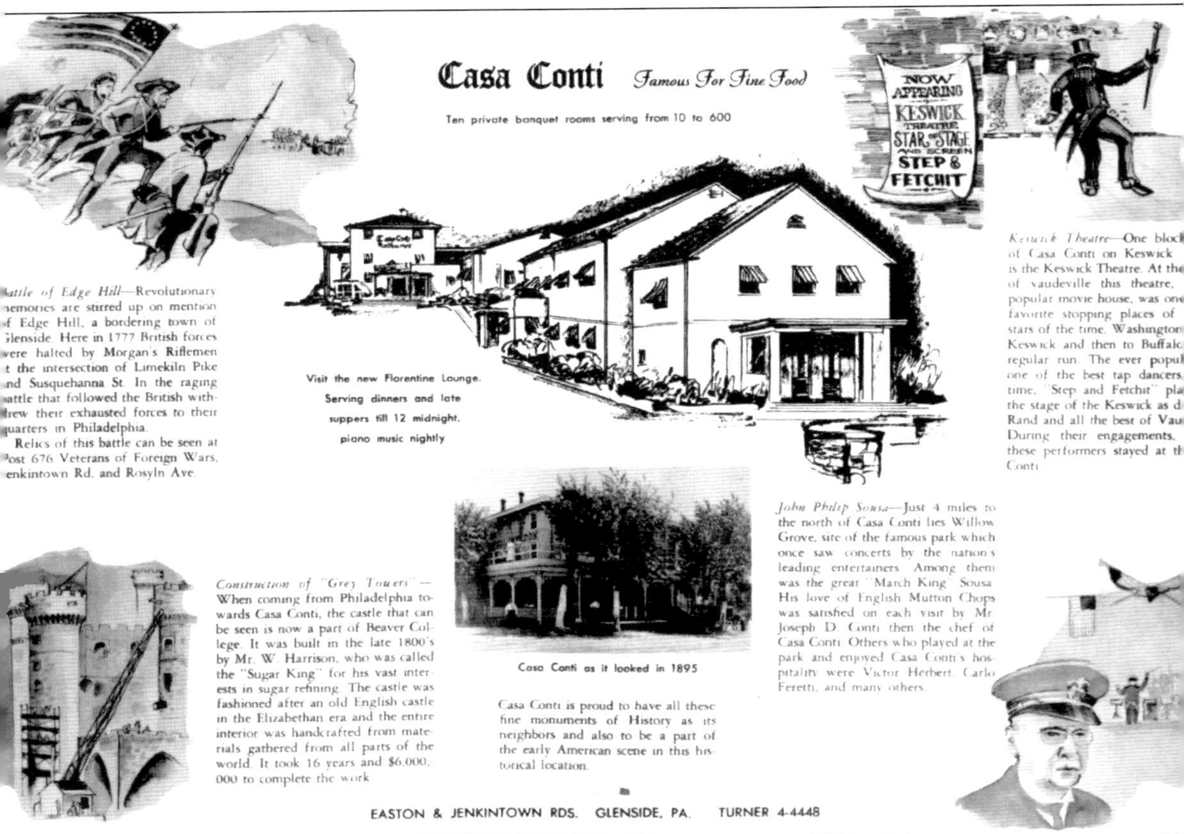

Local businesses were not shy about promoting the Keswick Theatre as part of the area's attractions, as shown in this Casa Conti advertisement from 1952. In this ad, the Keswick Theatre is already regarded as "historic." The ad also notes that the Battle of Edgehill was fought at the nearby corner of Susquehanna and Limekiln during the Revolutionary War. In the 1950s, it was easier to see the relics of a Revolutionary War battle at the local Veterans of Foreign Wars post than it was to find vaudeville posters for the Keswick Theatre. Melvin Koff actually found many movie and vaudeville posters in the dressing room area of the Keswick Theatre but was instructed by his wife, in no uncertain terms, to not bring them home. Probably because they posed a fire hazard when stored at the theater, these items were thrown away. The "Grey Towers" mentioned in the advertisement are now part of Arcadia University (then Beaver College for Women).

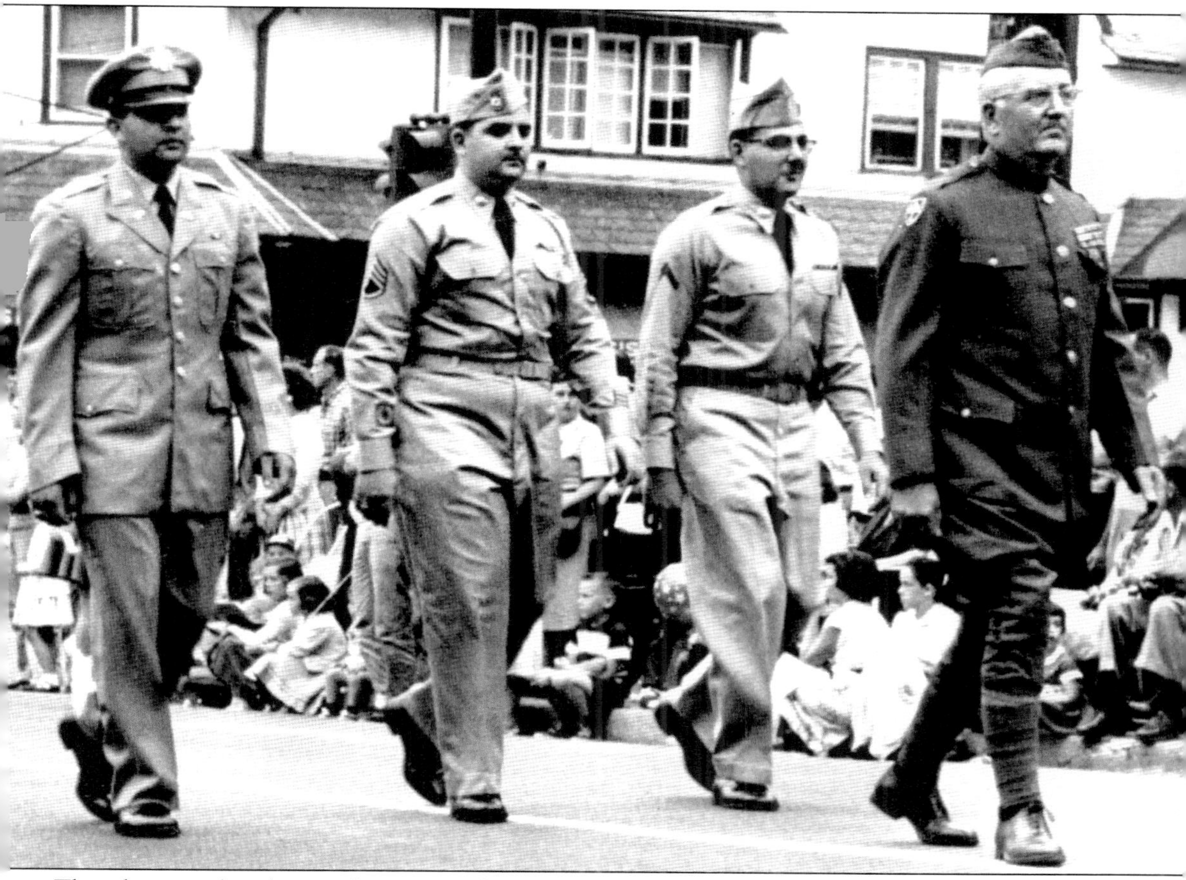

This photograph, taken at the corner of Keswick Avenue and Easton Road, shows the changes made to Edwin Johnson's original office building. The families of Glenside relied on each other, as happens in small towns. They stayed together through wars and floods, and through the Depression and its aftermath. One such family, the Conti family (owners of Casa Conti), is shown here on July 4, 1956, in the local parade. Pictured are Mr. Conti Sr., right, and his sons, from left to right, Frank, Joe, and Fred, leading the World War I veterans. The Glenside Fourth of July parade, which has been in existence for some 100 years, has the national reputation of being one of the most continuously held parades.

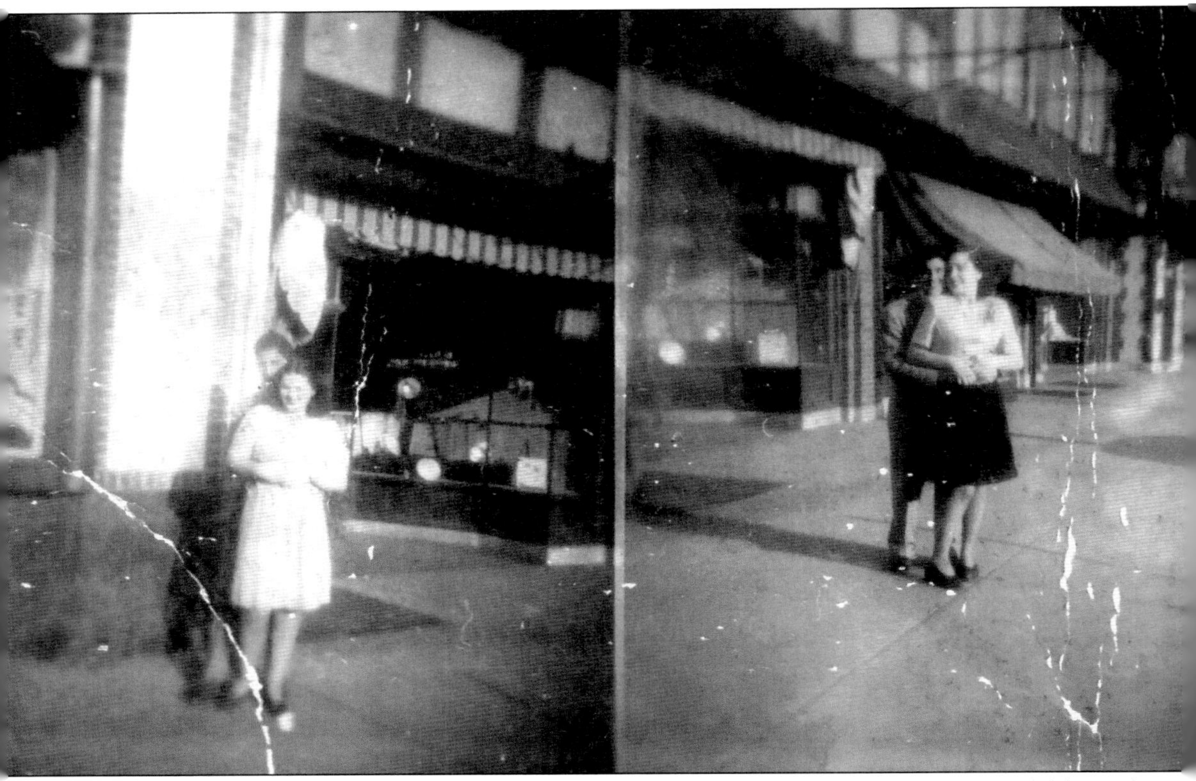

Through the late 1950s and into the 1960s, movies were an integral part of the social fabric of the life of children, teenagers, and adults. Movies were especially important to children. Taking children out for entertainment was an important ritual for families. Shown on the left are Millie Moffa and Joseph DeMarco on a date in front of the Keswick Theatre, and on the right Mary Moffa and an unknown friend. The Moffa sisters were daughters of an established Glenside businessman. A family tradition in the theater began when DeMarco and his brother Rocco ("Uncle Rocky") became ushers at the Glenside-Nixon Theatre. Millie and Joseph DeMarco got married. The family spent every New Year's Eve at the Keswick Theatre after having dinner at Casa Conti. Today, their daughter Janis DeMarco works at the Keswick Theatre as the concession and event manager. Two other daughters have worked part-time for the venue. Recently, two grandchildren, Alex and Lena, appeared on stage with Kevin Meany during his holiday Christmas show. The Gerding's photo shop is shown next door to the Keswick Theatre, on the left.

This program poses a slight mystery. Although the theater did not open until July, the program is dated March 25, and all of the movies advertised were released in 1955. Melvin Koff's daughters relate that he worked all day in Center City, Philadelphia, traveled home to the suburbs, ate, changed, and then went to work at the Keswick Theatre. This explains why there are two phone numbers on the program, one of which is local to Glenside and the other to Philadelphia.

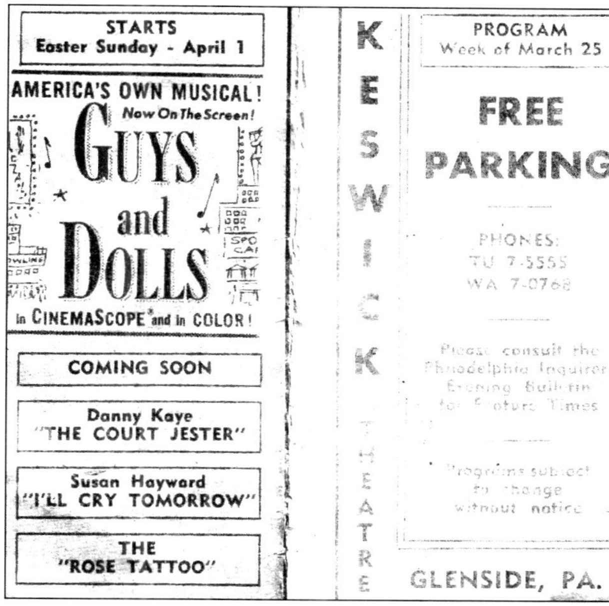

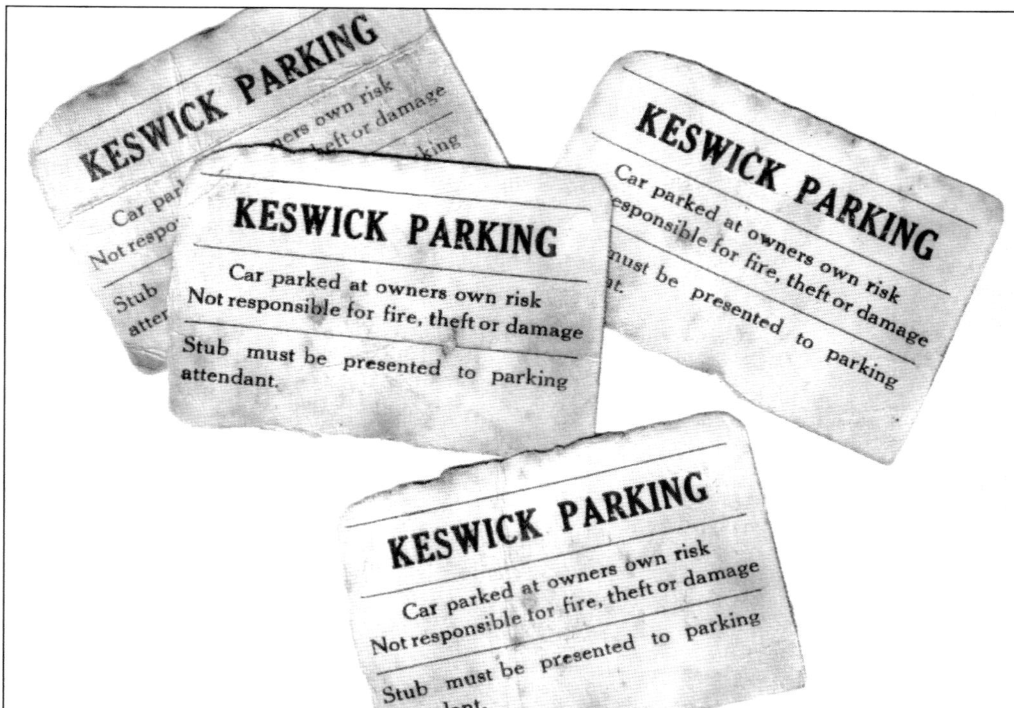

Free parking was still an important component in the Keswick's success, as parking space was less available at other venues. By the 1950s, the automobile was very much a part of the suburban lifestyle, much more so than it was in the 1920s. Many Glenside residents found jobs at the venue as parking attendants, ushers, or concession and ticket salespeople. A tale related about Melvin Koff's generosity is that if children did not have money for a ticket, they were given a little job to do in exchange for admittance.

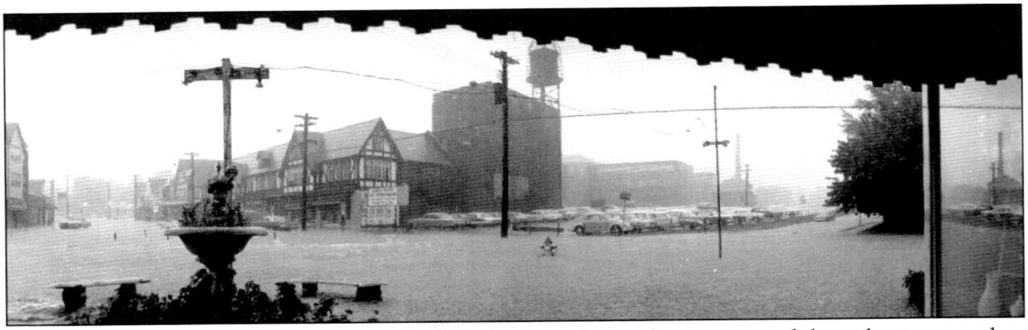

Penny's Flowers, the point from which this photograph is taken, is one of those businesses that grew alongside the Keswick Theatre. Vincent Pennypacker began his career selling flowers in front of the hardware store on Easton Road. His shop, initially located in the Keswick Theatre block, grew and expanded during its 50 years in business. Today, it graces the corner of Wharton Road and Keswick Avenue.

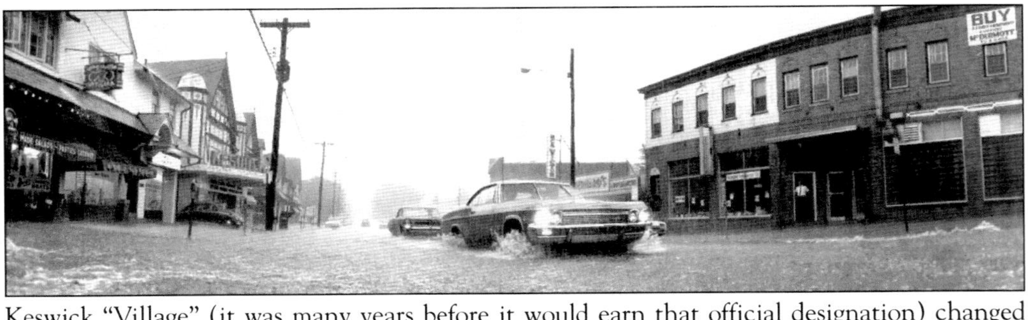

Keswick "Village" (it was many years before it would earn that official designation) changed a lot between the 1920s and the the mid-1900s. Glenside had many family-run businesses, including Gerhard Appliances, with the sign on the left directly across from the Keswick Theatre, and McDermott Real Estate, which served as the agent for the building with the "Buy" sign in the upper right corner. That particular building, having served by the 1950s as both a candy store and a tavern, had an organ in it that was used to entertain the patrons. The façade of these commercial buildings changed further over the next 20 years. The most striking difference was the elimination of the display windows protruding onto Keswick Avenue.

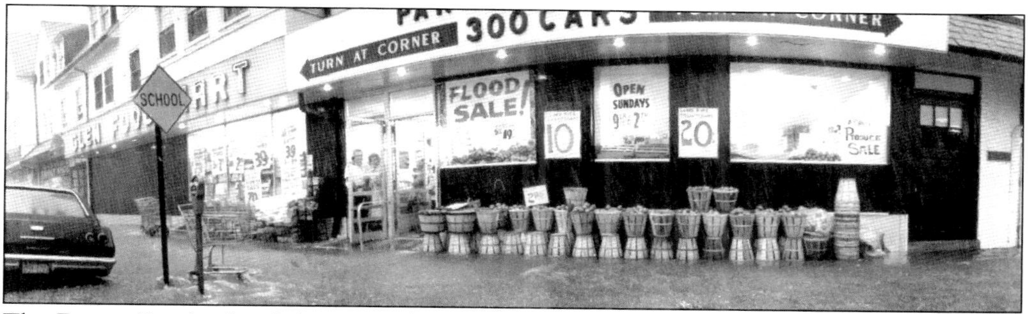

The Easton Road side of the original Johnson building also changed. The Glen Food Mart, shown here in 1967, wrapped around the Johnson Building. The food store was owned by Benjamin Blumenthal, who had purchased the theater in 1952, just days before the fire. Note the "Flood Sale" signs in the window. The Blumenthal family supported the Glenside Landmarks Society's effort to save the venue.

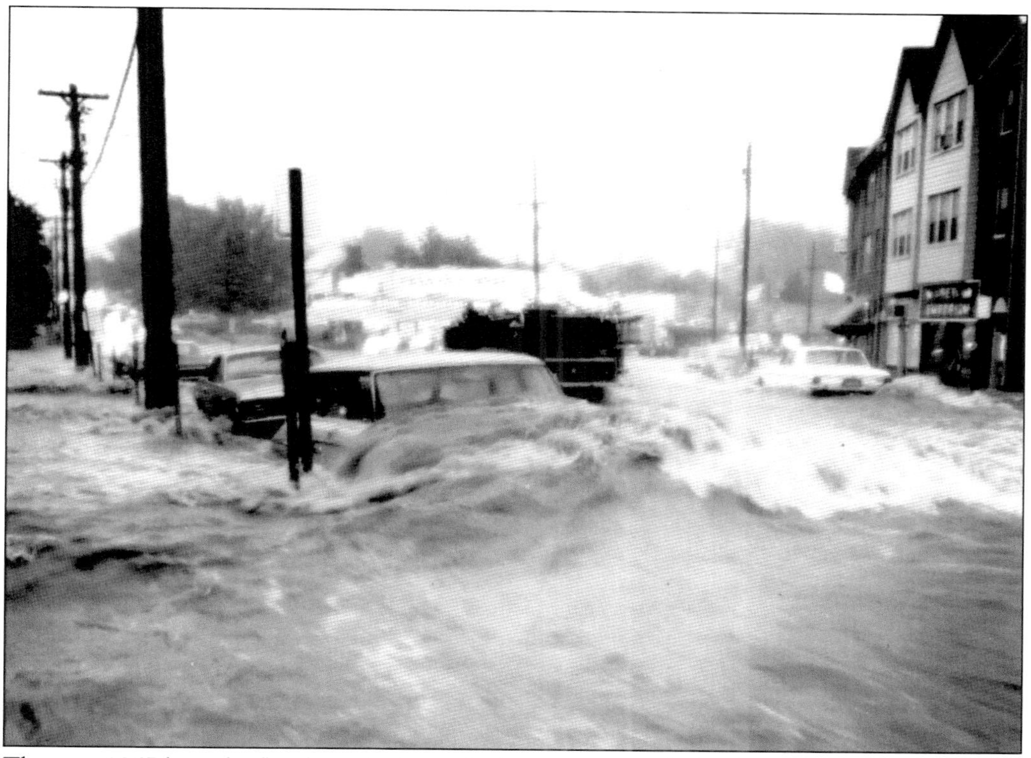

The year 1967 brought floods to rival the 1936 flood. As usual, the Keswick Avenue area was a collection point for the water. To make matters worse, there were two such floods, one in July and another in August. The station wagon in the photograph above is in front of the theater. In the far left distance is a small strip mall of shops and apartments, built by a developer who foresaw the growth of the area that would come with the reopening of the Keswick Theatre.

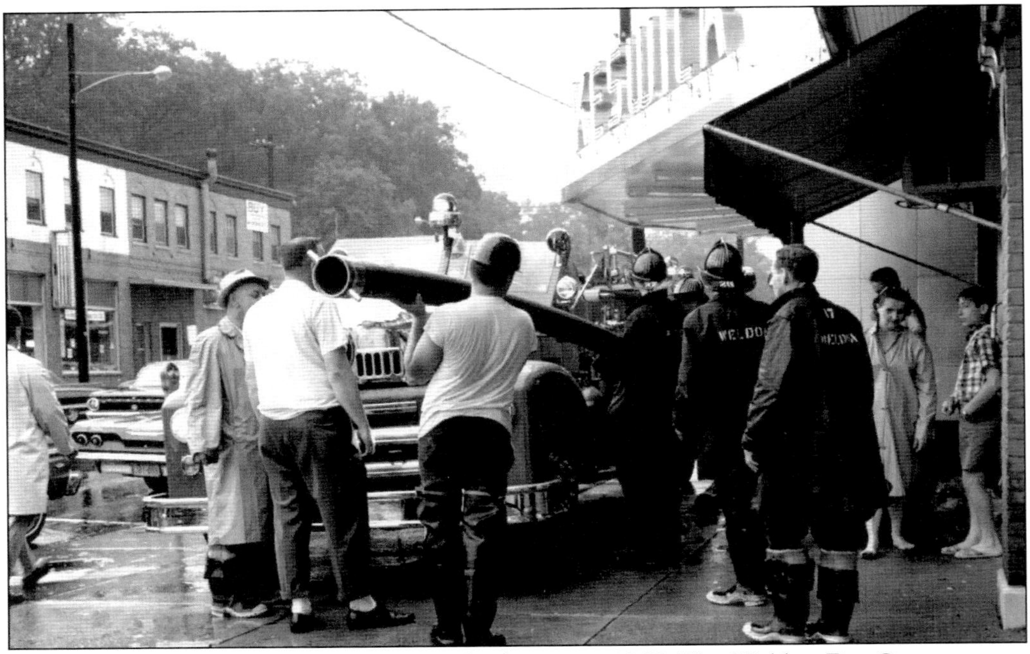

Firemen are shown in front of the Keswick Theatre in 1967. The Weldon Fire Company was called in after the flood to help pump the water from the building and the adjoining shops. Once again, the fire company came to the rescue of the theater, which, with the creek bed below it, floods during times of high water. Built as part of the Keswick's original design and maintained conscientiously to this day, a pump house works around the clock, keeping the stream of water moving.

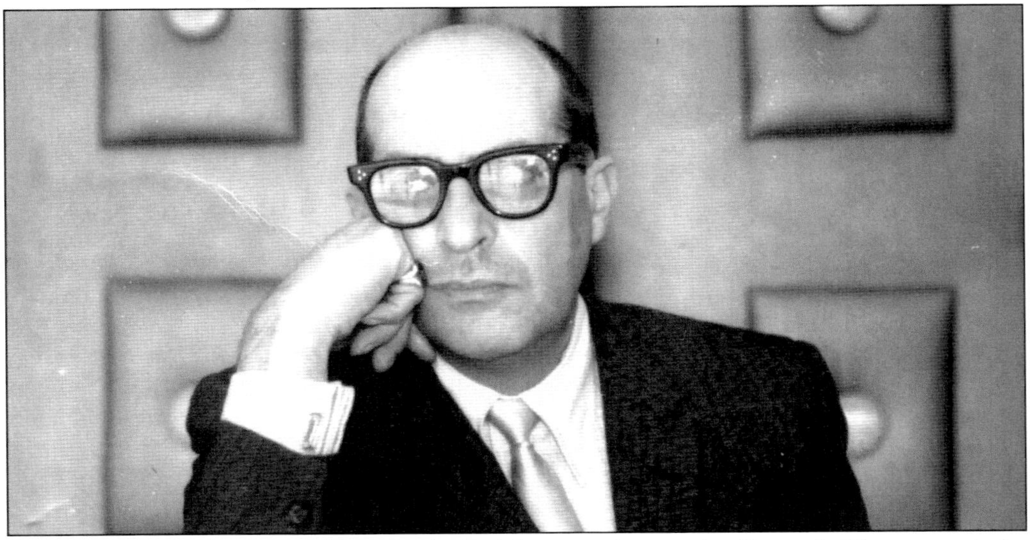

Melvin Koff, by the time of his death, had kept vigil over the Keswick Theatre and the surrounding shops for almost 25 years. His generosity was legendary, his business acumen was proven, and his ability to keep the building viable was exemplary. The Keswick Theatre had been established in the community for almost 50 years. With Koff's passing, the Keswick Theatre once again looked for direction and leadership.

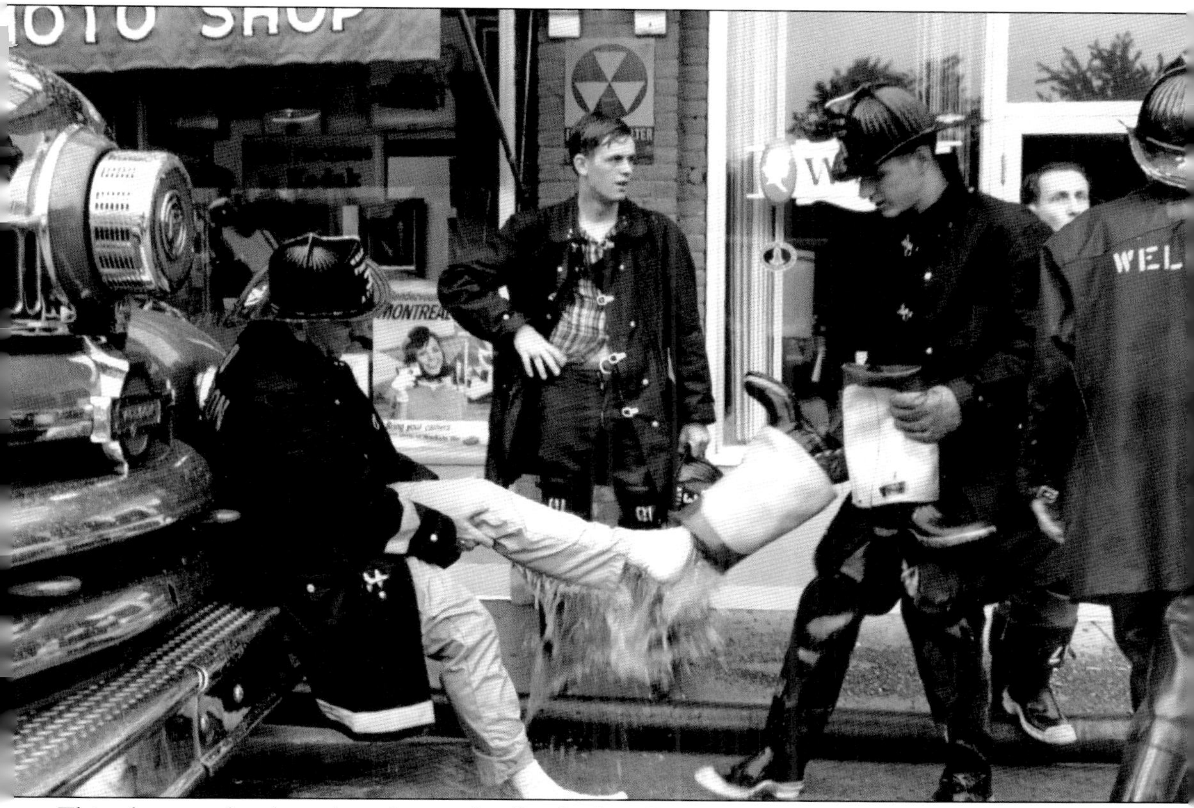

This photograph, also taken during the flood of 1967, is representative of the community. Volunteer firefighters have come together to save the buildings. Dick Gerding's photo shop is in shown the back left. Gerding's photographs and negatives of the history of the area were destroyed in the flood, which also affected the rear retaining wall of the theater. The business in the back right is a beauty salon, which Melvin Koff nurtured by working out a reduced rent for the owner. The bomb shelter sign speaks to a day and age when the Keswick Theatre was deemed one of the few buildings in the area strong enough to protect citizens in case of a nuclear attack. This coming together of citizens to help each other strangely foreshadows what the community would be asked to do in a few years' time.

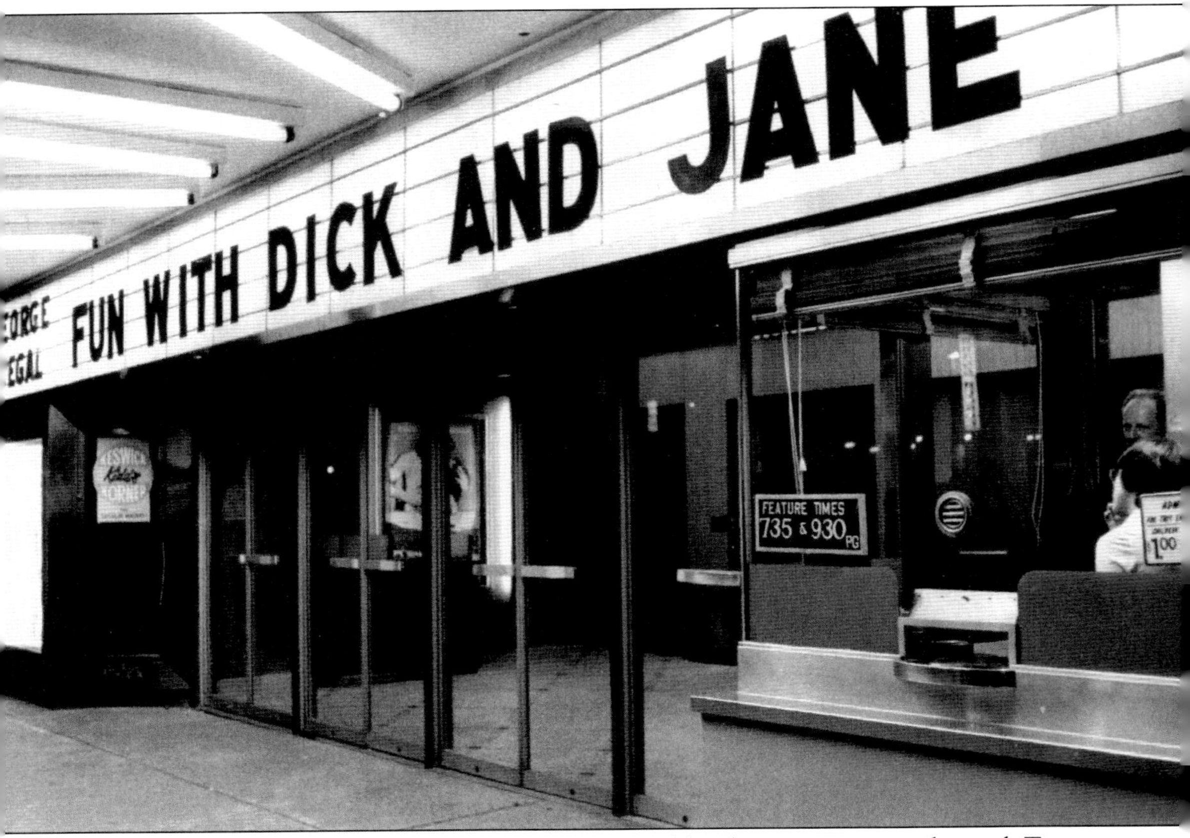

As the 1960s moved into the 1970s, the dynamic of family entertainment changed. Teenagers went to concerts and malls; parents watched television. With the advent of cable, videocassette recorders, home entertainment systems, and live entertainment at mega-concerts, the movie houses saw a decline. Families, especially those with two working parents, began to value their time together at home as something very special. Soon, multiplexes (venues with many small movie-screening rooms) became the answer to the dwindling audiences. Plans were on the drawing board to turn the Keswick Theatre into a multiple-room theater toward the end of Melvin Koff's stewardship. This photograph, taken in 1980, shows the Kiddie Corner sign, the prices of admission greatly discounted to as low as $1, and no waiting lines. The view also shows the redesigned outer lobby.

Three

A Performing Arts Center

After Melvin Koff passed away, Abington Federal Savings and Loan Bank purchased the shops, apartments, and theater building as part of a plan to build a branch bank in the area. The plan called for demolishing the auditorium and seating space of the building to make room for more parking and green space that were required by the zoning ordinance.

Although the plan included saving the façade, the primary function of the theater would be lost forever. In late 1980, the Glenside Landmarks Society stepped in and managed to save the building from demolition. However, by July 1981, the Keswick, now with 1,248 seats, was again in need of funding. The programming had begun to change as well. Magician and scientist Richard Gustafson was presenting Vaude 81. Meanwhile, Denis Cooke recalls attending a concert by Kenn Kweeder & His Secret Kids at the venue. The admission was $4. This experience inspired Cooke for the first time to contribute to the theater's revitalization.

With a six-month lease extension, the Glenside Landmarks Society looked to hire a fund-raiser. Then, "Three private businessmen stepped in to secure the building until May, 1982," according to a newspaper report. The businessmen organized as the Telford Industrial Authority.

By 1982, the Keswick was down to the wire again. The Glenside Landmarks Society managed to obtain the building on June 30, 1982, formed a nonprofit organization called the Keswick Theatre, and in 1983 reported some successes, including regular booking of the venue. Still, the venture was $18,000 in debt and looking to improve operations. Board member Tom MacCabe, who later became the owner of the venue, is quoted in the February 21, 1983, edition of the *Philadelphia Inquirer* as saying, "It can be a total living arts center that can benefit the people . . . by giving them an opportunity to participate in the fine arts. It's too important to not make it work."

In 1983, the Glenside Landmarks Society obtained certification for the building from the National Parks Service. The theater was listed on the National Register of Historic Places. In the application, Paul Bunting notes: "The Keswick Theatre's social significance stems from its having been a unique neighborhood theater which has played an unusually important role in its community's development. Serving an area that anthropologist Margaret Mead has described as 'an atypical American Suburb' (because of the way it has maintained its own distinct identity with a small town flavor)." This is most directly seen in the support given by more than 300 individuals and businesses in the form of time, money, energy, in-kind support, and patronage during the Glenside Landmarks Society's stewardship of the venue.

Full-season subscriptions were sold from 1981 through 1986, and the Keswick was a busy venue. Then, on June 26, 1986, the *Philadelphia Inquirer* reported that the "Lady Keswick" had been sold at public auction. Ginny Wiegand wrote, "For almost 60 years, the faithful came—through Depression, through war and peace and prosperity, through the crazy 60s, the selfish 70s and the yuppified 80s. Now, the once-grand Keswick Theatre is closed up tight and falling apart." Cheltenham Bank, the only bidder, had acquired the property.

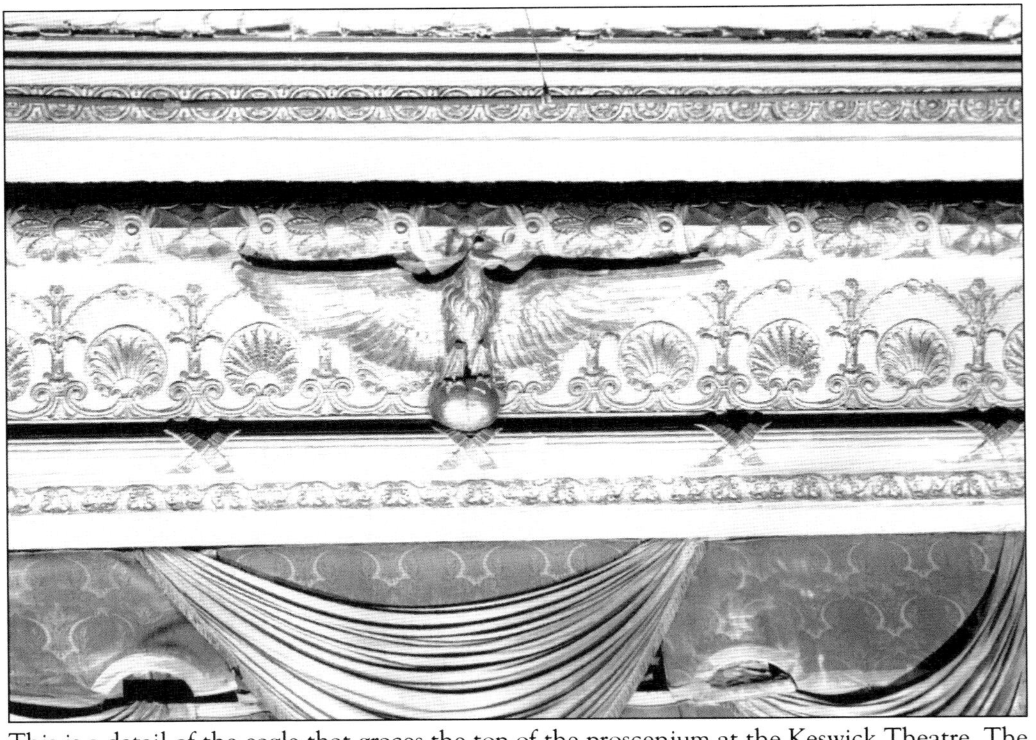

This is a detail of the eagle that graces the top of the proscenium at the Keswick Theatre. The plaster image has survived despite fire, flood, redesign, and curtains being mounted over the stage. For 75 years, the eagle has graced this point of the building, watching over the stage.

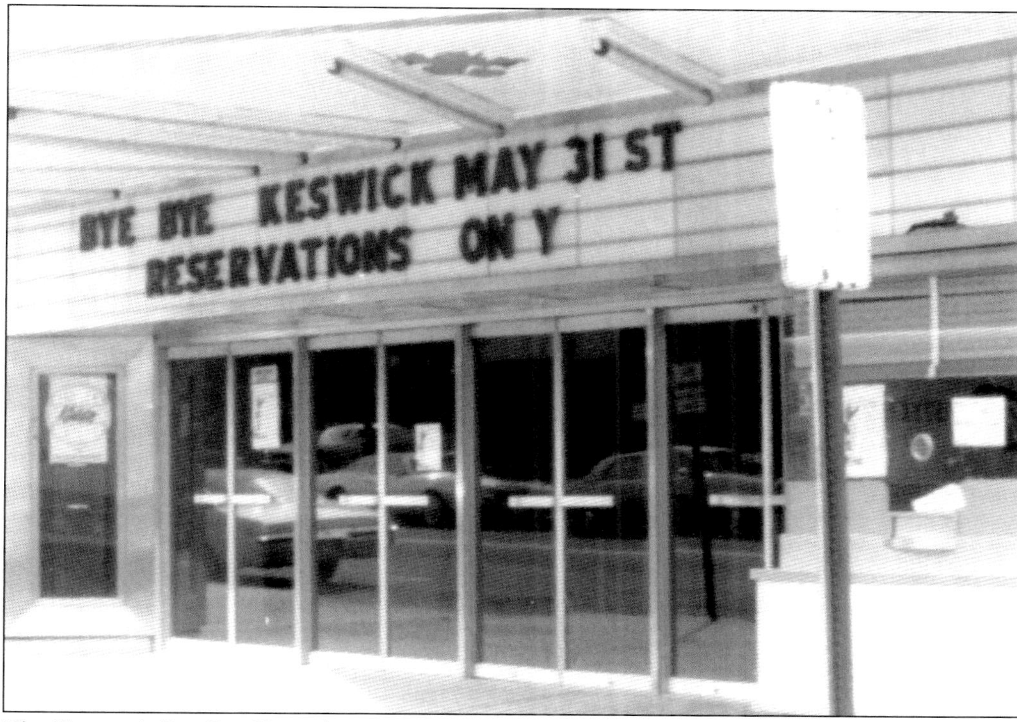

The Kiwanis's *Bye Bye Keswick* event turned into a grass-roots effort by concerned citizens to save the venue for its intended purpose: the performing arts and film. From this gathering of melancholy folks ready to say goodbye came a battle cry to save the Keswick. The building once again wrapped its arms around the local citizens, and many came forward to assist with the effort. The event was held May 31, 1980, and by June 6, 1980, the township had agreed to listen to the plan of the newly formed Glenside Landmarks Society to save the venue. The township commissioners also agreed to grant variances to the bank for the parking and green spaces if the group could come up with the funding necessary to purchase the building. The demolition order was held.

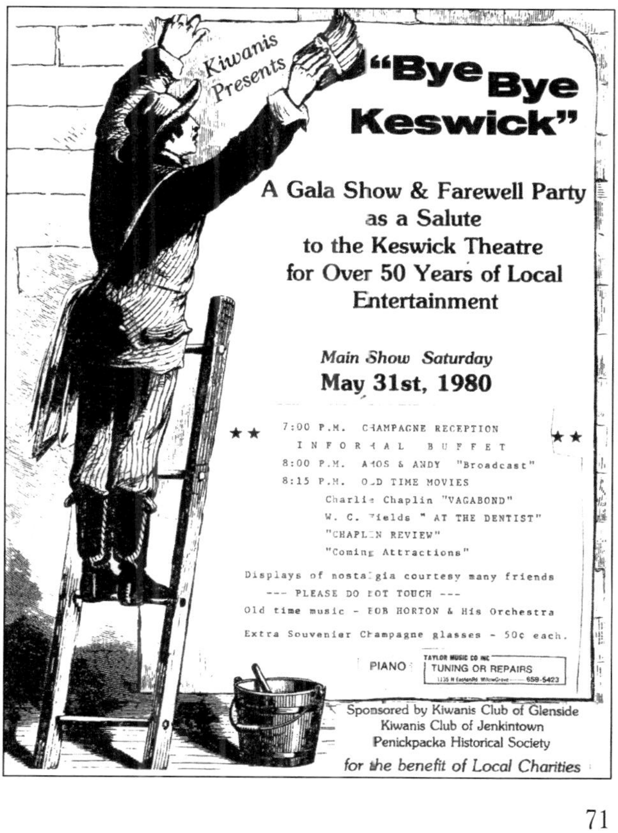

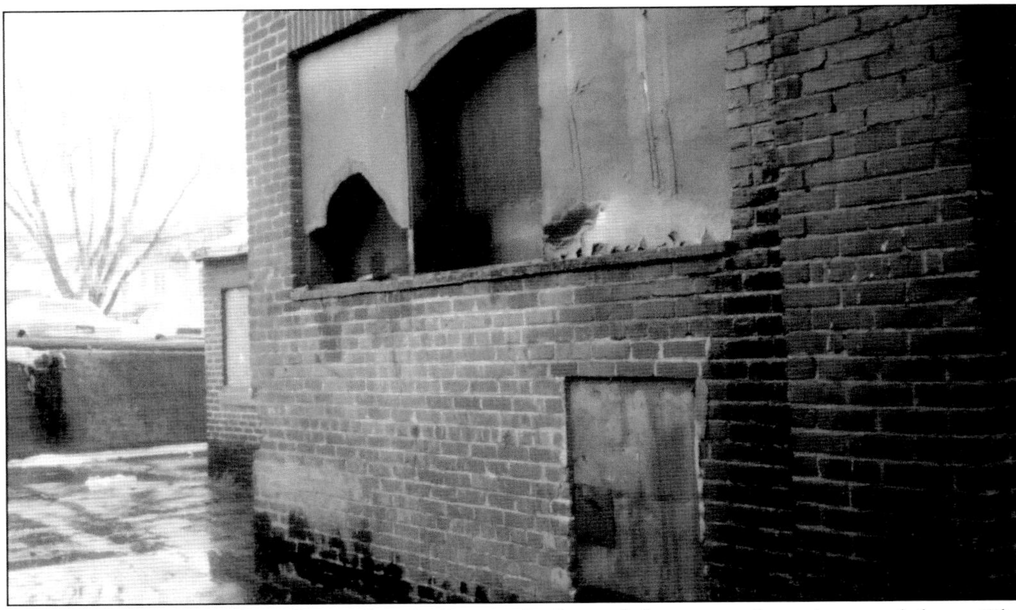

By July 9, 1980, the Glenside Landmarks Society had raised the money for a six-month lease. The township granted the variance just days before the demolition was originally scheduled to begin. The facility, however, had grave problems, as shown in this photograph of the original icehouse.

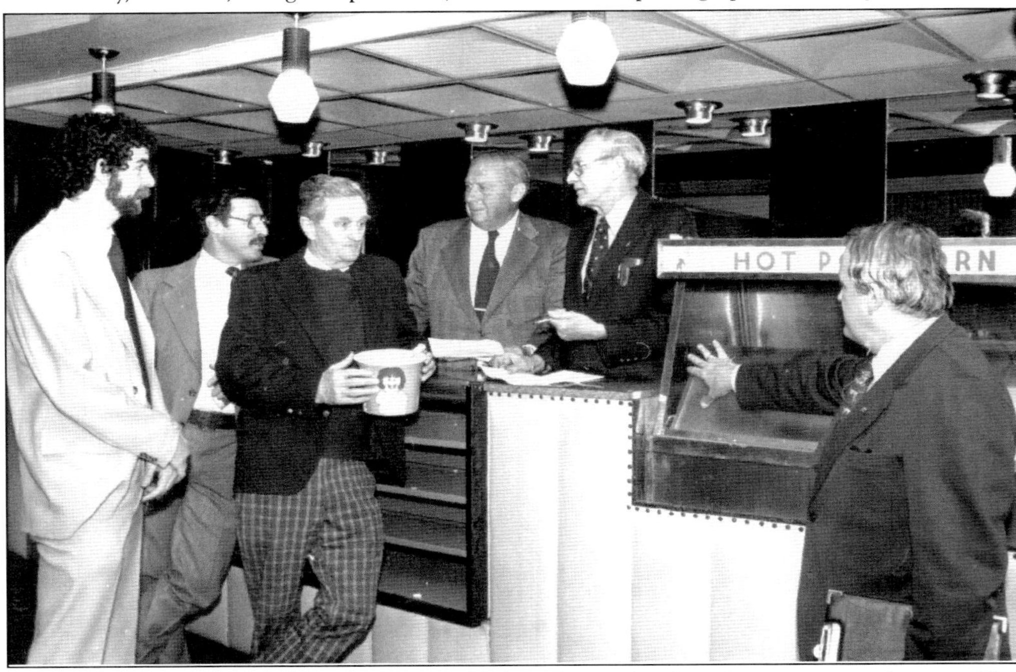

On December 12, 1980, the manager reported to the media that the venue was showing films every weekend. The battle was not over, however. The society needed to raise the money to purchase and renovate the building—reportedly about $2.4 million in all. Shown here at the concession stand are members of the Kiwanis Club that held the *Bye Bye Keswick* show, many of whom went on to lead the effort to save the venue.

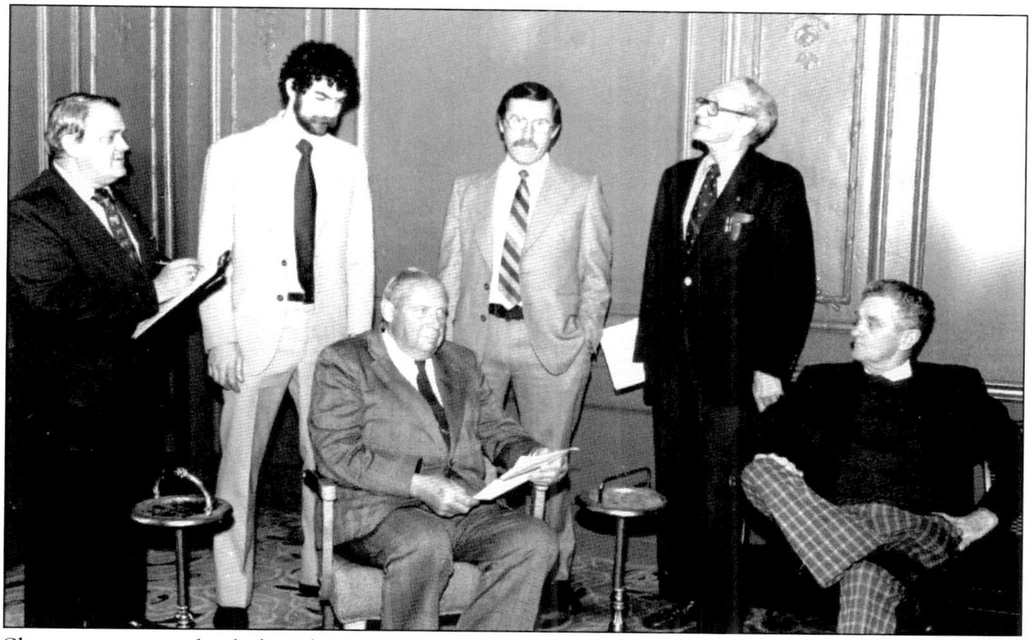

Shown again in the ladies' lounge, above, and in the projection booth, below, are the same five men. They represented a core of concerned citizens including Edwin Johnson's nephew N. Bruce Weir, Margaret Wyn Betz, Leon Clemmer, Craig Nicholson, and the Blumenthals, Alexanders, Brackinridges, Gerhards, Pennypackers, Clarks, Zumpanos, and Henders. The building had been separated, for the first time, from the other property on the block. Rental revenues and other sources of income would not help support the theater. Previous owners had the ability to supplement their finances with this income.

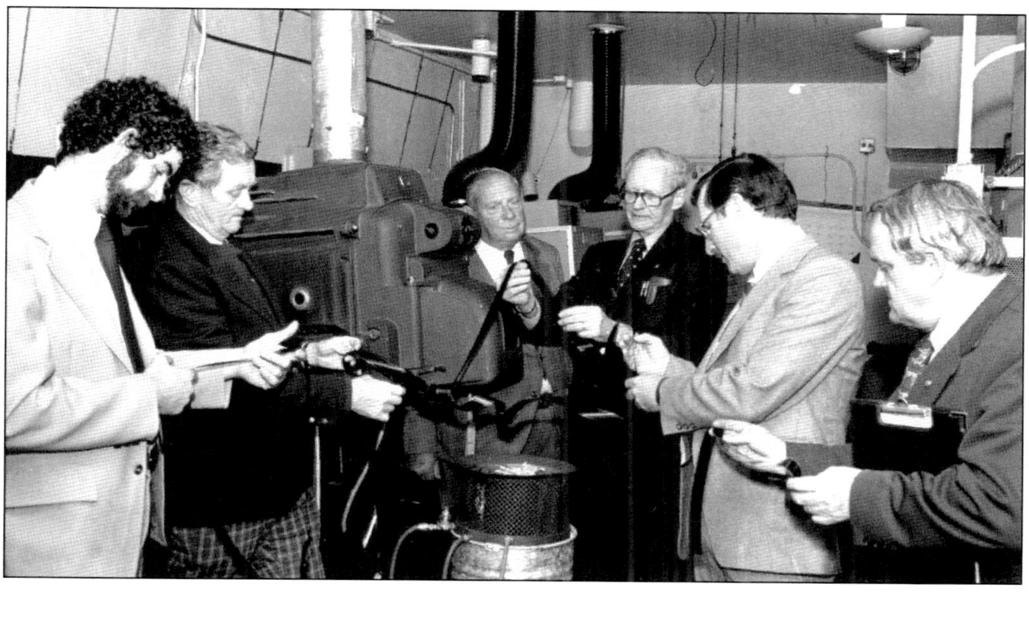

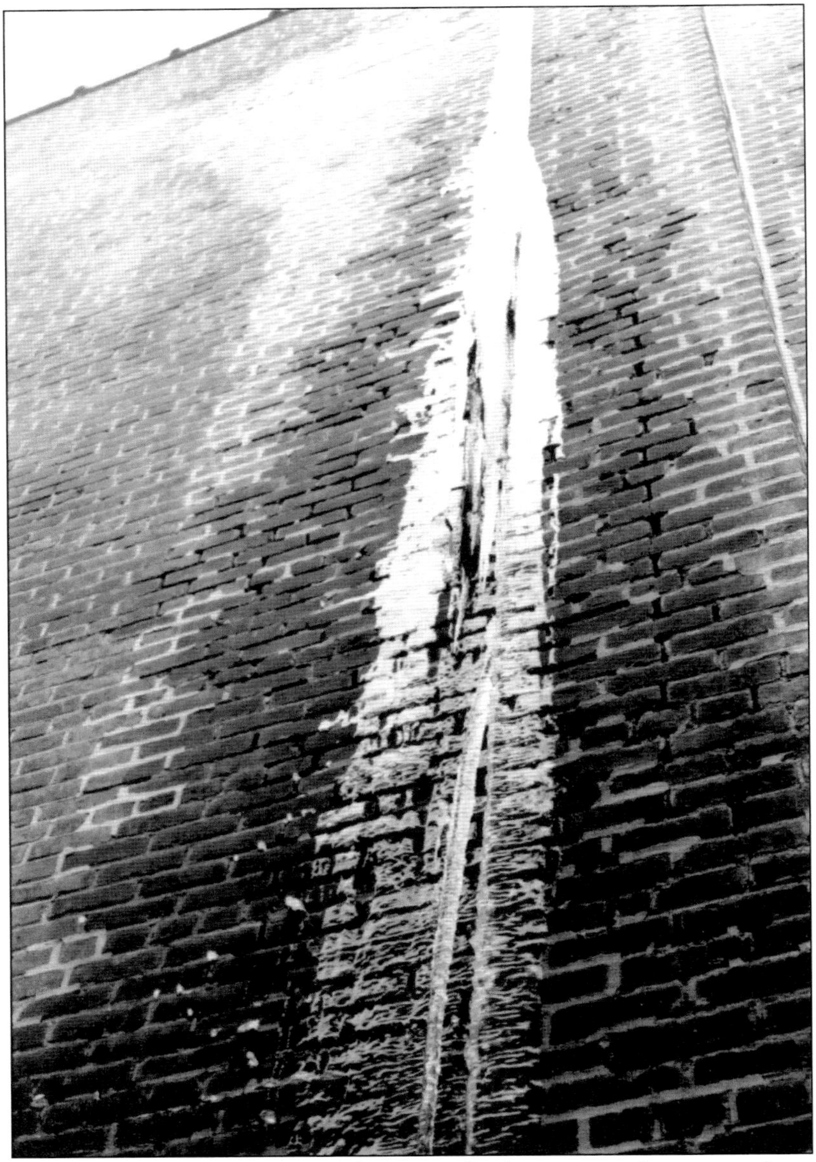

This image of ice penetrating the wall of the Keswick Theatre stage house is indicative of the magnitude of work that the venue needed. Repairs were necessary to the roofs (eight in all), and inside finishing work was needed to restore the theater to its original beauty. Despite the obstacles, an optimistic completion date of 1984 was set. The time was ripe, historically, for this movement. The 1978 tax credit laws made ventures such as this financially beneficial to private investors. As the "grand palaces of gaudiness" began to turn 50 years old, an entire generation began to reach out to their past and the places that held so many memories for them, many of which were being replaced with parking lots and office buildings. (Such was the fate of Philadelphia's Earle, Mastbaum, Carman, and Stanley theaters.) A national trend toward downtown revitalization to attract visitors back into the cities was also in the news. Articles about the fate of the movie palaces appeared in *Time*, the *Saturday Evening Post*, and *U.S. News & World Report*.

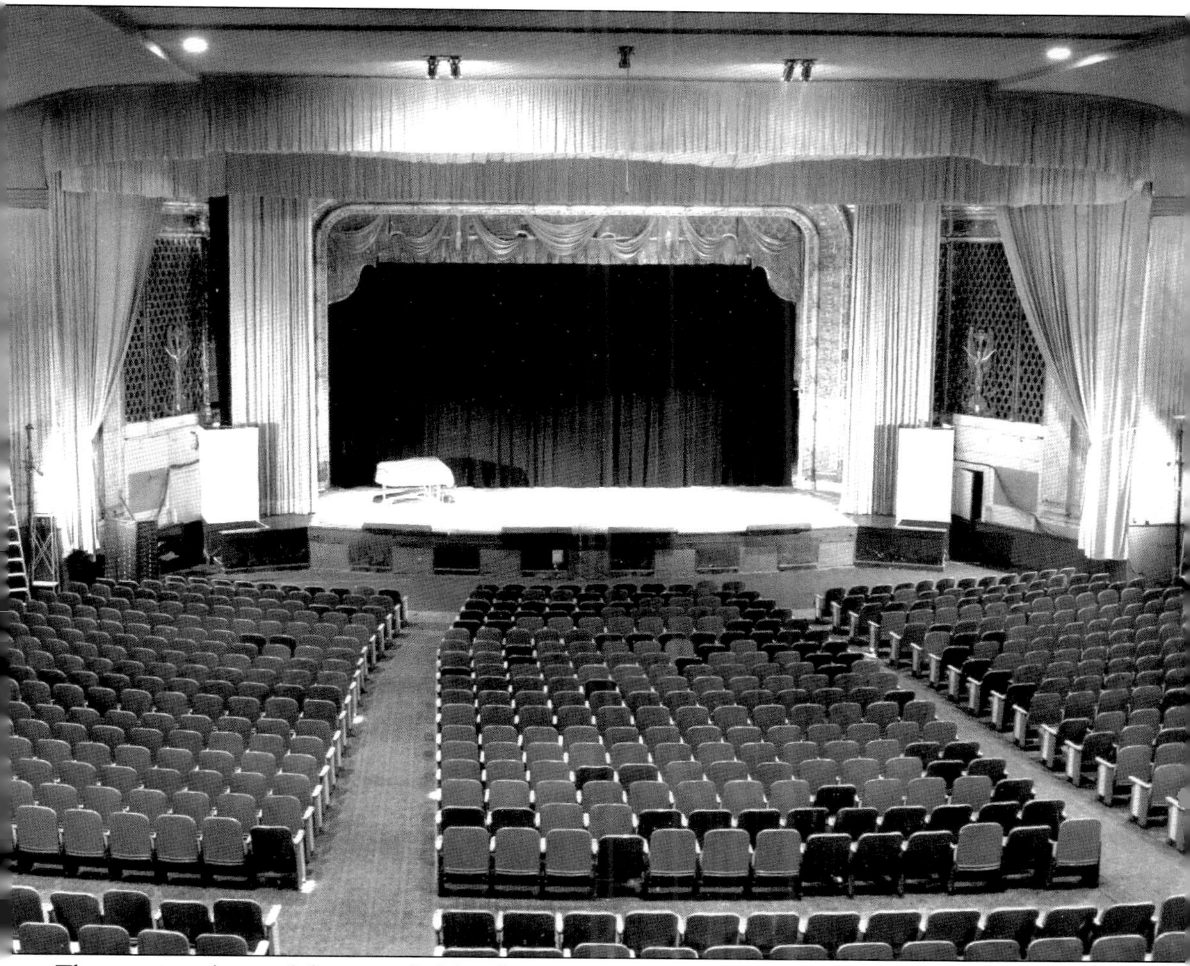

The movie palaces of days past held collective social memories for two generations, as they moved from vaudeville to film. Theaters were used for graduations, special social events, and romantic evenings. Teenagers grew up there, and their children followed. Tearing the theaters down was not like removing a blighted factory—it was tearing away at the heart of these generations. Words like "splendiferous," "gaudy," and "gilded" began to reach into the hearts of Disney fans and of would-be Clark Gables and Marlene Dietrichs. The League of Historic American Theatres was founded, and its work was aimed at saving these venues. Perhaps George Rapp, an owner of the Chicago architectural firm that designed theaters, summed it up best in a May 5, 1980, article in *Time*. He said the theaters were "a shrine to democracy, where there are not privileged patrons." Rapp designed the Omaha Orpheum, the St. Louis Theatre, and the Penn Theater in Pittsburgh, venues that reached from sea to sea. Saving each building was a serious victory for those involved.

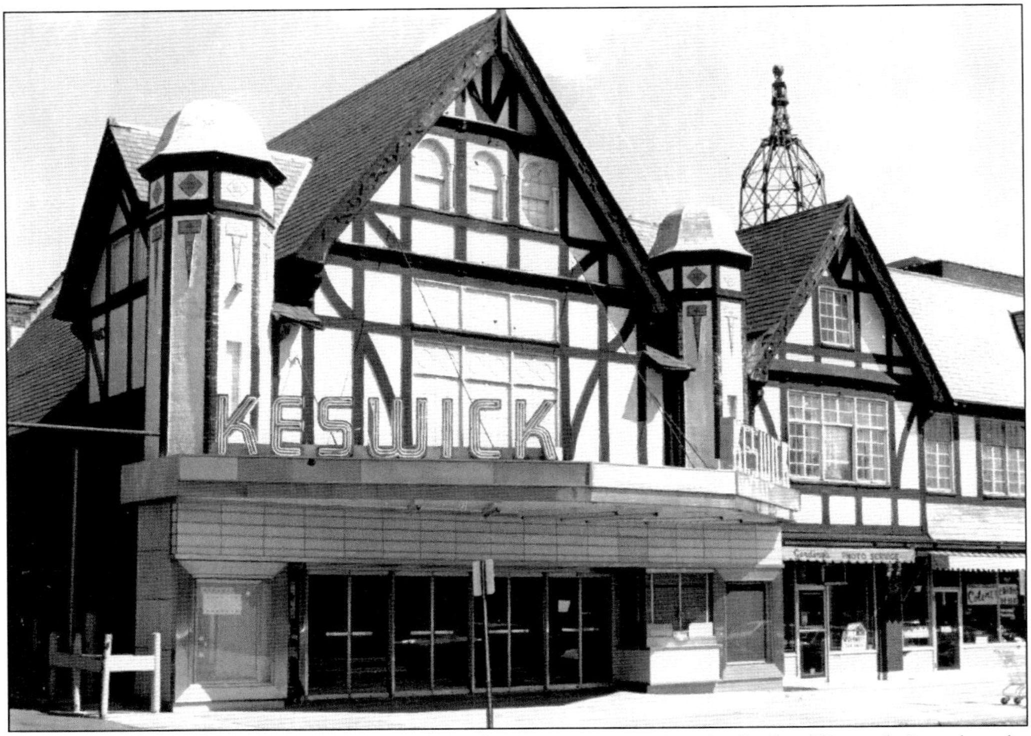

A closed and shuttered building—this was the environment to which the Glenside Landmarks Society members brought their efforts. They faced a strong structure with major problems that had caused it to deteriorate in value. The theater was built at a cost of $500,000; the building and stores were sold in 1952 for $315,000 (after a major fire); to hold off the theater's demolition, the bank was looking for $150,000 in 1980.

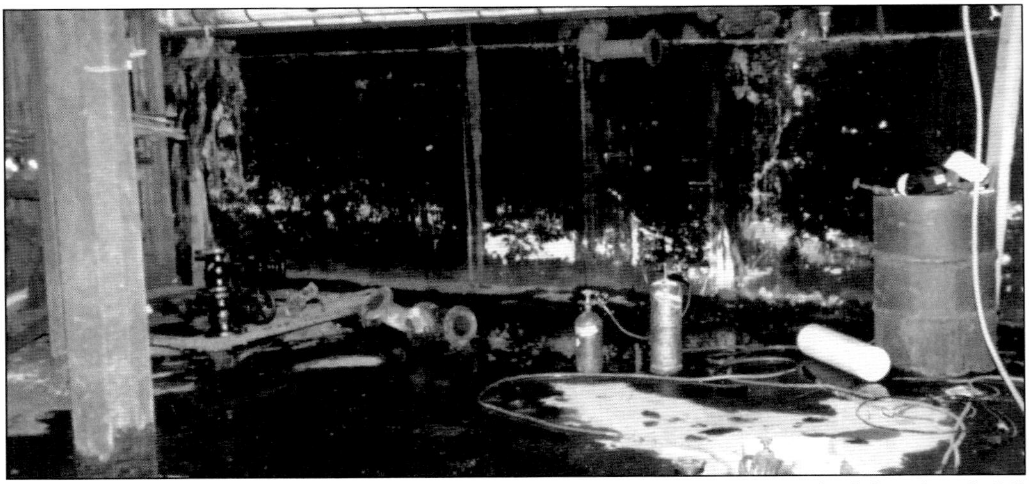

The basement is shown here in disrepair. The people undertaking this effort had their hands full in just bringing the building up to code and staffing it with personnel who could care for it on a regular basis (such as making sure the pump house was in working condition). It was several years before the necessary staff could be put in place, and thus, the building was likely opened only on an as-needed basis.

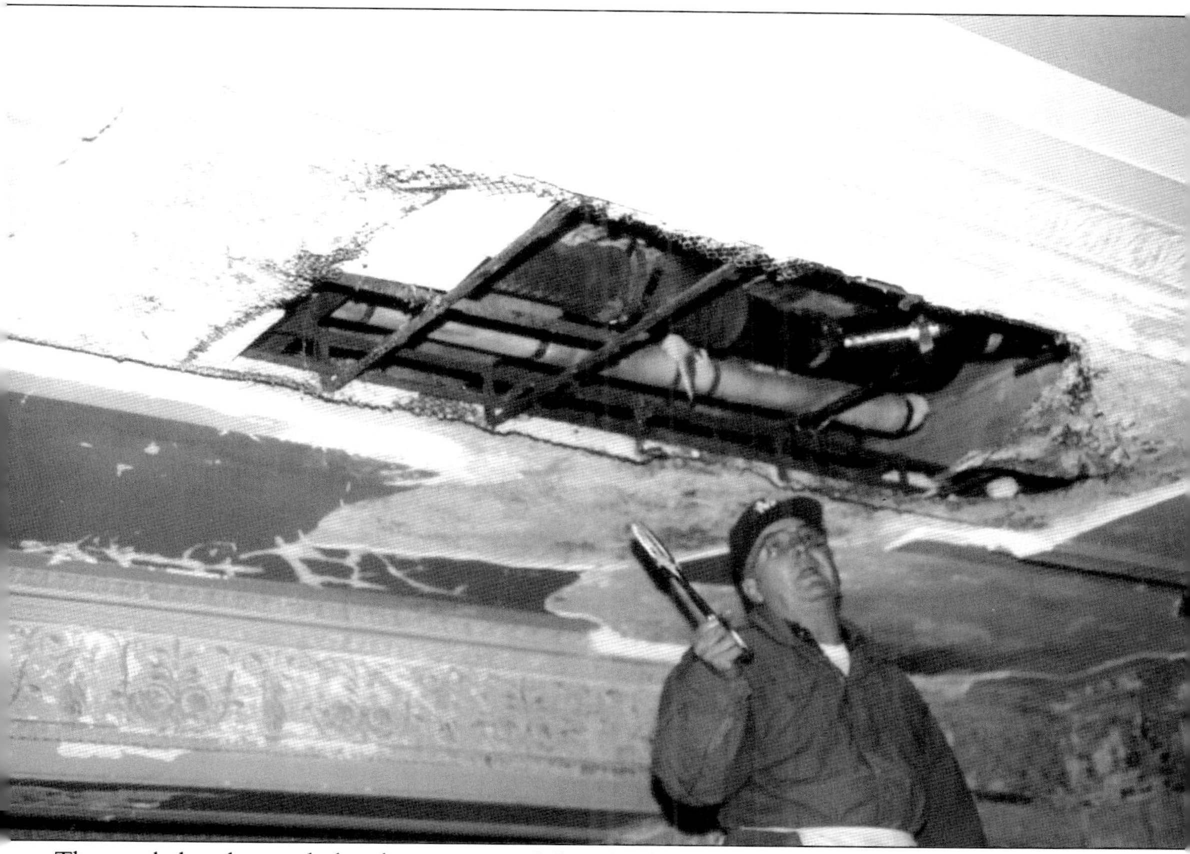

The puzzled and overwhelmed expression of this plumber is what has become known as "the Keswick look." Repairing the building remained the greatest obstacle. Just heating the venue was an economic crisis. Charles Schrader, who worked with the original society, began seeing events at the venue when he was seven years old. Vince Pennypacker, also involved, was fourteen years old when the venue opened. Lawyers, accountants, business owners, magicians, and tradespeople all came together for this common goal. George Shelps, who was involved in the film industry, secured refurbished projectors, as the originals had been sold off by the bank prior to the building's acquisition by the Glenside Landmarks Society.

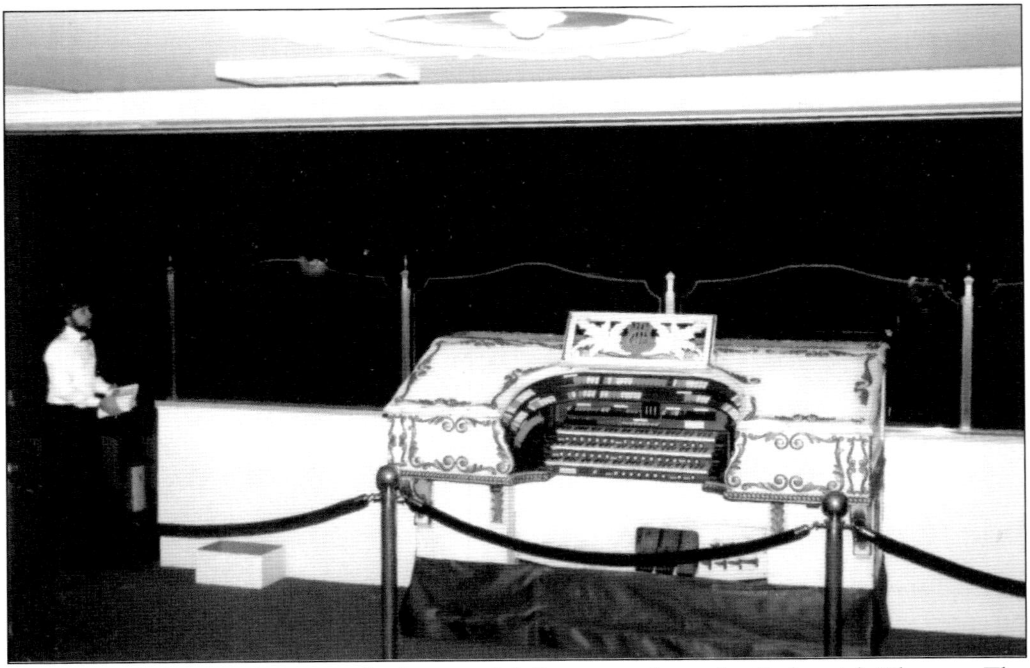

The Keswick became home to the historic Moller organ from the Sedgewick Theatre. The Sedgewick, a historic venue in the Germantown section of Philadelphia, was also in the process of being saved. However, its auditorium had been gutted and the organ had remained in storage. The organ found a home at the Keswick, albeit in the lobby for a year or so.

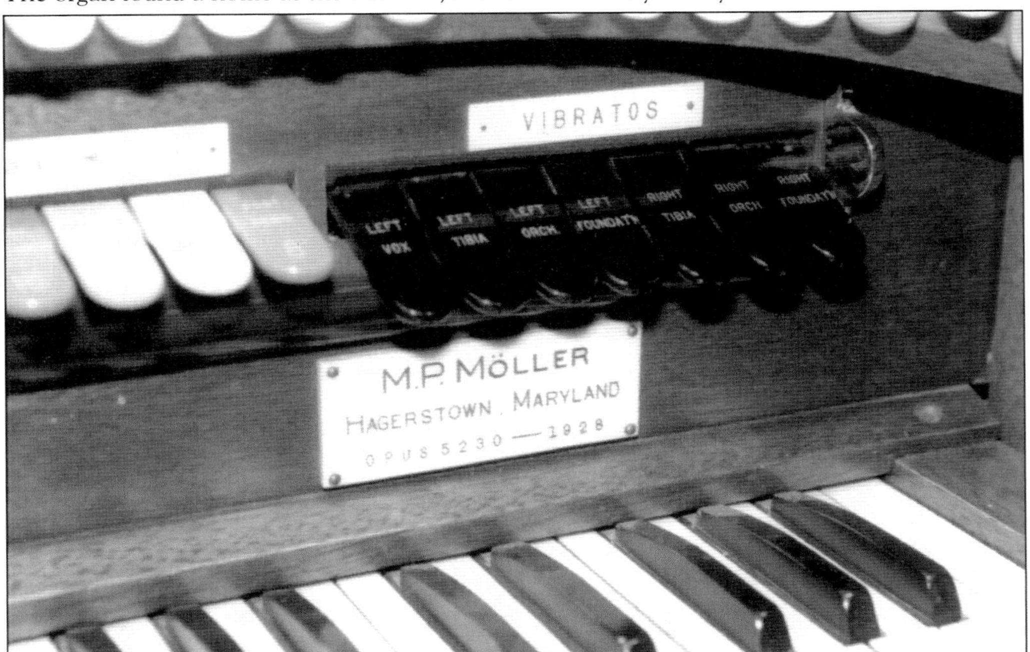

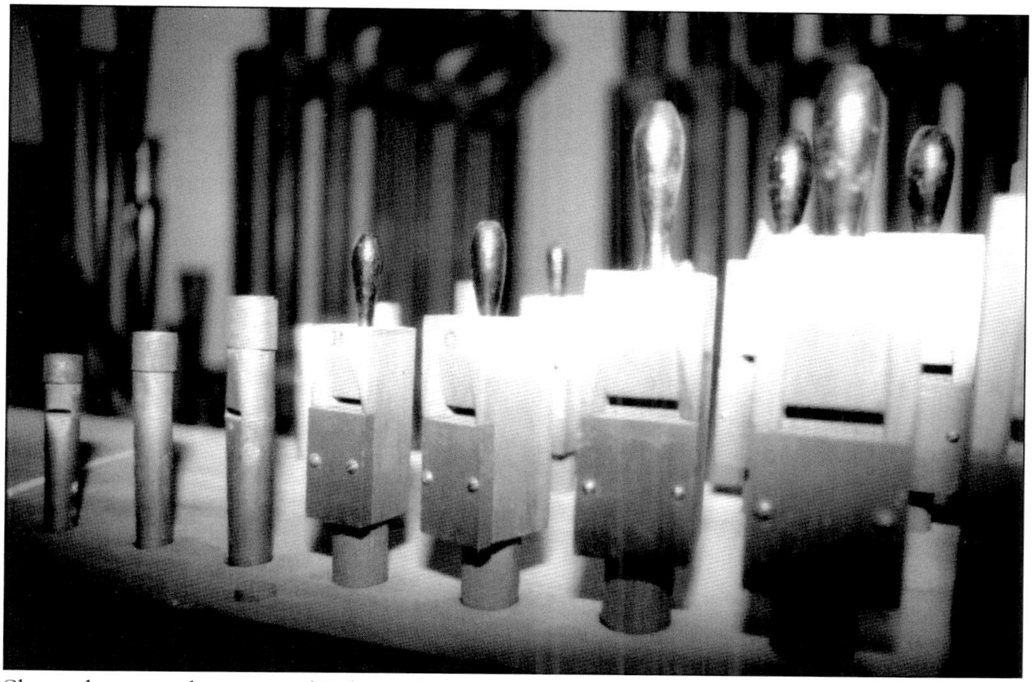

Shown here are the organ whistles and pipes that made their way into the organ chambers of the theater behind the gilt screens. The history of the organ restoration mirrors some of the other tribulations of the Keswick's restoration during this nonprofit period. The Delaware Valley Organ Society made the organ available, but the instrument went without restoration for many years while the various groups got organized. Now installed, the organ was rededicated in May 2004. Like the Keswick Theatre, it is both an engineering and an architectural marvel in need of care and attention.

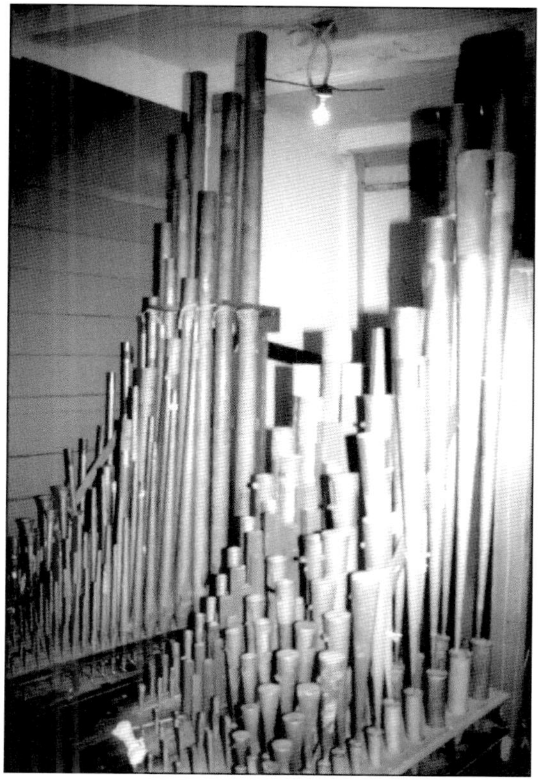

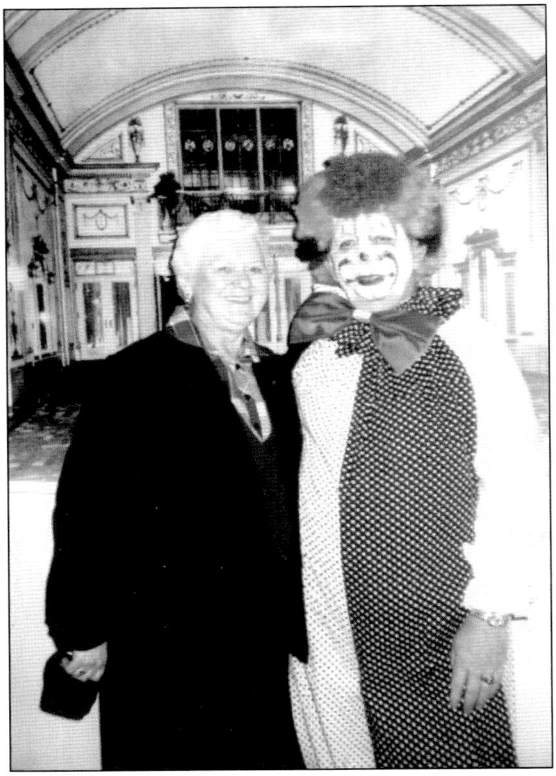

The Glenside Landmarks Society gathered up its most interested members and, despite internal turmoil during the six-plus years that it had possession of the building, accomplished its prime objective: saving the theater from demolition. Through the dedicated work of its members, the society established a performing arts group that presented local talent to the community. Shown at the left are local residents Peg and George Bodman, who volunteered to take tickets. George Bodman has served in this capacity for over 15 years. Shown below is Joan Gustafson, wife of Richard Gustafson. The Gustafsons were leaders in the Glenside Landmarks Society's efforts and, later, were owners of the venue.

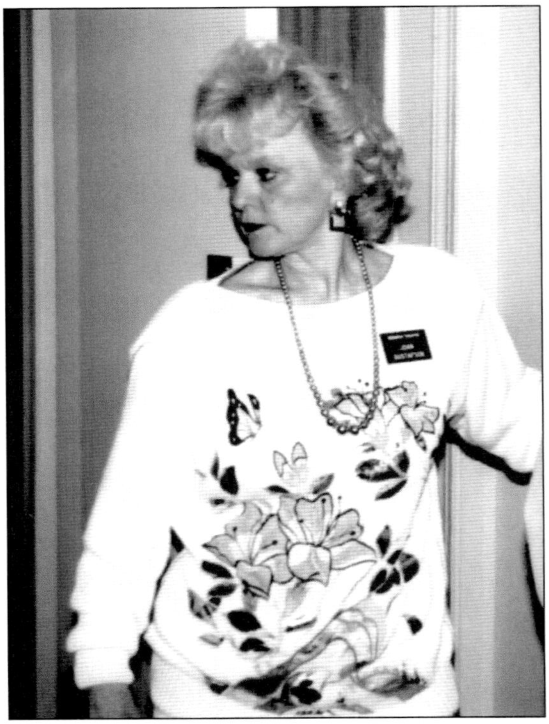

On December 13, 1987, the *Philadelphia Inquirer* reported that "Five owners stood around a kerosene heater in the lobby of the Keswick Theatre." The five were Harry Barbin, John Drury, Richard Gustafson, Elliott Hirsh, and Tom MacCabe. Due to family and business bligations, Drury left the venture early on. Pictured here are Debbie Hirsh and Elliott Hirsh at work in the venue. In the early days, the owners did any jobs that were necessary to make the venue successful.

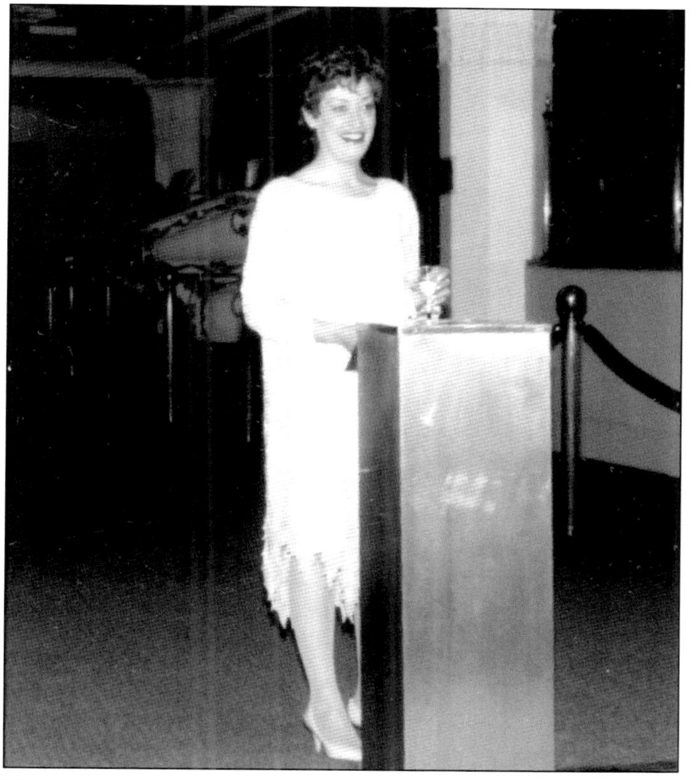

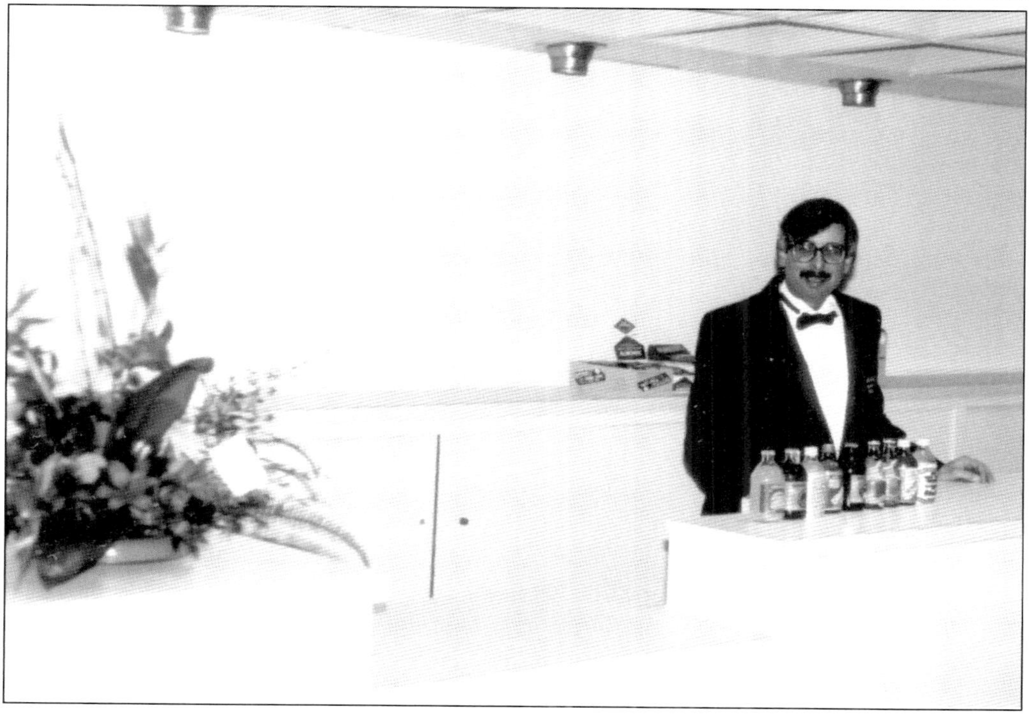

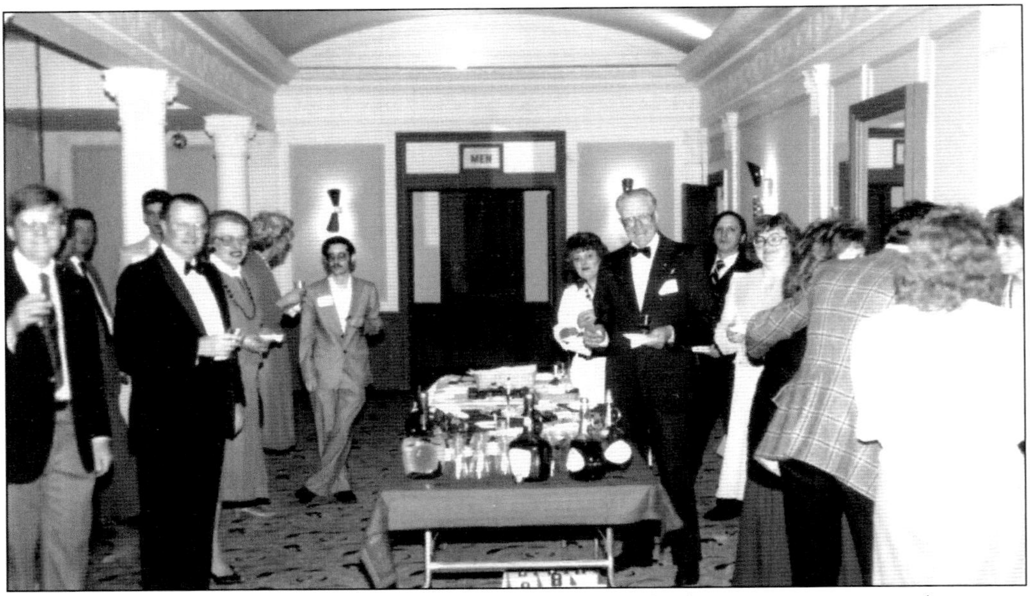

By March 1988, the owners had decided to open the Keswick Theatre as a commercial venture. Shown is the opening reception in progress in the mezzanine. Harry Barbin stands in the foreground, second from the left.

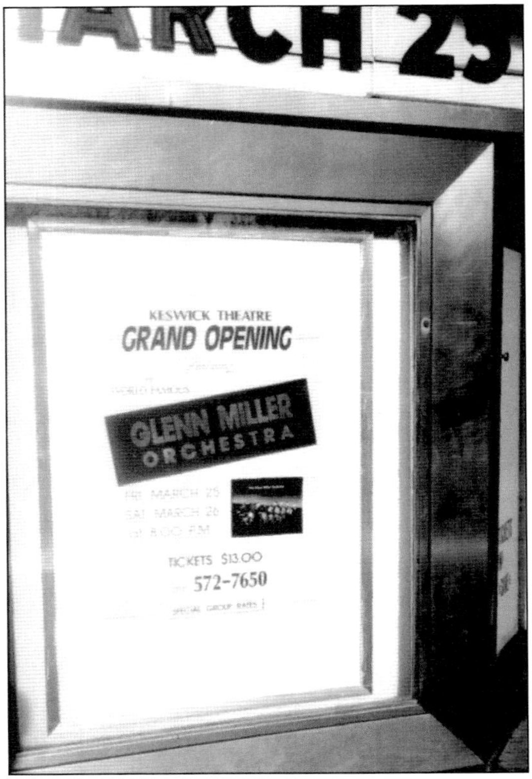

With careful business planning and much time volunteered by those specializing in financial, legal, and technological matters, the venue began to flourish. Over time, it became the "jewel of Glenside" once again. Taking a practical approach to show business, the new owners focused not only on the business of the show but also on venue management.

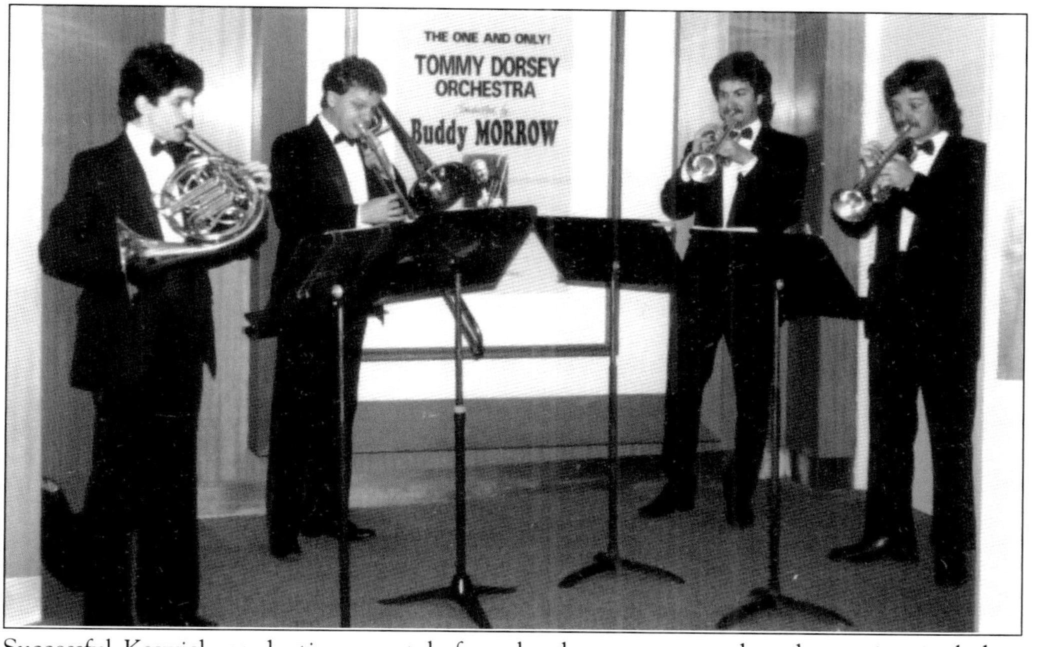

Successful Keswick productions, rentals from local promoters, and anchor series, including annual performances of *The Nutcracker*, with Dance Elite of Doylestown, and *Jesus Christ Superstar*, with Midnight Productions of Bucks County, brought stability and growth to the Keswick Theatre. The closing of the local Devon Music Fair and the ability to open the venue to even more local promoters continued the success of the venture.

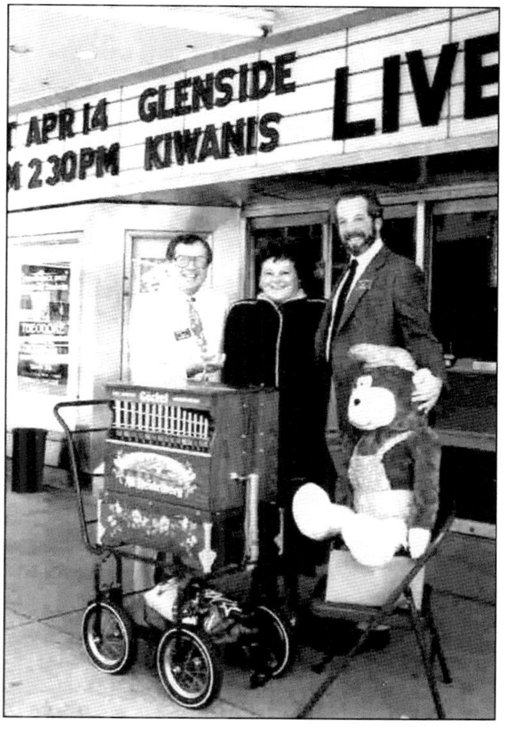

When Roy Snyder, right, was hired in 1988, the venue had a full-time person to concentrate on promotion and booking. Snyder eventually became executive director and a partner. The venue saw steady positive growth during the intervening years. The building eventually was placed on the Pollstar list of the top 50 theaters with a capacity under 5,000.

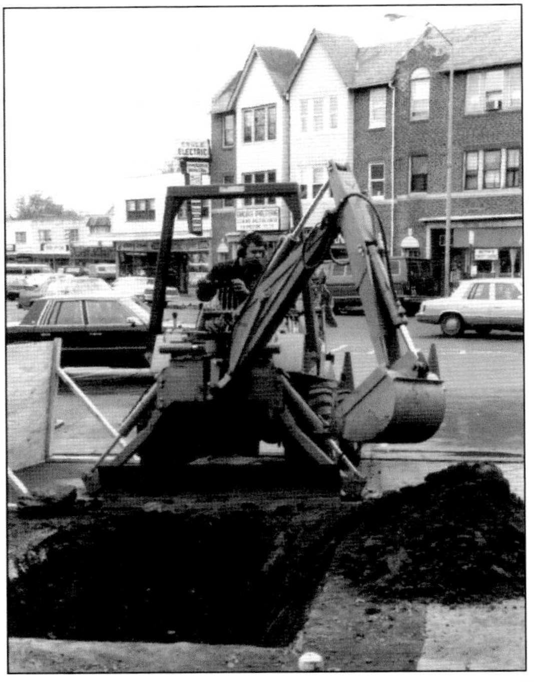

From 1993 to 1995, Abington Township once again turned its eye toward what was now dubbed Keswick Village. Brick walks were installed. Shops were given facelifts, and businesses were encouraged to move into the area.

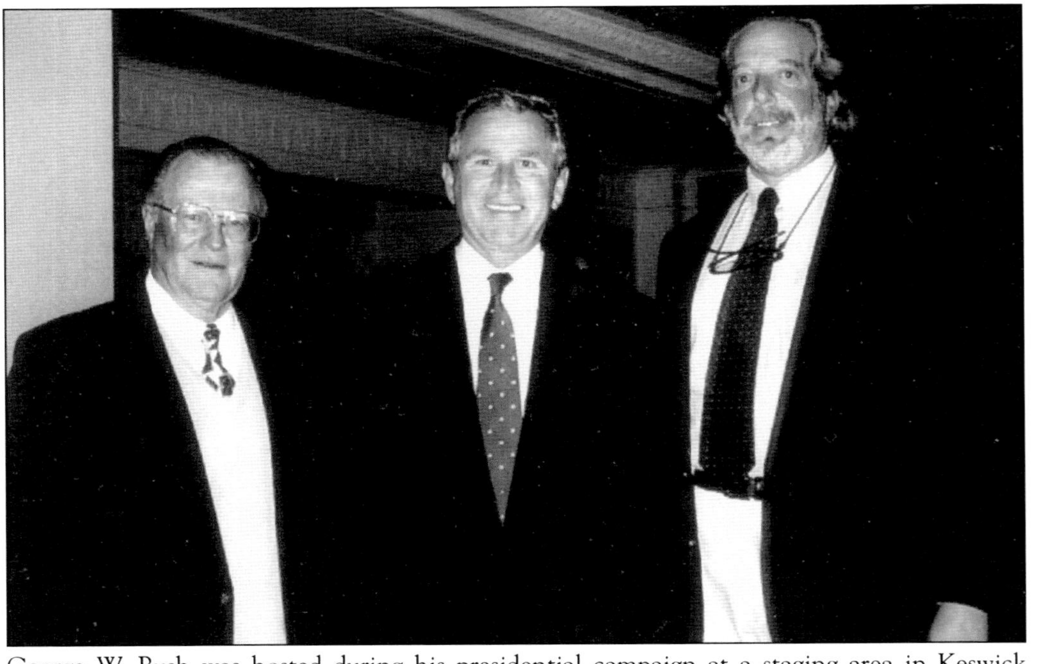

George W. Bush was hosted during his presidential campaign at a staging area in Keswick Village. He stopped in on his way through the building to meet with Harry Barbin, left, and Roy Snyder, right. The visit was another first for the venue. It included snipers on the roof and agents in the building. Typical of the spirit of the Keswick, four hours after Bush left, the theater was open to the public with a sold out *Capitol Steps* show that had been scheduled months earlier.

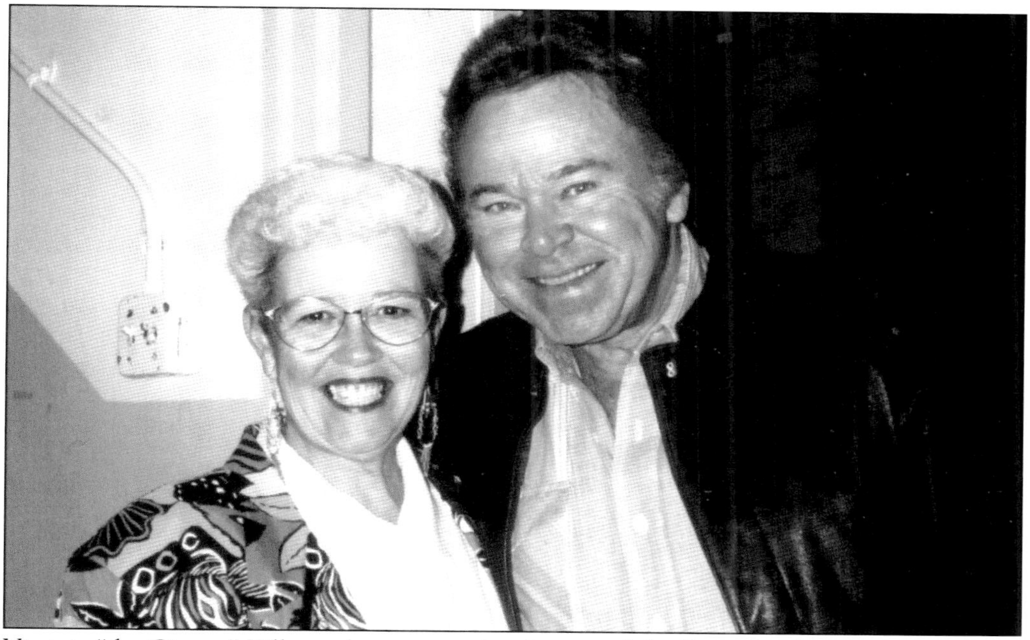

Virginia "the Ginster" Killeen, then group sales director of the Keswick Theatre, is shown with Roy Clark backstage. She joined the Keswick Theatre as a volunteer usher for the Glenside Landmarks Association. After being hired, she served the theater in many capacities, including box office duty and front-of-house management, often wearing two hats at once. Her husband, Thomas Killeen, became facilities engineer for the venue after retiring from PECO Energy. Through all the changes, the Keswick Theatre group has tried not to forget its community roots.

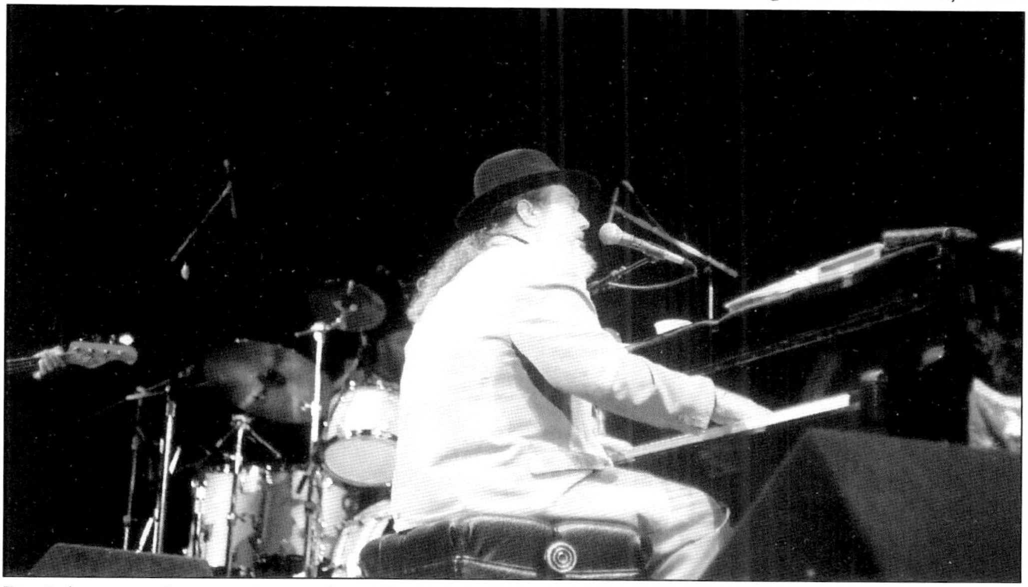

Dr. John gets the people on their feet with his magic music. His performances in the venue are representative of the most special dynamic of the Keswick Theatre. The hospitality of the venue lends itself to a comfortable environment. The warmth of the theater makes everyone—patrons and performers—want to return.

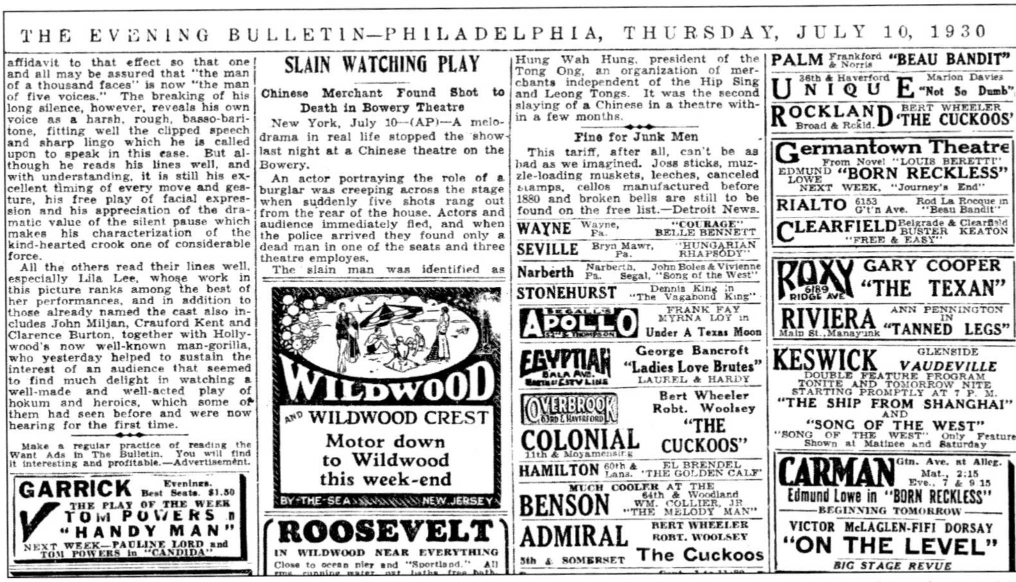

THE EVENING BULLETIN—PHILADELPHIA, THURSDAY, JULY 10, 1930

affidavit to that effect so that one and all may be assured that "the man of a thousand faces" is now "the man of five voices." The breaking of his long silence, however, reveals his own voice as a harsh, rough, basso-baritone, fitting well the clipped speech and sharp lingo which he is called upon to speak in this case. But although he reads his lines well, and with understanding, it is still his excellent timing of every move and gesture, his free play of facial expression and his appreciation of the dramatic value of the silent pause which makes his characterization of the kind-hearted crook one of considerable force.

All the others read their lines well, especially Lila Lee, whose work in this picture ranks among the best of her performances, and in addition to those already named the cast also includes John Miljan, Crauford Kent and Clarence Burton, together with Hollywood's now well-known man-gorilla, who yesterday helped to sustain the interest of an audience that seemed to find much delight in watching a well-made and well-acted play of hokum and heroics, which some of them had seen before and were now hearing for the first time.

Make a regular practice of reading the Want Ads in The Bulletin. You will find it interesting and profitable.—Advertisement.

GARRICK Evenings. Best Seats. $1.50
THE PLAY OF THE WEEK
TOM POWERS in
"HANDY MAN"
NEXT WEEK—PAULINE LORD and TOM POWERS in "CANDIDA"

SLAIN WATCHING PLAY

Chinese Merchant Found Shot to Death in Bowery Theatre

New York, July 10—(AP)—A melodrama in real life stopped the show last night at a Chinese theatre on the Bowery.

An actor portraying the role of a burglar was creeping across the stage when suddenly five shots rang out from the rear of the house. Actors and audience immediately fled, and when the police arrived they found only a dead man in one of the seats and three theatre employes.

The slain man was identified as Hung Wah Hung, president of the Tong Ong, an organization of merchants independent of the Hip Sing and Leong Tongs. It was the second slaying of a Chinese in a theatre within a few months.

WILDWOOD AND WILDWOOD CREST
Motor down to Wildwood this week-end
BY-THE-SEA NEW JERSEY

ROOSEVELT
IN WILDWOOD NEAR EVERYTHING
Close to ocean pier and "Sportland." All

Fine for Junk Men

This tariff, after all, can't be as bad as we imagined. Joss sticks, muzzle-loading muskets, leeches, canceled stamps, cellos manufactured before 1880 and broken bells are still to be found on the free list.—Detroit News.

WAYNE Wayne, Pa. "COURAGE" BELLE BENNETT
SEVILLE Bryn Mawr, Pa. "HUNGARIAN RHAPSODY"
Narberth Narberth, Pa. John Boles & Vivienne Segal, "Song of the West"
STONEHURST Dennis King in "The Vagabond King"
SEGALL'S APOLLO 52nd & Thompson FRANK FAY MYRNA LOY in Under A Texas Moon
EGYPTIAN BALA AVE. George Bancroft "Ladies Love Brutes" LAUREL & HARDY
OVERBROOK 63RD & HAVERFORD Bert Wheeler Robt. Woolsey "THE CUCKOOS"
COLONIAL 11th & Moyamensing
HAMILTON 60th & Lans. EL BRENDEL 'THE GOLDEN CALF'
MUCH COOLER AT THE BENSON 64th & Woodland WM. COLLIER, JR. "THE MELODY MAN"
ADMIRAL 5th & SOMERSET BERT WHEELER ROBT. WOOLSEY The Cuckoos

PALM Frankford & Norris "BEAU BANDIT"
UNIQUE 36th & Haverford Marion Davies "Not So Dumb"
ROCKLAND Broad & Rckld. BERT WHEELER 'THE CUCKOOS'
Germantown Theatre From Novel "LOUIS BERETTI" EDMUND LOWE "BORN RECKLESS" NEXT WEEK, "Journey's End"
RIALTO 6153 G't'n Ave. Rod La Rocque in "Beau Bandit"
CLEARFIELD Belgrade & Clearfield BUSTER KEATON "FREE & EASY"
ROXY 6189 RIDGE AVE GARY COOPER "THE TEXAN"
RIVIERA Main St., Manayunk ANN PENNINGTON IN "TANNED LEGS"
KESWICK GLENSIDE VAUDEVILLE
DOUBLE FEATURE PROGRAM TONITE AND TOMORROW NITE STARTING PROMPTLY AT 7 P. M.
"THE SHIP FROM SHANGHAI" AND "SONG OF THE WEST"
"SONG OF THE WEST" Only Feature Shown at Matinee and Saturday
CARMAN Gtn. Ave. at Alleg. Mat., 2:15 Eve., 7 & 9:15
Edmund Lowe in "BORN RECKLESS"
—BEGINNING TOMORROW—
VICTOR McLAGLEN-FIFI DORSAY "ON THE LEVEL"
BIG STAGE REVUE

The Keswick has taken the journey of being one of many theaters—as evidenced in this 1930s advertisement—to becoming one of the few that have survived. The key is in the community. People like Allyson Cochran and Mary McCalla, who attended the first show or danced in the first recital and now usher at the venue, are what define the Keswick Theatre.

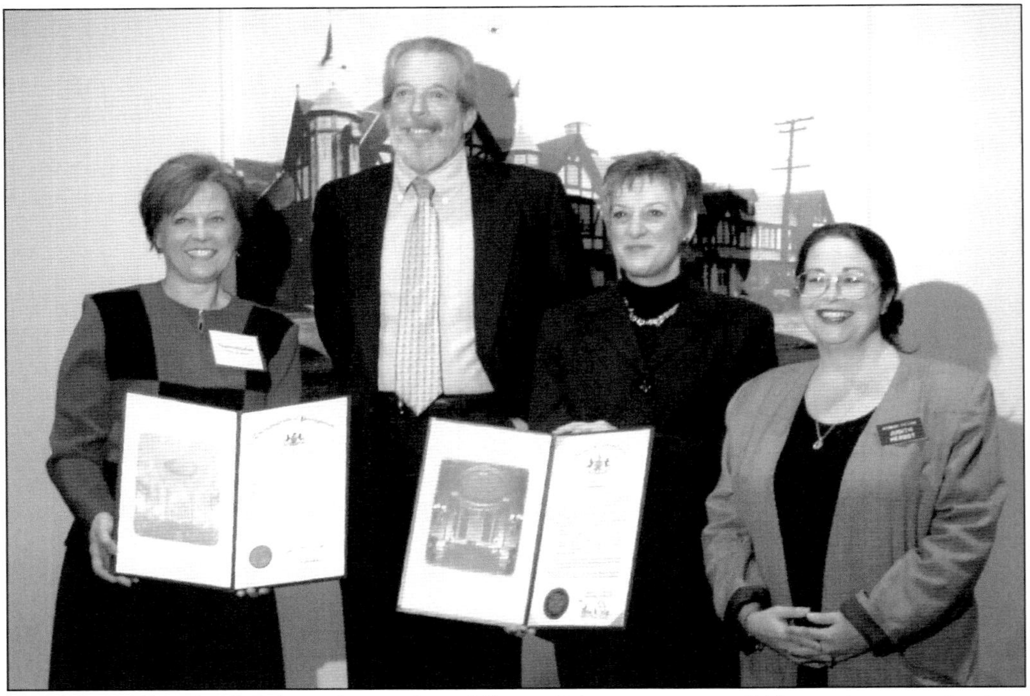

State Rep. Ellen Bard, left, and state Sen. Allyson Schwartz present 75th-anniversary citations to Roy Snyder and Judith Herbst, far right. Both citations have one thing in common: they speak of the past and of the venue, mentioning it not just as a historic site but also as an integral part of the community of Glenside and the Philadelphia region.

75th Anniversary

THE KESWICK THEATRE

(FIRST OPENED CHRISTMAS DAY 1928)

REQUESTS THE PLEASURE OF YOUR COMPANY

AT THE

75TH ANNIVERSARY RECEPTION

FRIDAY, DECEMBER 26

TWO THOUSAND AND THREE

COCKTAILS, HORS D'OEUVRES, DESSERTS AT 7:30 PM

R.S.V.P. BY DECEMBER 16TH

215-572-7650x213

In February 2002, the Keswick attracted the attention of Jack Utsick Presents. This veteran international concert promoter purchased the venue. Partners in Jack Utsick Presents Northeast and resident staff of Keswick Entertainment Group continued to develop programming, as the Keswick entered into its next phase as a regional performing arts center. This development in the history of the theater is reflective of the changing times in entertainment and the theater's ability to adapt. Below, the dance by Harry Brackinridge's daughter Isabella Brackinridge Barthelmeh represents the underlying strength, the bricks and mortar, of the Keswick. Above is the invitation to the reception marking the 75th-anniversary of the theater.

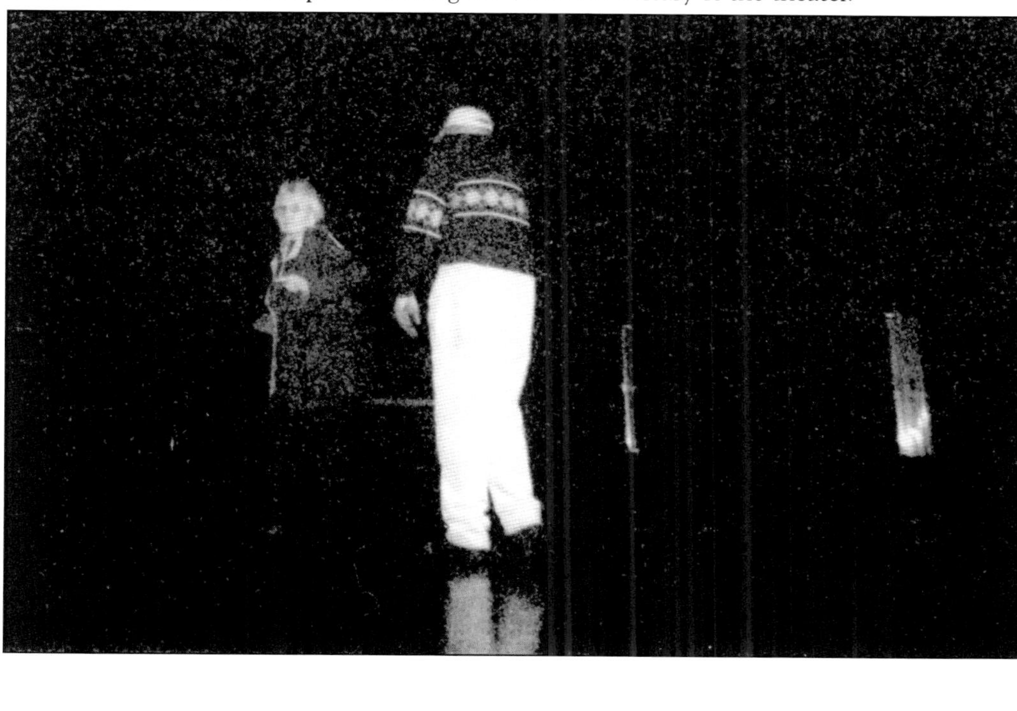

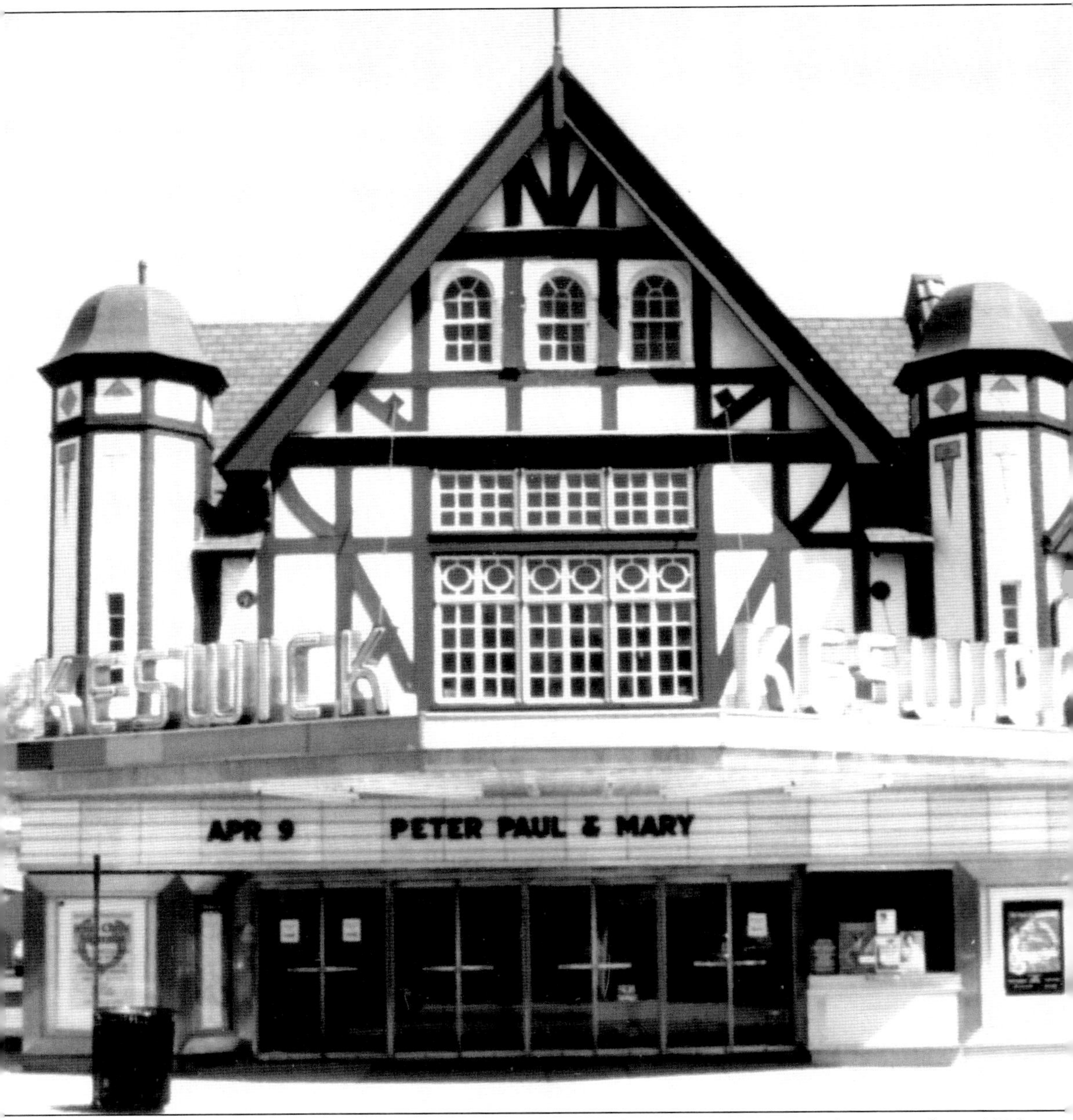

This is the front façade of the theater *c.* 2000. Note that in comparison with images from 1928 and later, the neon sign has been improved. The façade was restored in 1994. The sign in the poster case on the left is for the annual *Jesus Christ Superstar* series. The Kiddie Corner board, on the left, has been replaced with an upcoming event list. The outside ticket window, no longer in use, has upcoming event posters in it. The beacon and flagpoles are gone. The slate roof has been replaced with more modern material, as the expense of reroofing with slate was exorbitant but the leaking had to be stopped to preserve the inside plasterwork. The turrets remain, but access to the spiral staircases is closed up.

Four

BRICKS AND MORTAR

The architecture of the Keswick Theatre is part of its unique charm and interest to patrons, artists, and community members. The venue, in its three distinctive stages, created specific responses from the community. Many people remember different aspects of the venue. This chapter will deal specifically with the challenges of working with the original building, the changes that have been made, and the effects of the building's architecture on its different uses. Something in the character of the building elicits an emotional response from those who visit it, whether they have come for the first time, have visited continuously over the years, or have returned after a long time away.

Recently, tours of the building have been held. The most memorable tour included a gentleman who had played in the creek as a youngster, watched the building being constructed, and seen "Big George," hired to put the ice in the tunnels, as a "strapping young man." (Big George later became both an Abington Township police officer and a volunteer firefighter.) Also on the tour was Isabella Barthelmeh, who came with her niece, Harry Brackinridge's granddaughter. Members of the Delaware Valley Organ Society entertained everyone. A woman who grew up in the area and watched movies here when she was in her teens, just before the 1980 closing of the venue, came for a visit while she was home for the holidays. Families brought children and grandchildren to see the backstage area; some of these children had performed on the stage or had come to see school shows. These people brought their individual stories together with one consistent theme: emotional tales of the theater's place in their life.

Part of the reputation of the building has been its connection to Horace Trumbauer's famed architectural firm. However, a study of the building's history has revealed that a number of architectural visions went into its construction, reconstruction, and continued restoration. Perhaps because Trumbauer had experience in palatial homes as well as institutions, the building has a warmth that tempers its grandeur. This warmth is especially noticeable in the auditorium, where, whether through original design or the compilation of its structural history, the acoustics are praised.

The building's many spaces create a journey, each with stories to be told. Friendly ghosts are felt in certain areas; they have been sighted twice. The tunnels and stream water that run under the auditorium intrigue visitors. The height of the stage house and the design of the proscenium hold interest, as do the dressing rooms. Amazingly, the bathrooms (including, backstage, what is likely one of the world's largest urinals) are a subject of discussion. As an engineering marvel and an architectural treasure, the building has value in its very bricks and mortar.

This chapter highlights the compromises and challenges that this type of a venue presents in remaining vital. It emphasizes the journey that has transpired to renovate the building and illustrates the unearthing (sometimes literally) of some of the treasures that it holds. This journey at the Keswick Theatre is ongoing, and the hope is that the development of the building and the continued marriage of history and technology will never be finished. This is a trademark of the venue.

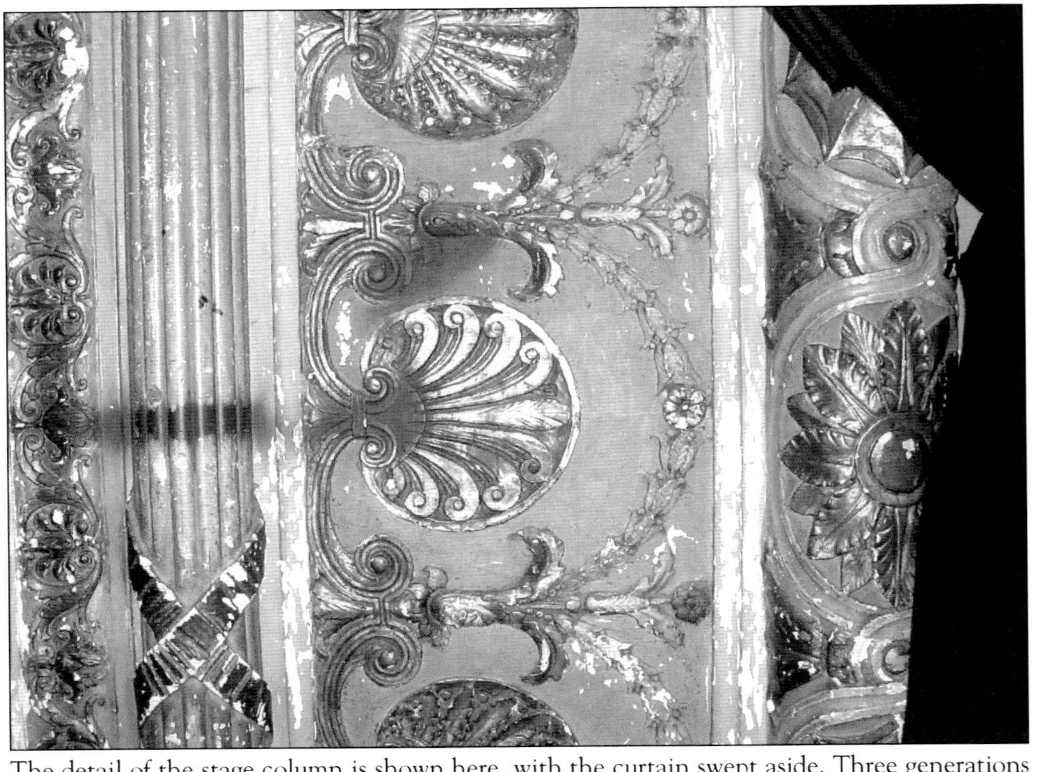

The detail of the stage column is shown here, with the curtain swept aside. Three generations of ownership have worked to uncover these hidden treasures: The Glenside Landmarks Society, G.B.M Wharton, and Keswick Entertainment Group/Jack Utsick Presents. The latter two entities have proven that restoration can work hand in hand with commercial enterprise.

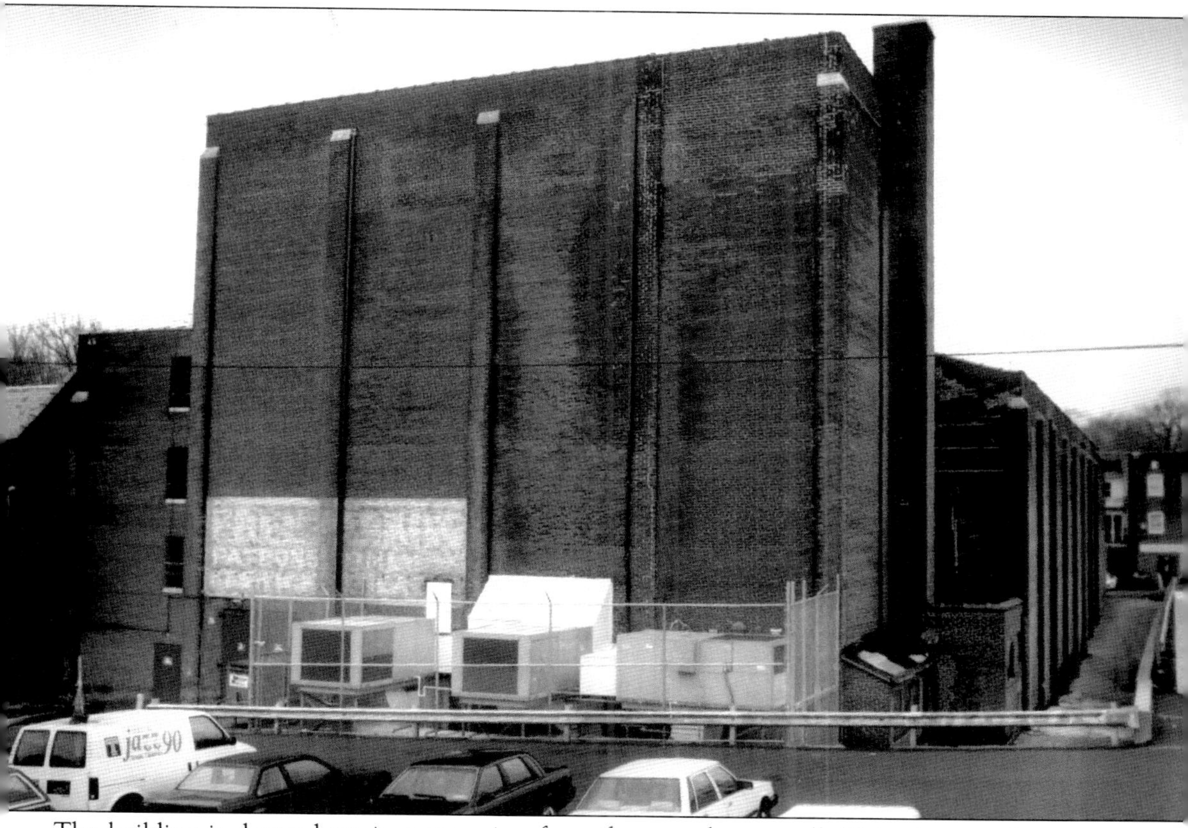

The building is shown here in a rare view from the stage-house wall. This photograph was taken in late 1992 to highlight the installation of a new ventilation system. The unit on the stage had been removed earlier, and until this point, the venue had been relying on the original boiler in the basement and a roof-top unit at the other end of the building. Patron comfort is a hallmark of any theater building. This system has been a blessing and a problem. The positioning of the outside units and their cost efficiency in operation are of great benefit to the operating companies of the building. However, the positioning of the units near the loading dock of the venue has created the need for some imaginative responses to loading in equipment for large shows. Technically complicated shows have been done with multiple tractor-trailers, with the cooperation of the neighboring businesses. As later photographs will show, this new system also created some unique problems on the stage. The front façade of the building is deceiving in showing the size of the venue; this view gives a better indication of its size. The long retaining wall to the right of this photograph created another unique challenge for the Keswick Theatre.

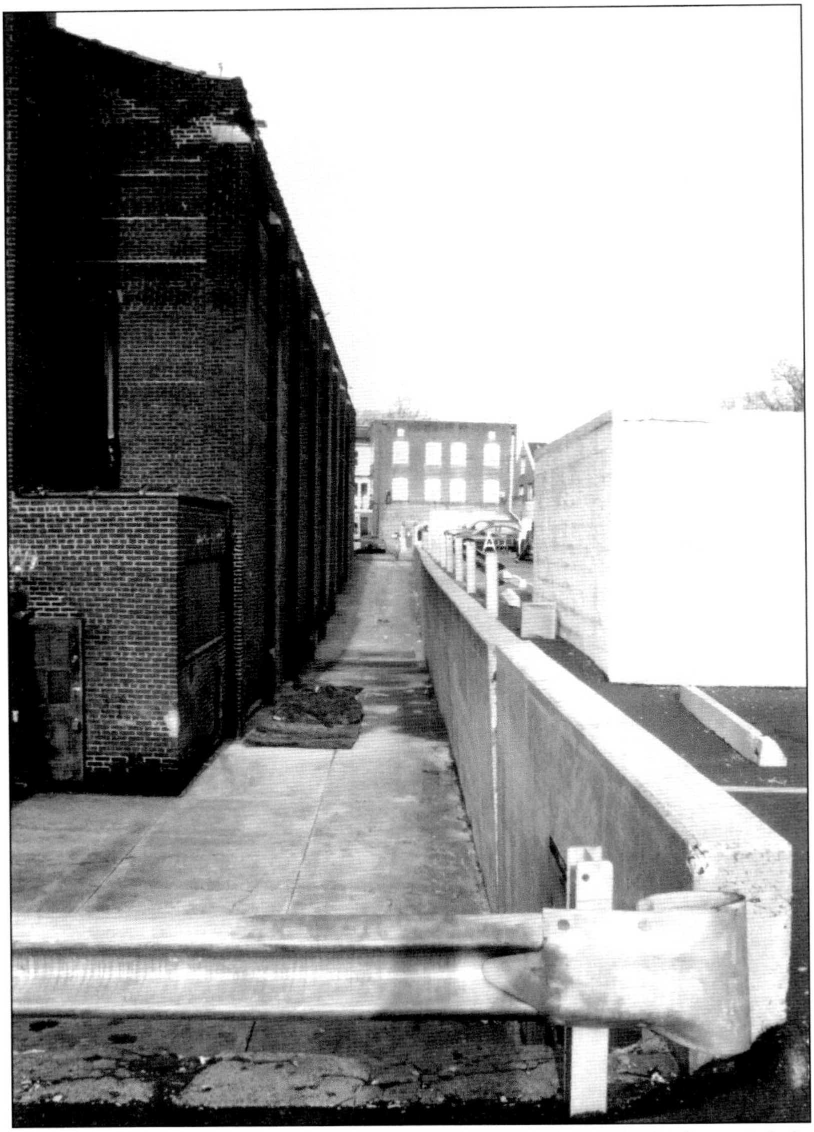

The length of the auditorium is illustrated in this photograph, with the house's left-side doors opening into the alleyway. Under the alley are the lower basement and the end of the tunnels that connect to the creek. Just to the right, on the other side of the guardrail, is where the original pump house stood. It is now accessible by a door in the retaining wall. As seen here, the retaining wall began to tilt toward the building sometime during the 1980s. The wall (later discovered to not be the original wall) was not the correct height for drainage runoff from the parking lot. The building would take water in from this side regularly during heavy rainfalls and snowmelt cycles. The water would come in directly through the walls. The original plaster walls were in serious disrepair under the false curtain and drywall that covered them, and pieces regularly fell through. Resulting damage to the plaster bled through onto the curtains in the form of lime deposits. The strategy was to begin with the exterior of the building and work inward. Eight roofs were to be restored or replaced, and the building was to be reappointed in phases, concentrating on the worst areas first.

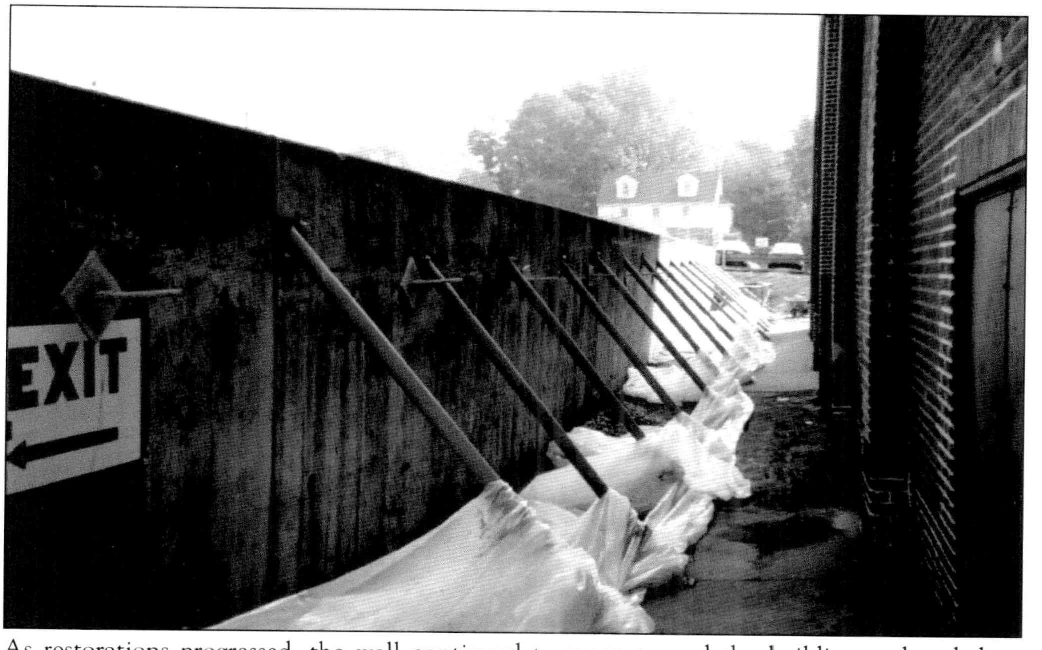

As restorations progressed, the wall continued to move toward the building and ended up having to be braced. Because the location of the wall impacted the main wall of the auditorium and stage house, the basement, and the tunnels, it was critical that it be replaced properly. Through observation of the small wall adjacent to this large wall, it was determined that the retaining wall was not of the same river stone makeup as this older wall and had been replaced at some point. Residents remember the wall falling down in the late 1960s or early 1970s.

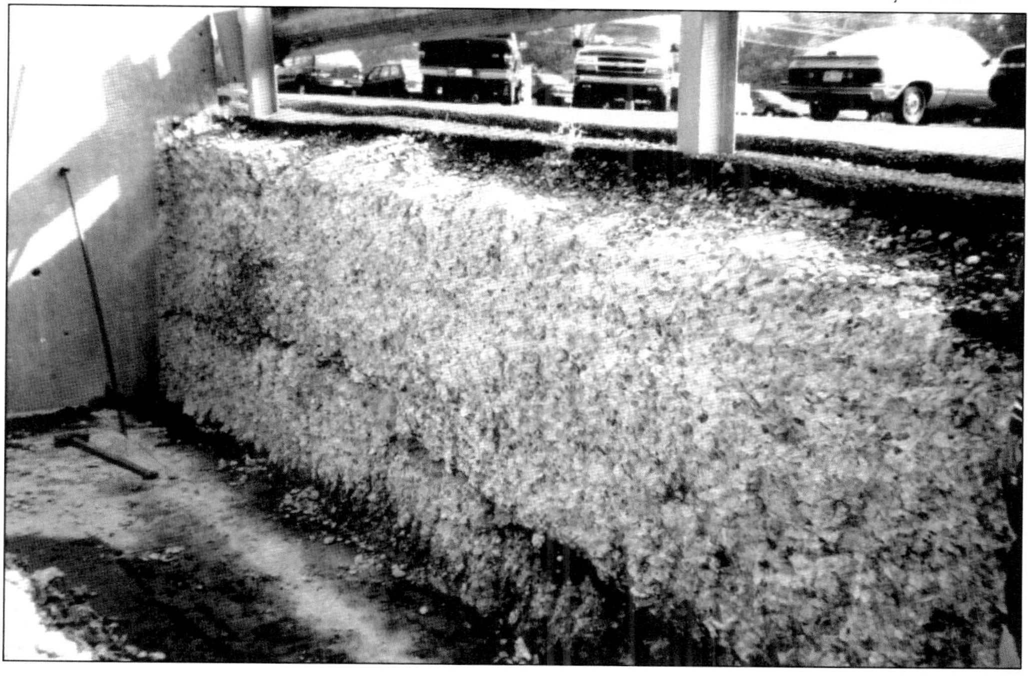

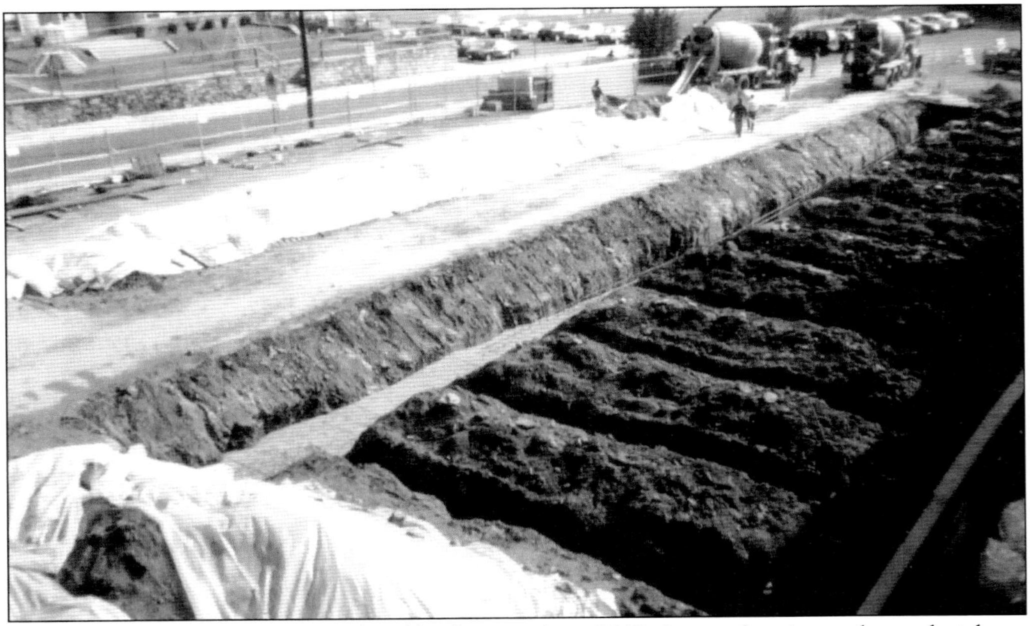

The wall was finally replaced and tied back properly in 2002. It was also given a better height to redirect runoff, and portions of the parking lot were graded to assist with the flooding problems. Both the new owner and the restoration fund financed the project, which cost over $350,000. The flooding has abated.

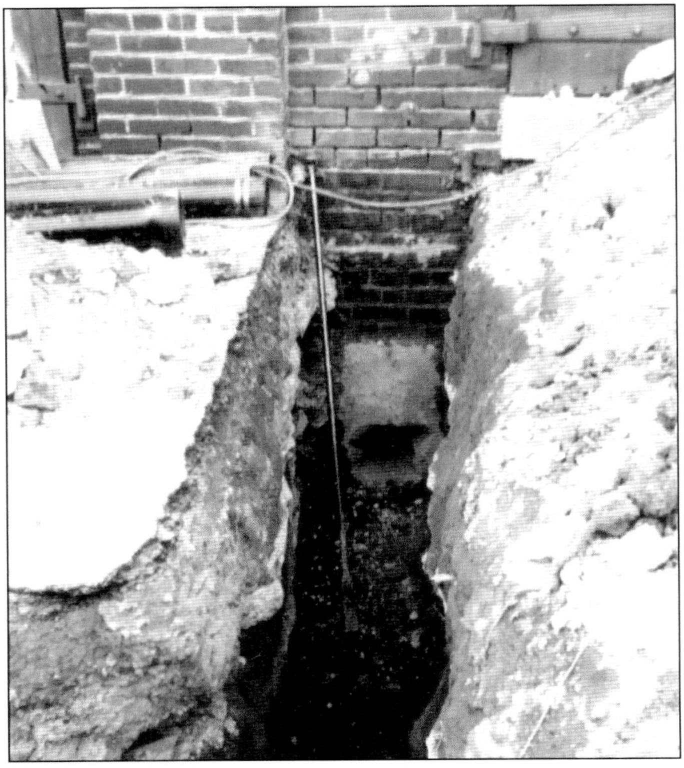

The previous owners, G. B. M. Wharton, had already handled problems relating to the stage-access side of the building. This photograph shows excavation being done to allow for a new standpipe for the sprinkler system and grading being done by the stage loading doors.

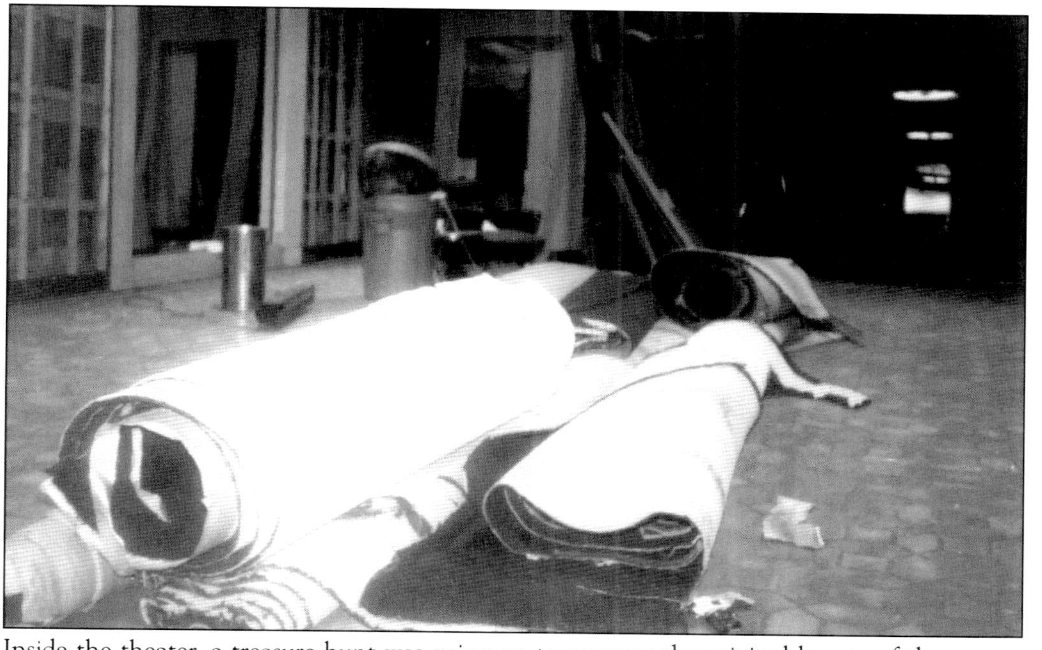

Inside the theater, a treasure hunt was going on to uncover the original beauty of the venue. This photograph shows the Moravian tile floor being uncovered. Note also the removal of the frames for the inner doors.

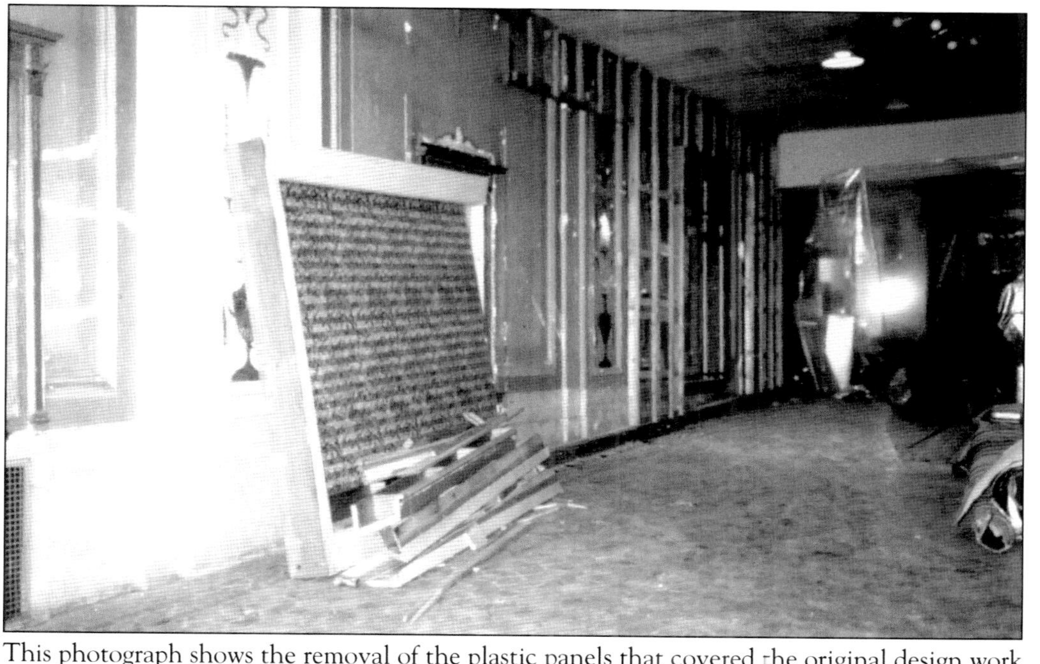

This photograph shows the removal of the plastic panels that covered the original design work of the lobby area. As Melvin Koff had envisioned, this work was uncovered and appreciated. It is uncertain during this phase of recovery what the impact will be of the loss of the work by David Supowitz and Shander Berger, which typifies the 1950s, relative to its value to the history of the building. Photographs will remain as a record.

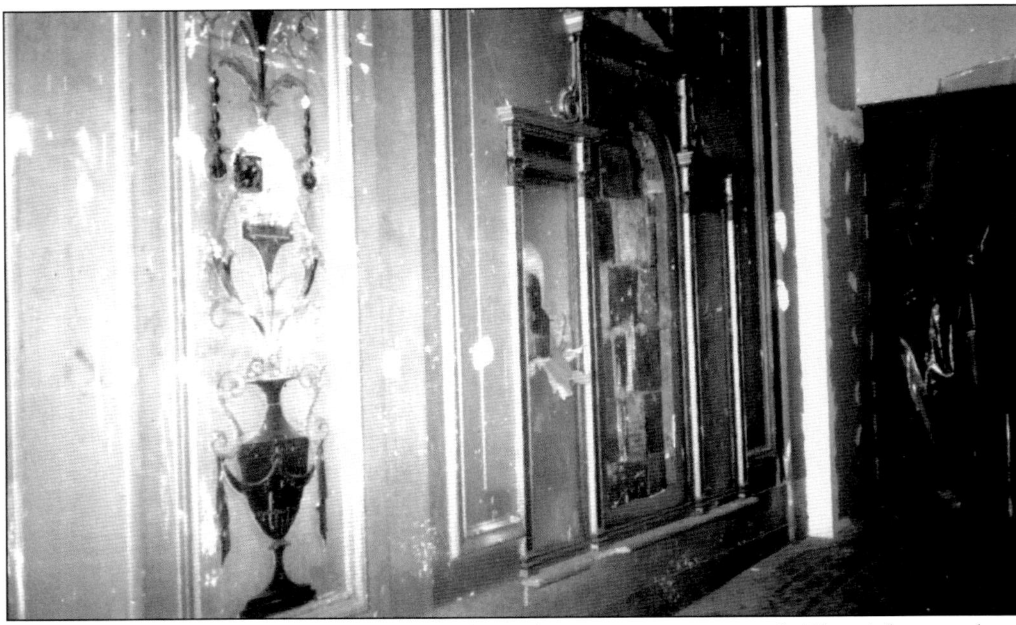

These two photographs show a closer look at the treasures uncovered. The Adams style of plasterwork contains motifs, which are a study unto themselves, that are carefully threaded through the plasterwork of the building. As seen, much of the damage that had been done required that the walls be stripped down to the terra cotta blocks that were below the ornate plaster and woodwork. Of note is that the lobby frames are of wood, not plaster. Also of note is that in both photographs and in the restoration of the venue, the *crux gammata*, or swastika (su-asti-ka in its original form) has been eliminated, most likely due to its relationship with the Nazi party. Other classical forms remain, such as the griffin and the egg and dart.

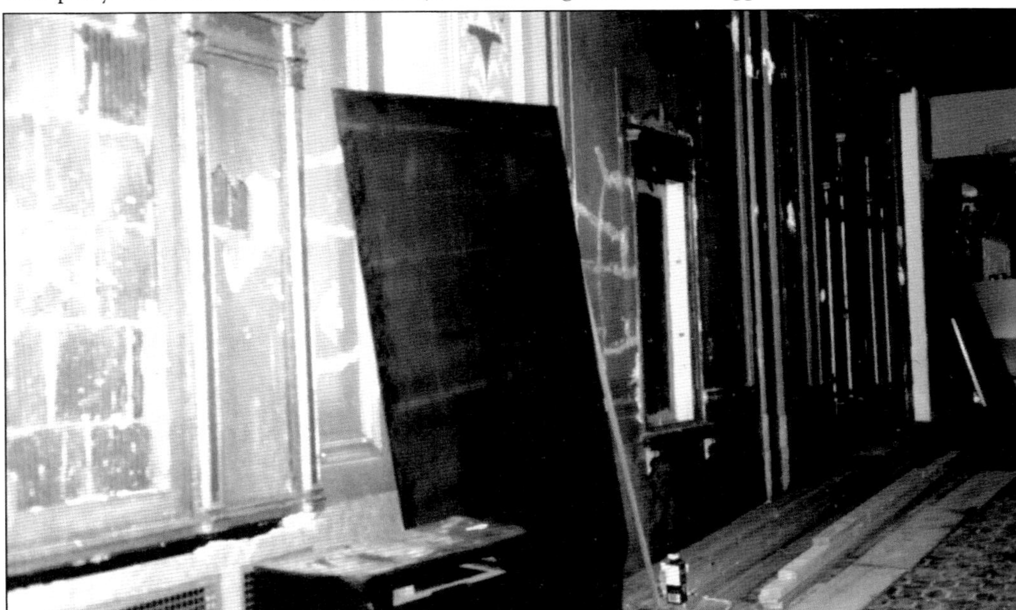

These panels in the lobby were designed for sponsorship activity. Note the grilles that were under the panels. These grilles served to hide the radiators. Due to the draft these spaces caused (the radiators had been removed), the areas were finished with drywall and plaster.

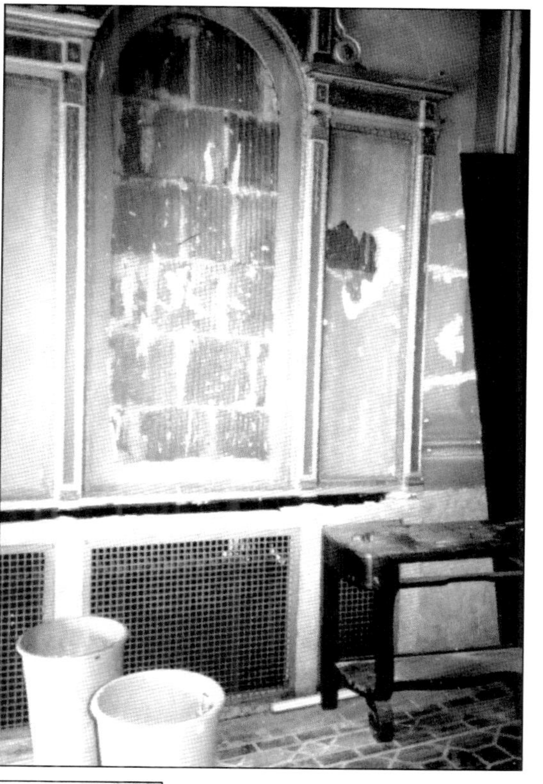

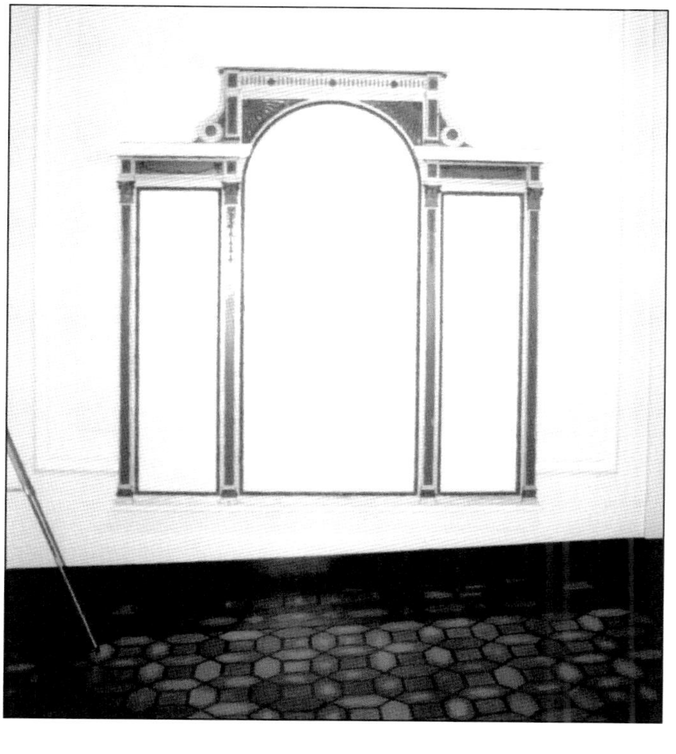

This photograph shows a restored panel in the main lobby and the uncovered Moravian tile floor. The restoration of this area was a compromise due to budget constraints. This portion of the lobby area was restored, but the false ceiling was retained due to mechanical problems, as well as the enormity of the renovations needed in that area.

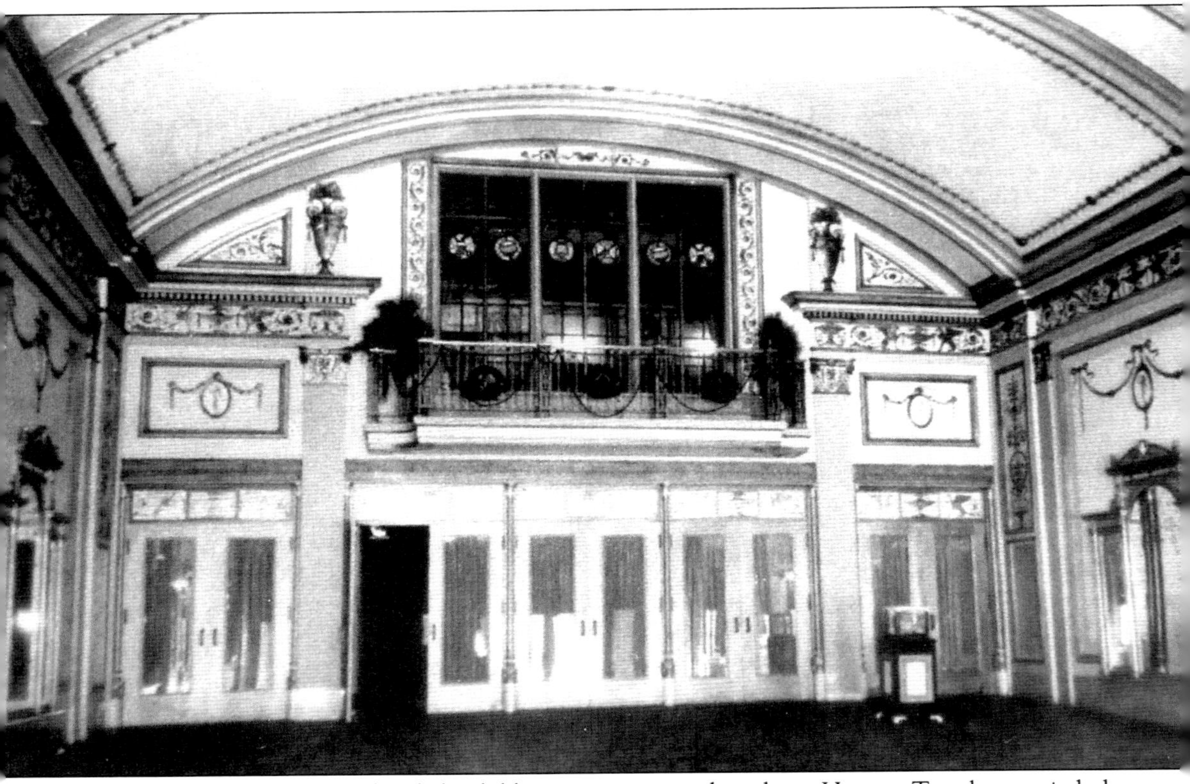

In this 1929 photograph of the lobby area, it is evident how Horace Trumbauer tied the Elizabethan and Adams eras together. The effect of an inner courtyard is seen in the tile floor, the balconies, and the street-side windows (not visible). The subtle plasterwork and design is of the Adams era. The left-hand wall has been restored up to the false ceiling, which was installed in the 1950s. A hole has been cut in the ceiling so that people can look up above the false ceiling and see some of the original work. The right wall suffers from the same fate as the ceiling above; it is covered over by the box office and the concession stand, which hide its decorative work. Despite all the renovations, one of the original doors into the main lobby remains behind the concession door.

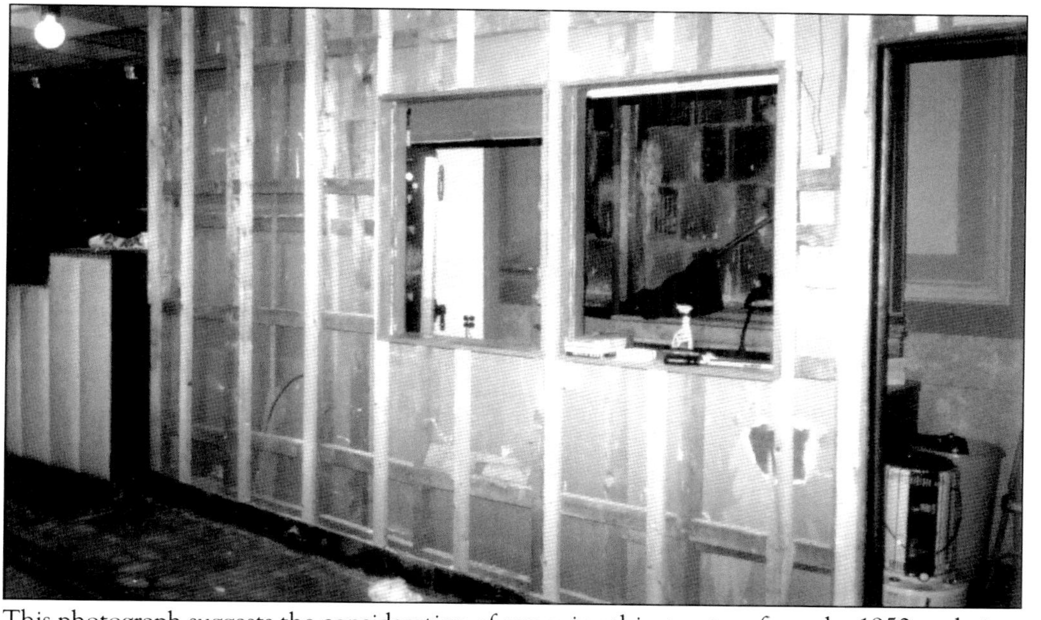

This photograph suggests the consideration of removing this structure from the 1950s redesign. It seems as if it might have been a moment's hesitation. Through the door, some of the original plaster design work still exists. However, mechanical problems of several kinds intervened once again. Piping for the boiler system had been raised up through the ceiling. A large old-fashioned safe took up most of the room and would have been costly to remove and dispose of. Plumbing had been installed in the concession stand, in the background.

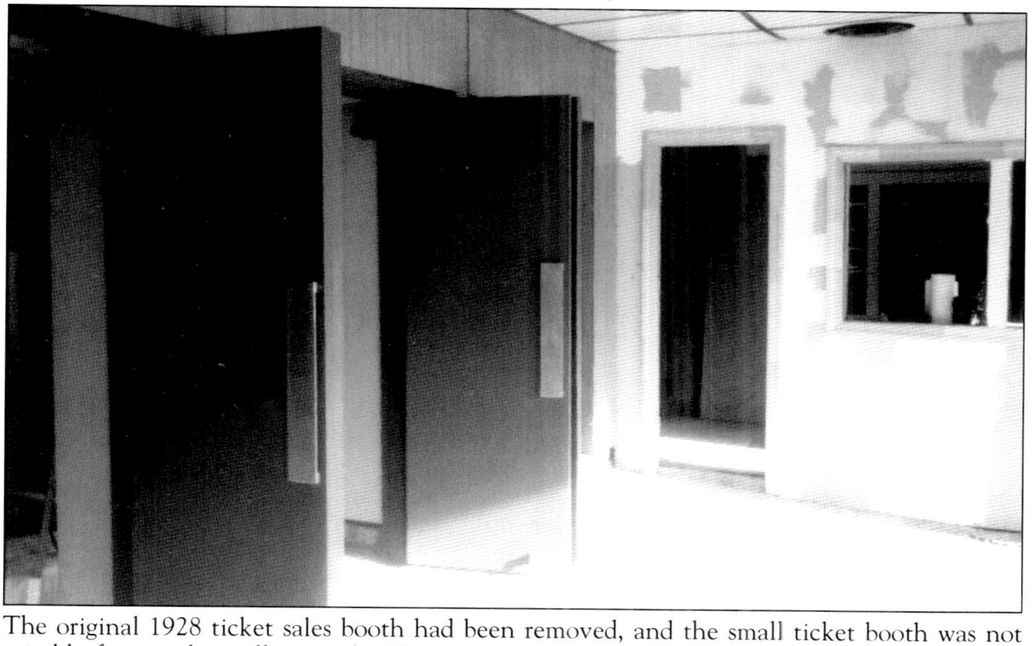

The original 1928 ticket sales booth had been removed, and the small ticket booth was not suitable for new box office needs. The compromise was to marry the two rooms. Again, the historic plasterwork that was present still exists; member of today's box office staff work alongside history. This room also covers one of the spiral staircases to the turret.

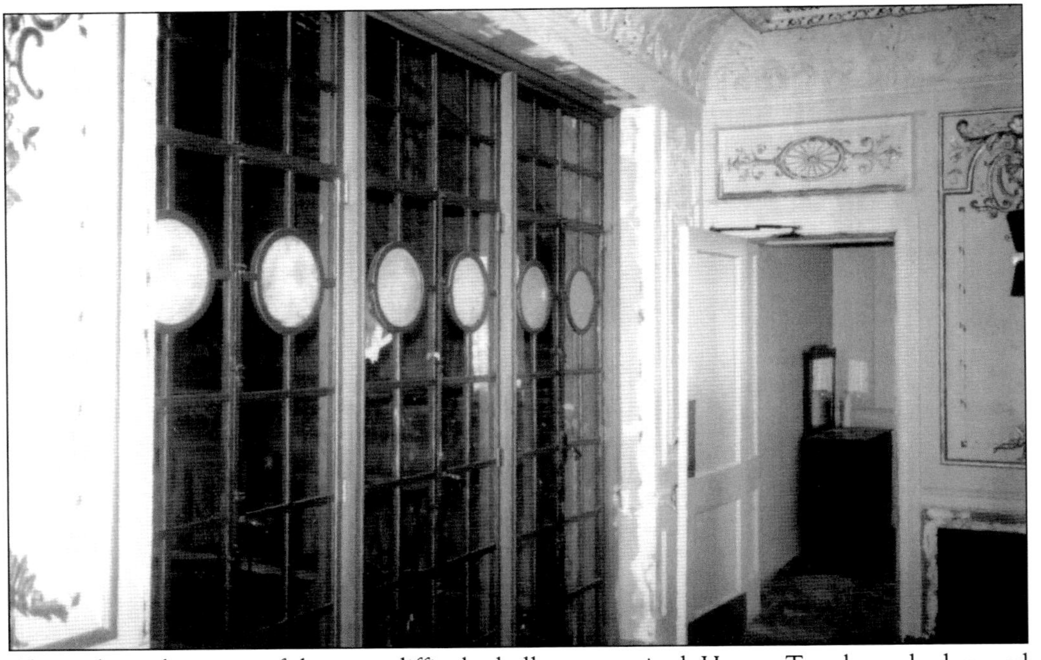

Above the ceiling, one of the most difficult challenges awaited. Horace Trumbauer had moved to quite another style of architecture for the ladies' lounge, as shown. The lounge windows looked out over the original vaulted ceiling. The door led to the ladies' room.

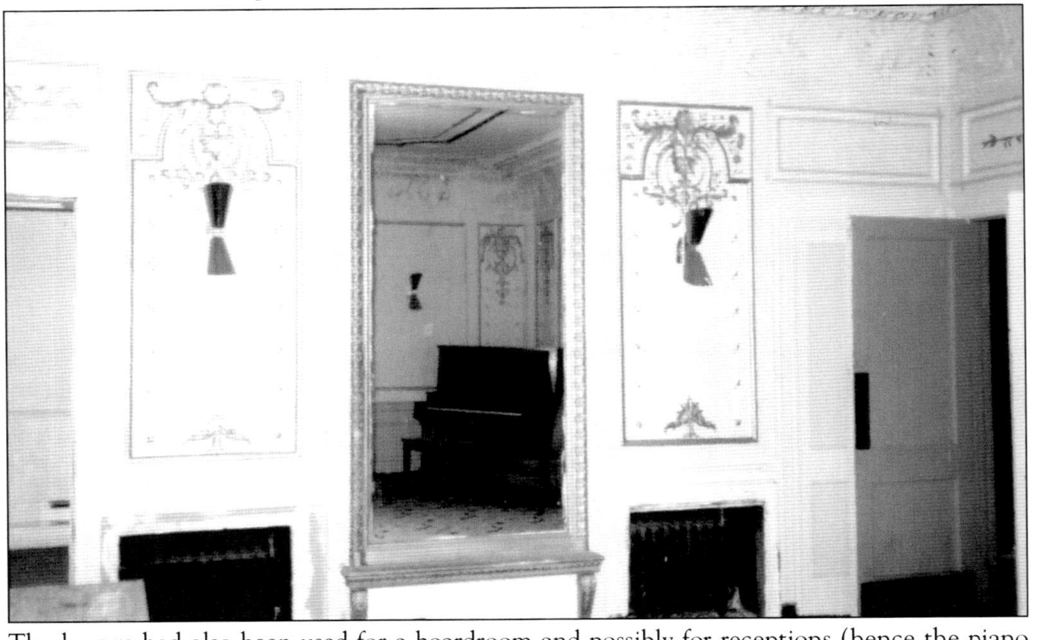

The lounge had also been used for a boardroom and possibly for receptions (hence the piano shown in the reflection in the mirror). However, with sensitivity to modern human resources problems, the owners thought that the room should not continue to be tied to the ladies' room if it was going to be used for office space, which, for a growing commercial enterprise, was at a premium.

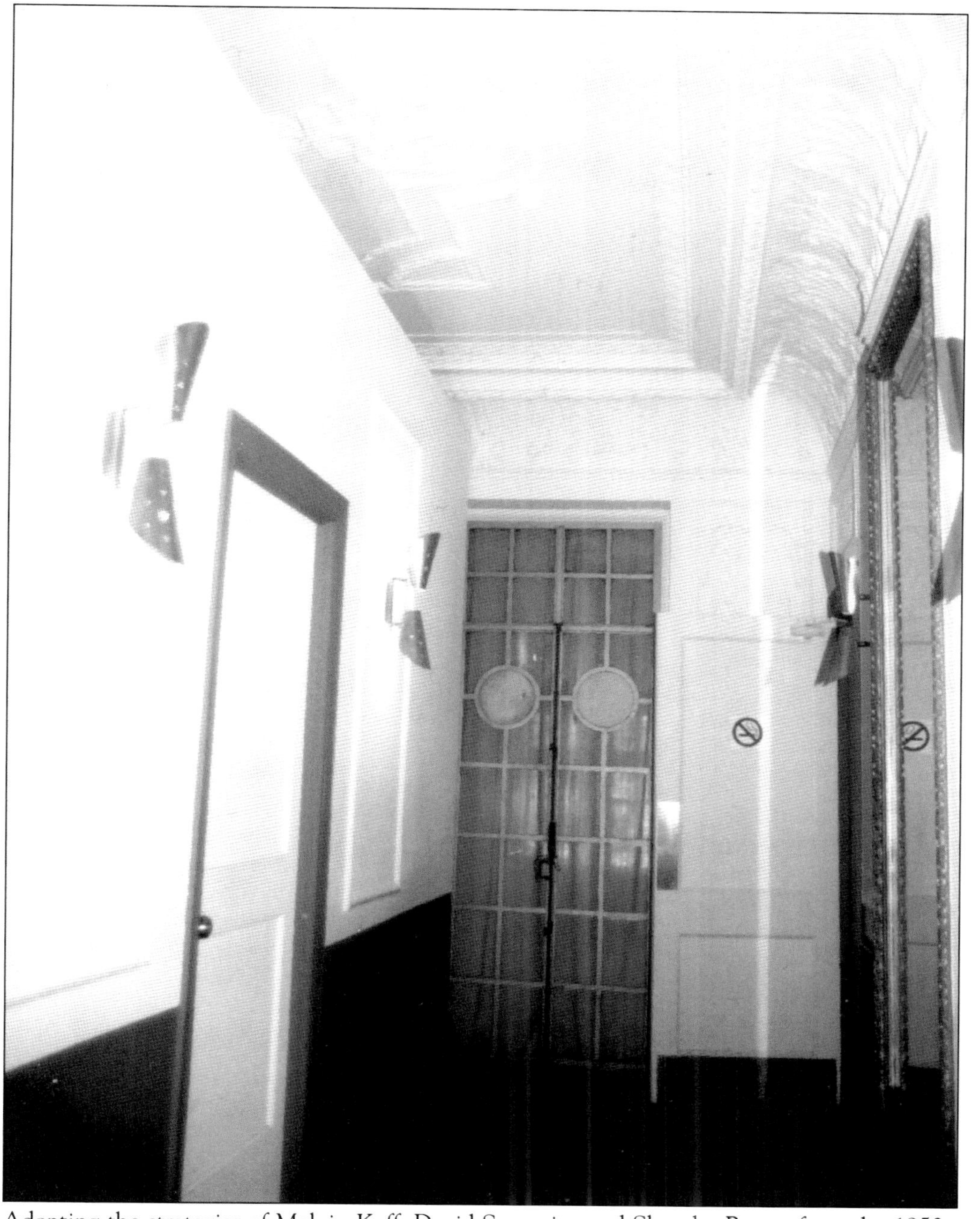

Adopting the strategies of Melvin Koff, David Supowitz, and Shander Berger from the 1950s, a drywall shell of a room was tucked into this area after the plaster was restored. Although this covered the beauty of the original room, it provided two items: a designated entrance to the ladies' room, with a hall and a large mirror; and the much-needed office space for the staff. Currently, eight people work in this space. Note that one set of doors remains as a reminder of the original design and as access from this side of the false ceiling. Renting outside office space was not part of the business model.

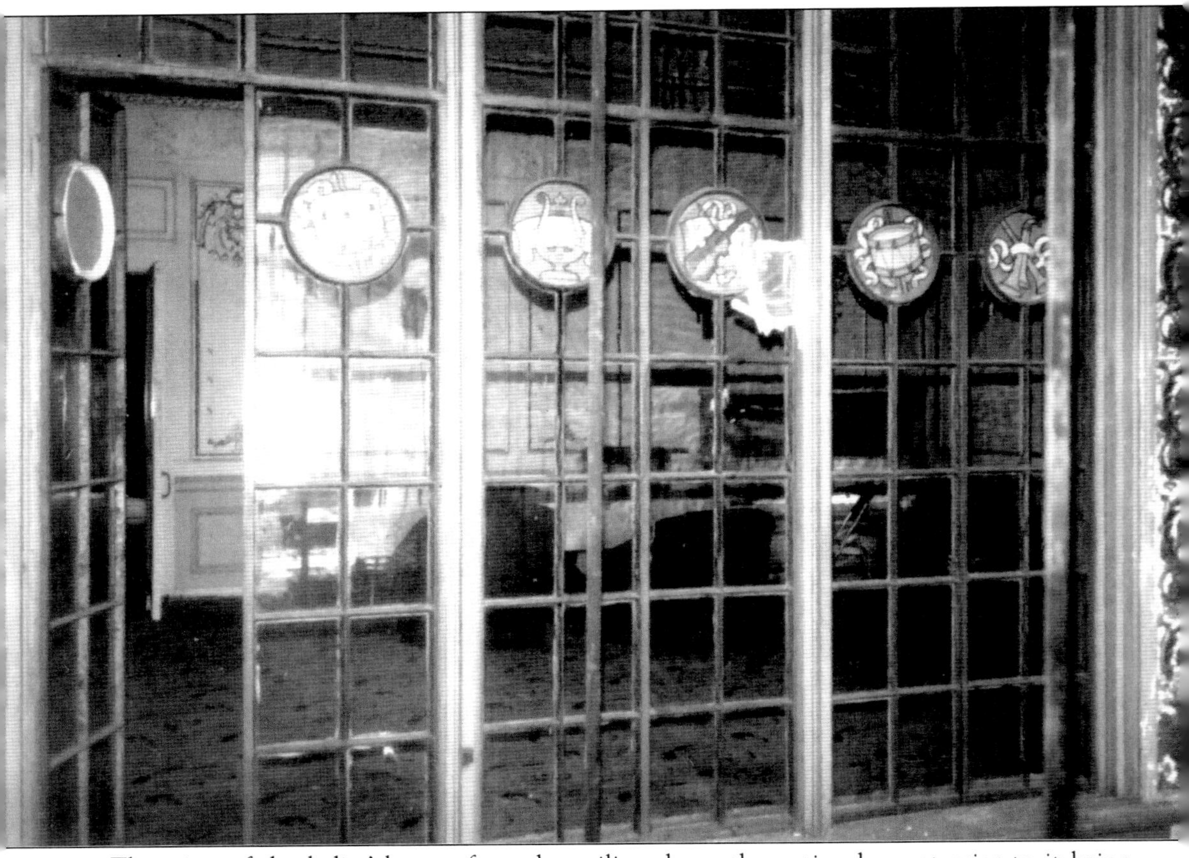

This view of the ladies' lounge from the ceiling shows the entire door set prior to it being covered up. Note that the balcony railings, as shown in the 1929 photographs, are gone. The room created a further liability in that unauthorized people could walk right out of the doors onto a false ceiling. Since renovations could not be completed at this time, it was decided that calling less attention to the area was better than advertising it. One side of the original ceiling was in extreme disrepair due to the leaking roof above.

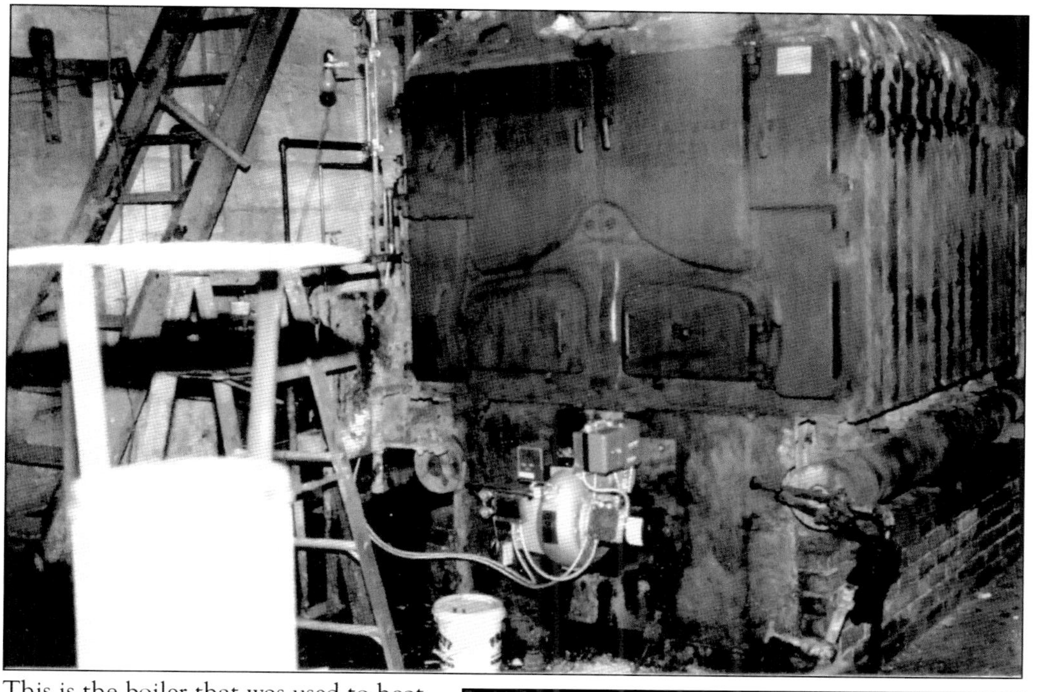

This is the boiler that was used to heat the theater from the time the 1950s unit was removed from the stage until the new ventilation system went into place in 1992. The major mechanical problem that plagued all of the owners was the heating and cooling issue. The rooftop unit that supplied the main lobbies and the upstairs was on the roof, and the ductwork ran across the false ceiling. The other unit sat on stage and needed to be removed, as it was an unforgiving 30-year-old giant that took up a large amount of stage space and made it impossible to purchase a variety of talent for live entertainment. The stage unit was removed, and the old boiler was put back into service for several years until money could be raised to replace the system. For several years, the local plumbers were almost in residence at the venue, working around the clock to try to keep the boiler running.

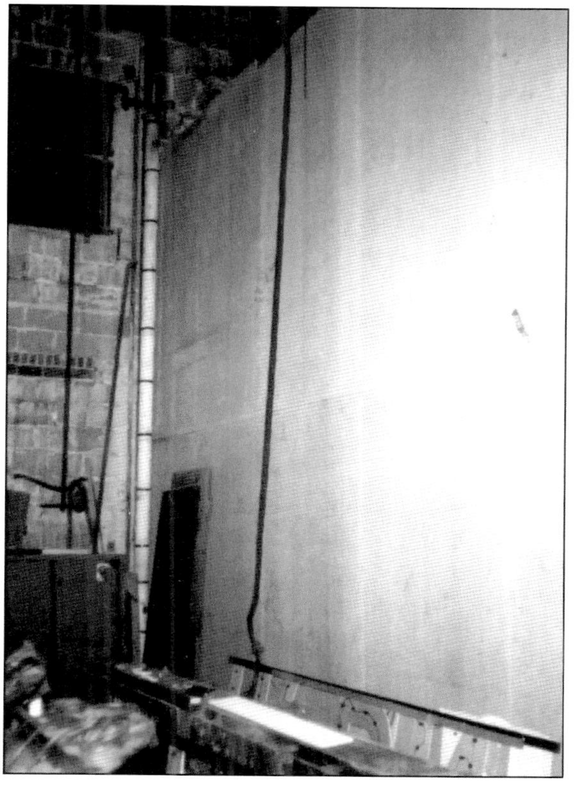

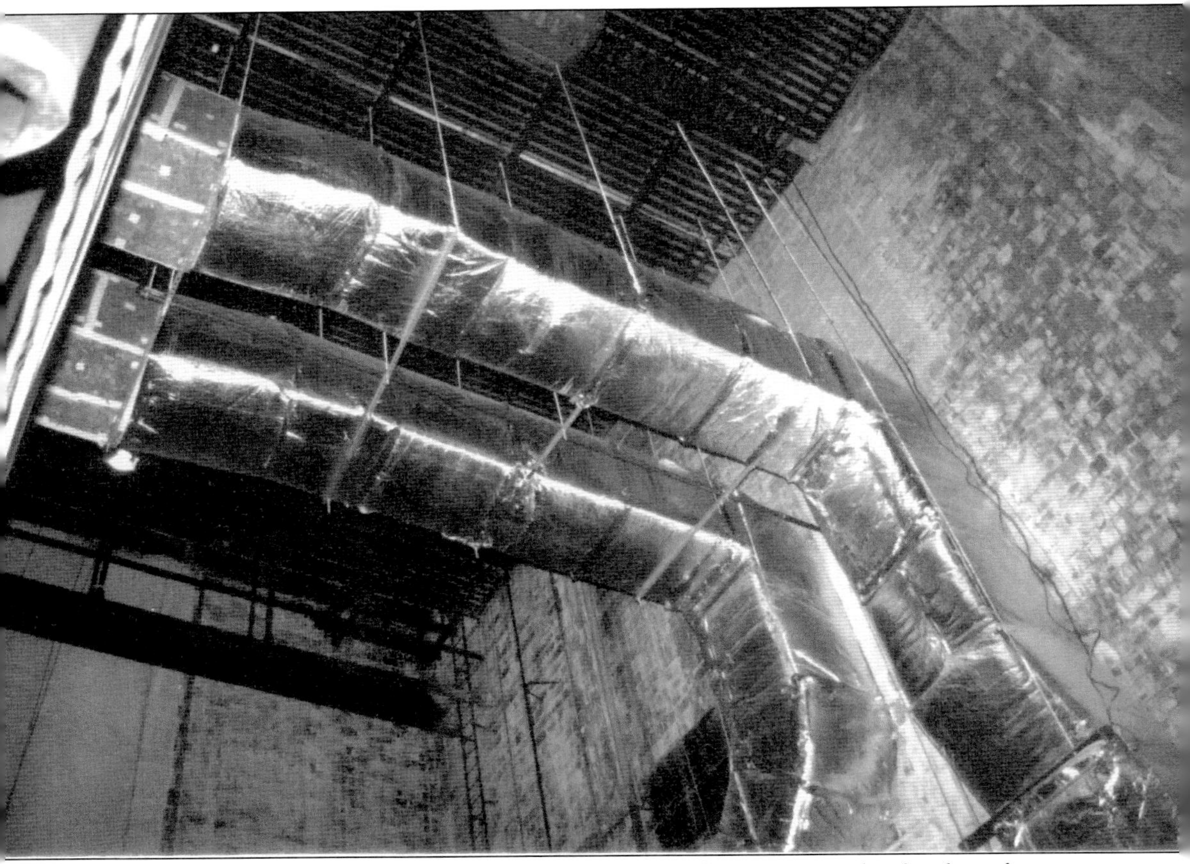

This is the new ventilation system. It is imaginative in design, as it took a few feet of stage space for the main duct. Ductwork was taken across the grid to heat the auditorium from the ceiling and to serve the backstage areas. The design has the ductwork going through the old trunk lifts, no longer in use, to heat the upstairs dressing rooms and the green room on stage left. Structural support was readily available from the grid.

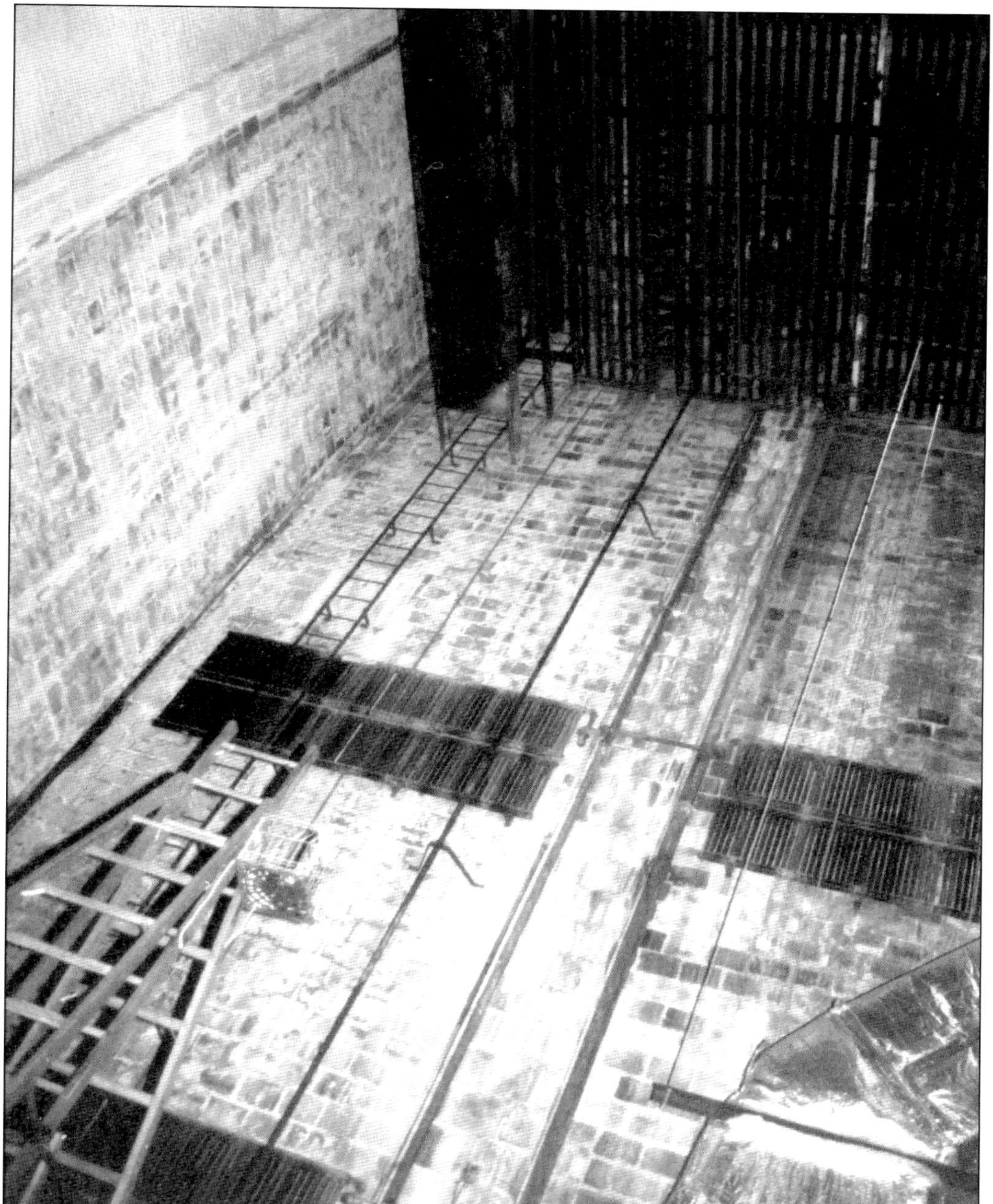

The removal of the ventilation system from the stage, though it intruded on some of the grid use, reopened not only floor space but also access to the ladder to the grid. The floor space was used to regain access to rooms that had been hard to get into due to the organ chambers and the small equipment room behind the stage thrust that had been added in the 1950s. The ability to use the grid for flying some of the lighting equipment and backdrops required by touring shows opened the venue up to new programming possibilities. Although the ductwork precludes some flying, the overall gain in programming is a win-win-win proposition: comfortable patrons, better programming, and space for equipment.

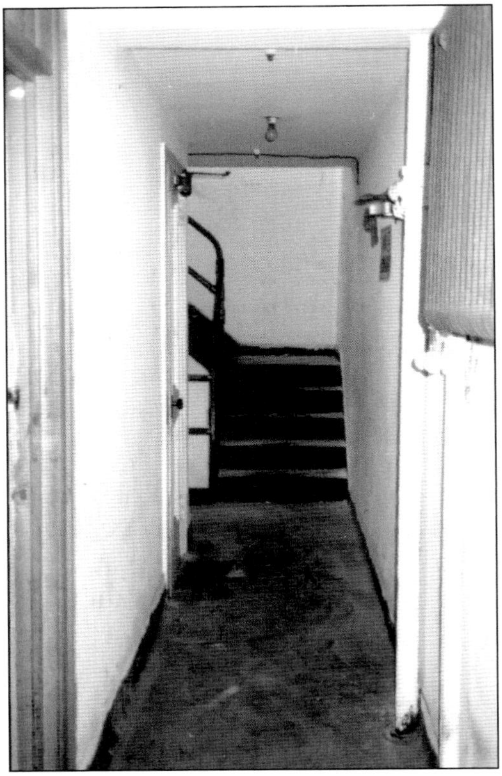

With improved programming came the needs of more high-profile acts. The dressing rooms were in shambles. Not needed during the movie era, they had been neglected, and had not been painted or maintained in some time. They still sported gooseneck lamps that were out of code, and where the electricity actually worked, it was poorly wired. There was no air conditioning until the new system was installed, the old radiators dominated the walls, and tin-top, poorly painted countertops, tentatively attached to the walls, served as dressing tables. Originally, the dressing rooms were given a cursory coat of gray and white paint, and base heaters and window air conditioners were installed. The Keswick owes a great debt to the many artists who patiently returned year after year and worked under these conditions (including the pay phone in the downstairs hall).

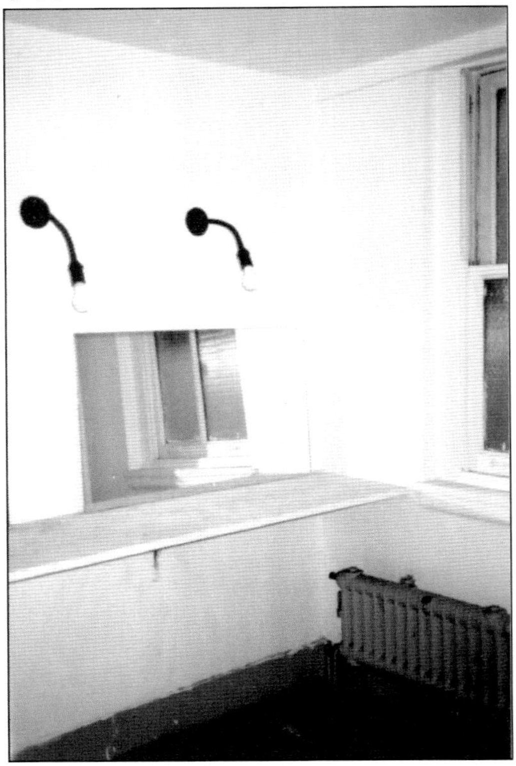

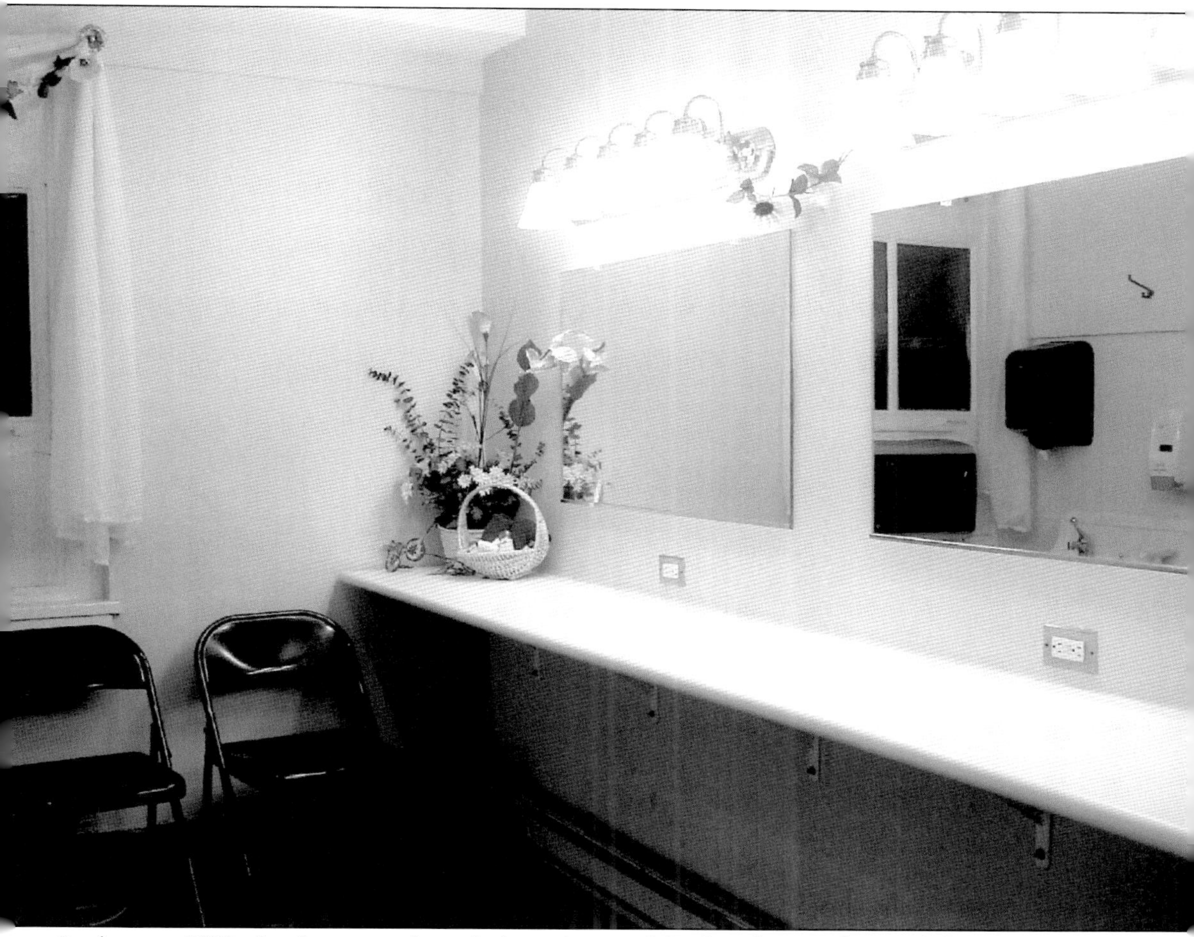

In the year 2000, the theater undertook the redesign of the first-floor and second-floor dressing rooms (the third floor, still with limited electricity, remains in c. 1930s condition) in an attempt to offer comfort and meet code regulations while using a décor reminiscent of the original building. The combined effect has pleased both new and returning acts. The first-floor bathroom and third-floor dressing rooms remain close to their original designs. The green room, originally supposed to have been the prop room, was utilitarian in its original design, and has been retrofitted to serve anywhere from one to sixty people on a busy show day. Phone lines have been installed, and the pay phone is gone. Two-way cable service is available, and high-speed service will follow to keep up with the growing technology needs of groups that are on the road 20 or 30 weeks of the year.

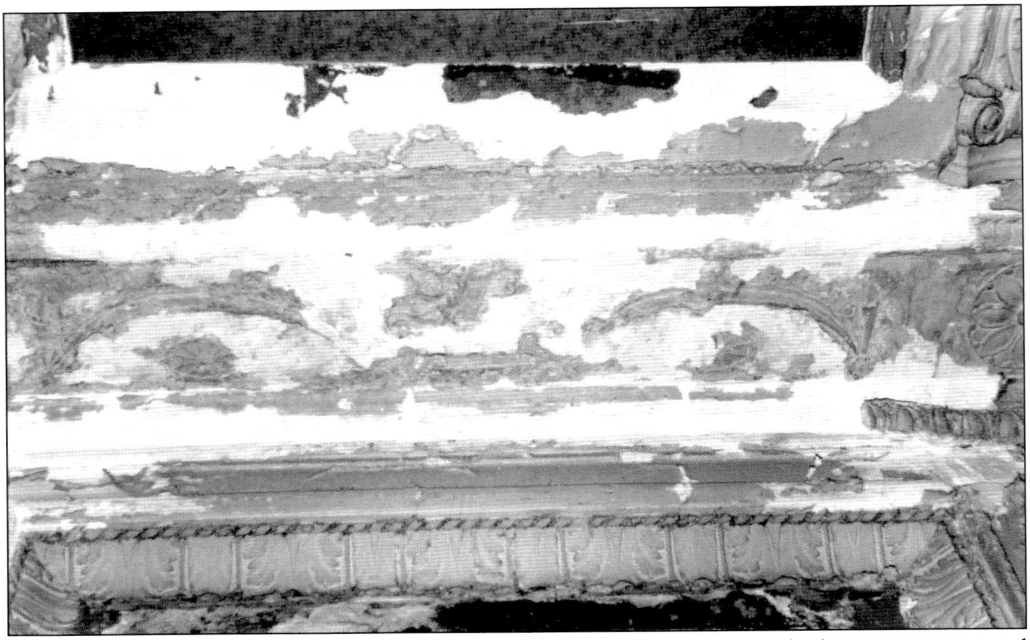

This closeup image of the disrepair of the plasterwork is indicative of what was uncovered during the initial restoration of the venue. While hiding the work under false coverings may have preserved the original design and perhaps the color scheme, it kept the eye from seeing what was happening—specifically, the water damage to the areas.

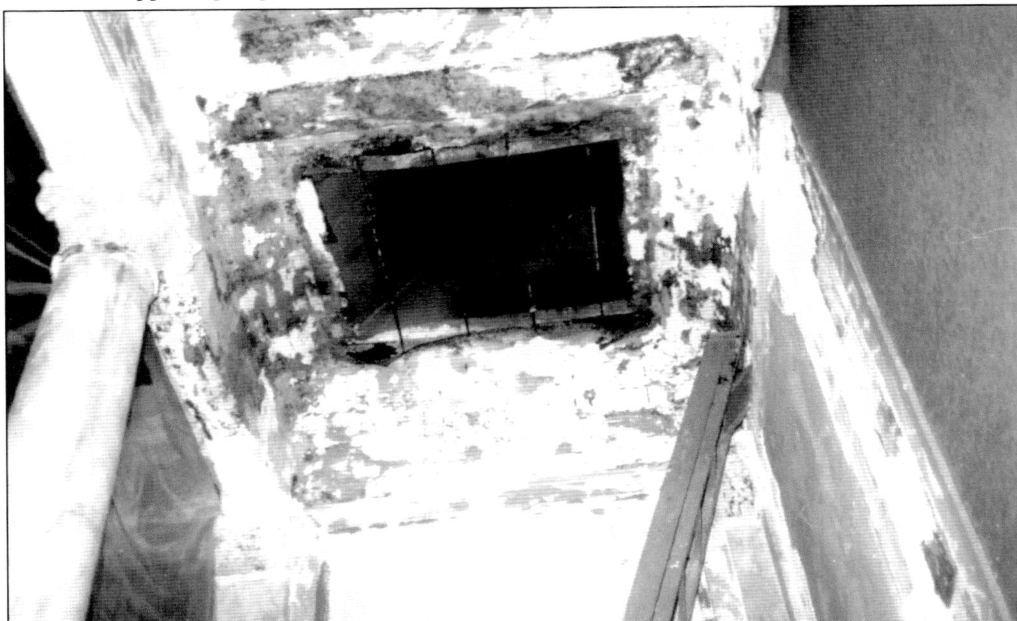

This photograph, taken from a little farther away, shows an opening to the mezzanine's vaulted ceiling that has since been covered over. The original opening had a removable grille in it to allow access for service to the electrical and plumbing systems. The area is now accessible from the ceiling of one of the offices. Of note in this closeup is the scagliola finish on the columns.

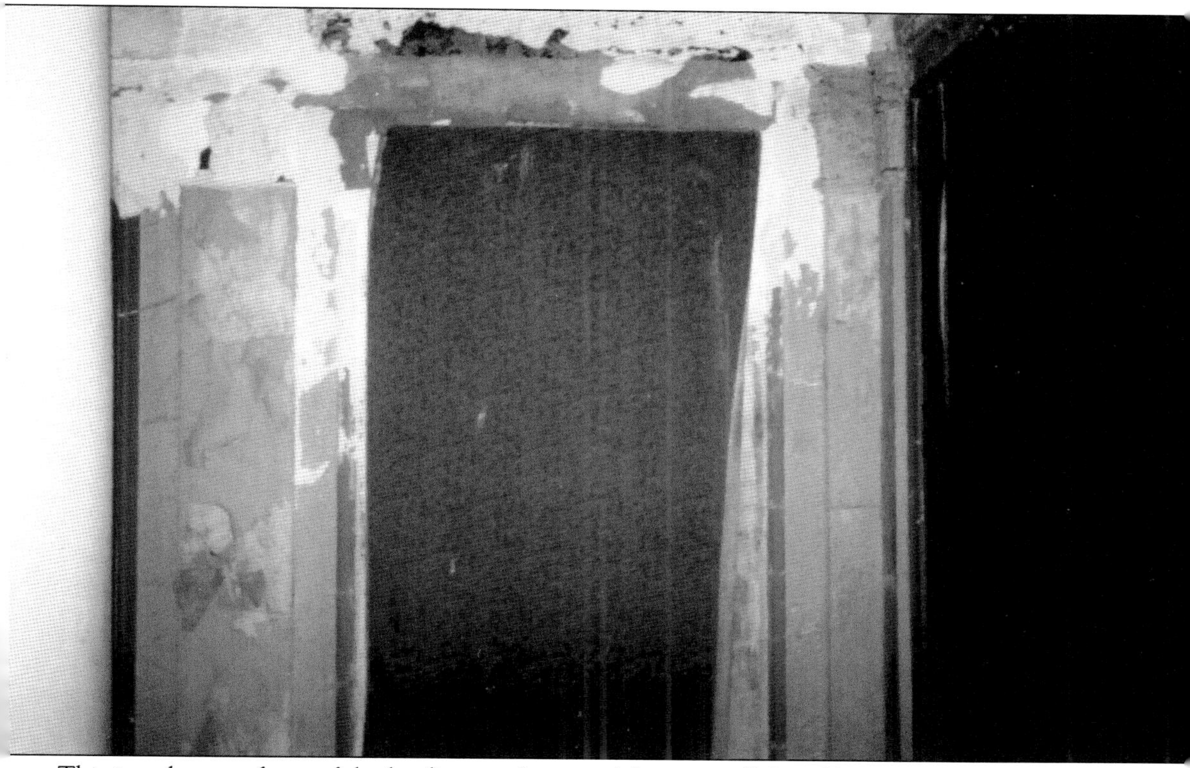

This is a closeup of one of the landings at the top of the stairwell. In addition to the tragedy of the disrepair that is noted here, the fabric inserts are shown. The original descriptions of these panels note that they contained either fabric or art glass designs, or both. Again, the scagliola finishes and marble are evident. Both were in such poor repair that they have been covered over until they can be appropriately refinished. To the left side of the photograph is where one of deMerlier's original murals would have hung. The group seeking historical certification of the venue was the first to see this vast disrepair. This would have been a sobering sight for those trying to balance programming, history, and finance.

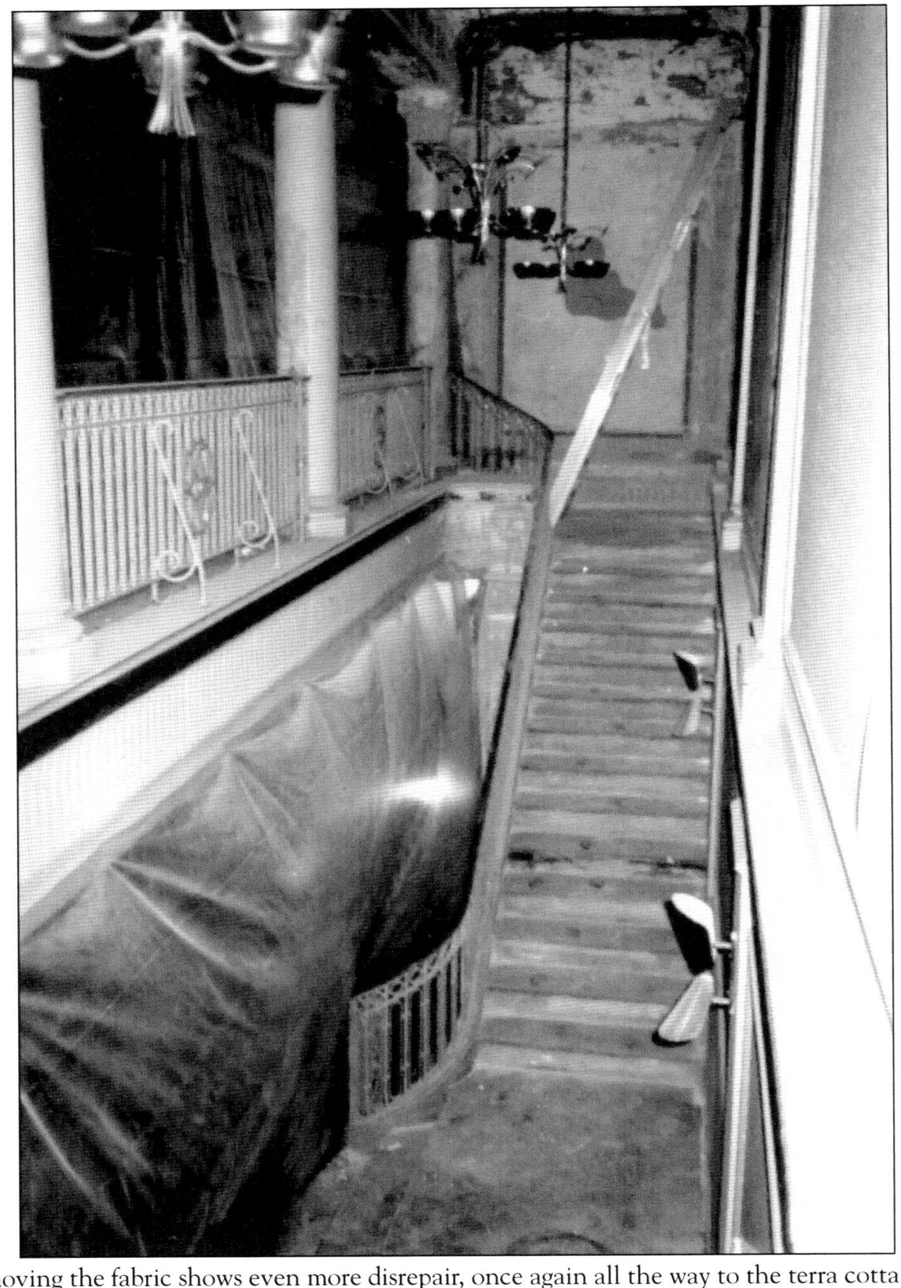

Removing the fabric shows even more disrepair, once again all the way to the terra cotta block. Luckily, the original staircase balustrade was intact. The marble steps had been covered by carpet for many years, most likely as a precaution against slip-and-fall incidents, and also as a part of the modernization process. The steps needed refinishing as well. The lighting fixtures, although not of the 1920s, were retained because they are reflective of the movie house era.

Photographs of the stairway renovation show the enormity of the project these organizations faced in restoring the building. The renovations, both by the Glenside Landmarks Society and by G. B. M. Wharton, took years to complete. They included not only the application of plaster and paint but also the exploration of hidden rooms and spaces. Decisions needed to be made about priorities and finances. Except for short periods of time when, due either to work or financial troubles (usually involving how to pay the heating bill), the venue had some type of programming for the community. On the second floor, behind the public spaces, are the technical booth, which runs about half of the width of the auditorium, the original manager's office, and the ushers' waiting room. The technical booth is still in existence. Other spaces, like the ladies' lounge, are now staff offices. The building houses 14 full-time staff people, and on a busy day, up to 40 more part-time people.

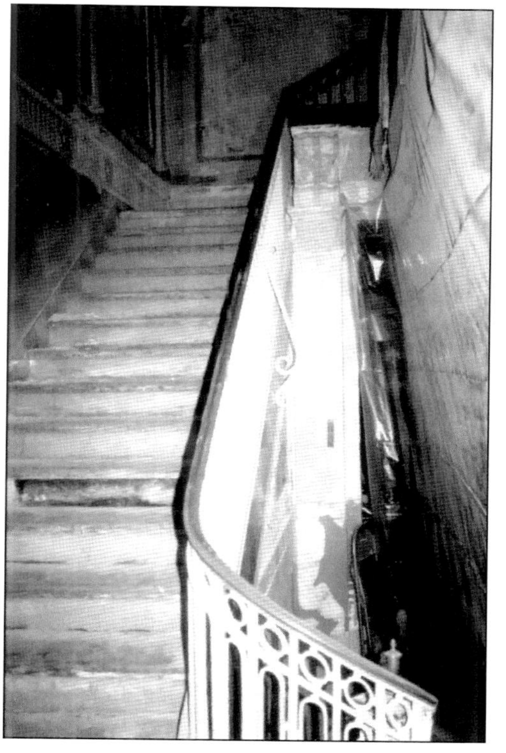

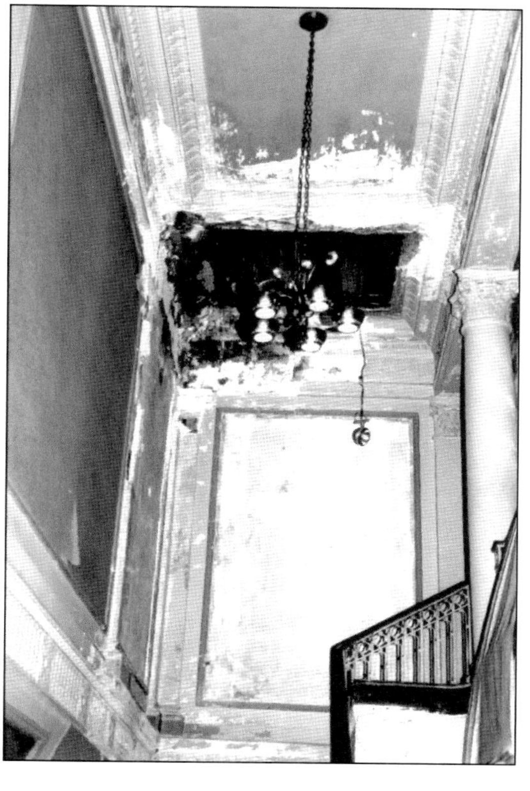

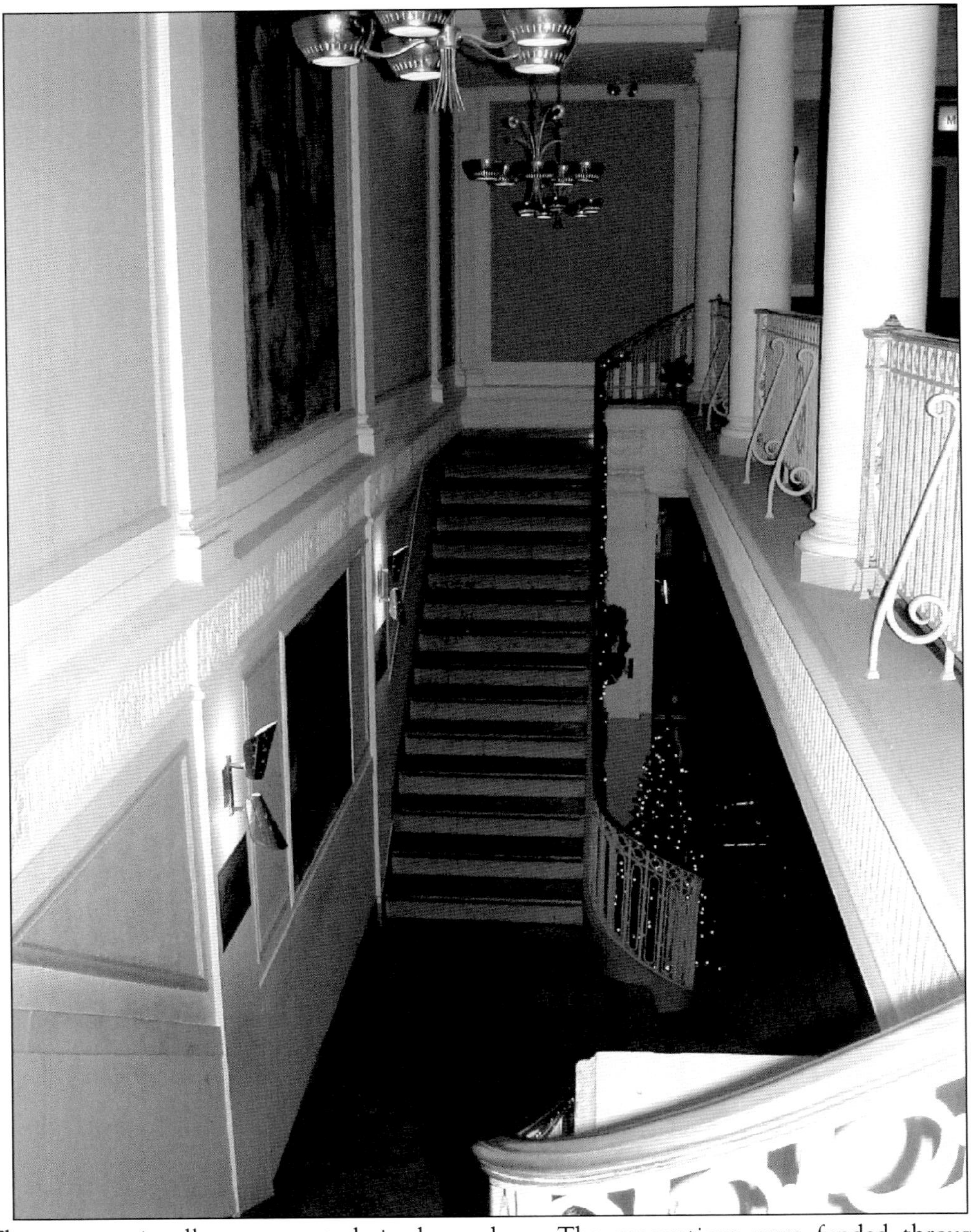

The same stairwell, as renovated, is shown here. The renovations were funded through contributions and through commercial enterprise. The ventilation system was partially funded through a grant received in 1992. It is impossible to tell what the total cost was of all the renovations, as it took many organizations to complete them. It is estimated to be close to $5 million. An example that puts the cost into perspective is that a single restoration of plasterwork at the top of the steps (one sill and four moldings) cost close to $2,000. Yet the restoration is only in its infancy. These were the sums expended to make the building habitable so that it could continue to be saved. The ongoing care and maintenance of the building has been part of the stewardship of each organization that has operated it.

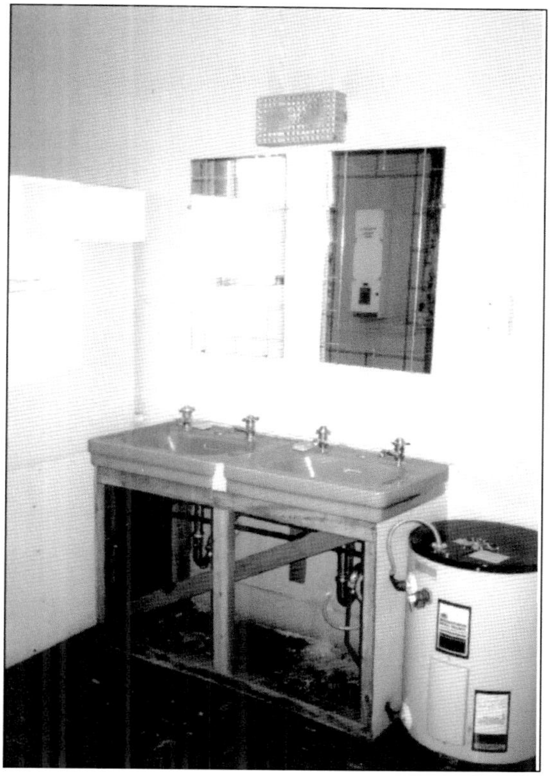

As happens in any public space, amenities became a focal point—and sometimes a point of contention. In relating the history of the Keswick, these two photographs of the bathrooms before and after renovation are an integral part of the equation. During renovation, the ladies' room was expanded from three stalls to five; yet there still seem not to be enough. Unfortunately, the waste pipe for the venue runs under the Moravian tile floor. Engineering will play an immense role in the next redesign, as the floor will not be excavated.

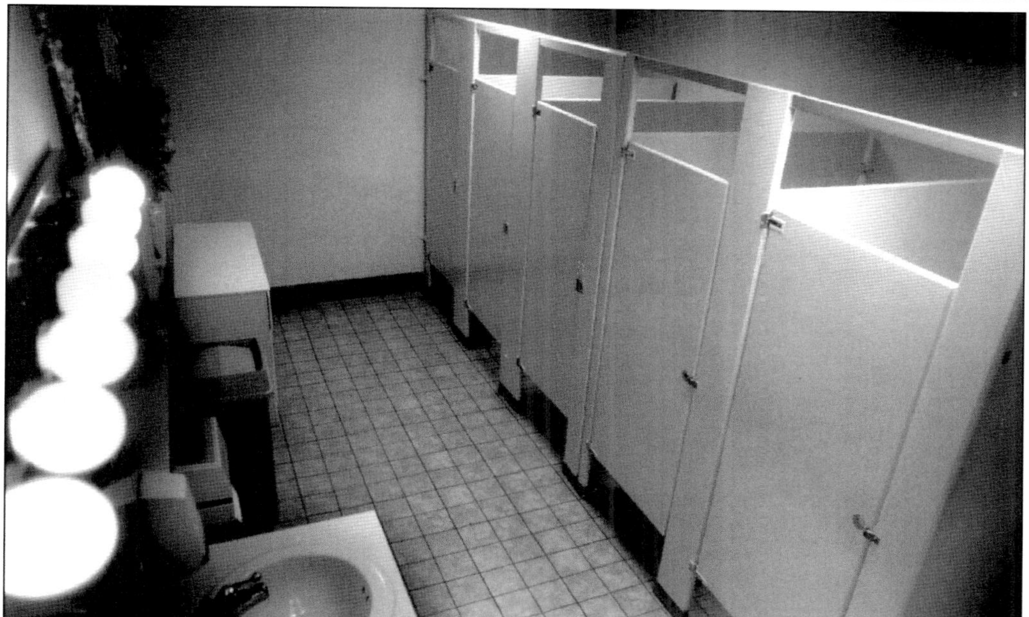

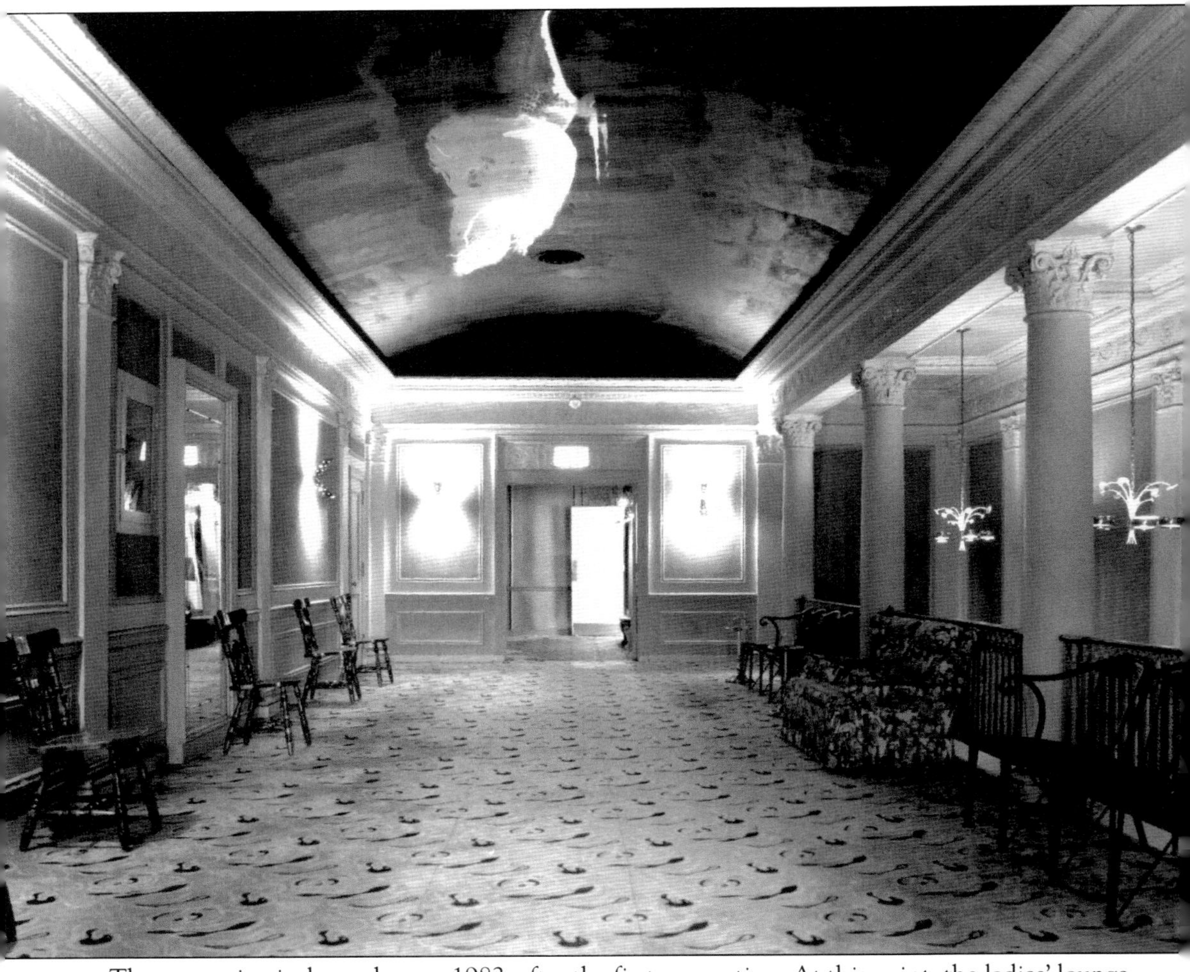

The mezzanine is shown here *c*. 1982, after the first renovation. At this point, the ladies' lounge had not yet been redesigned into office space. The current piece of artwork, the mythical screens, also was not yet in place. The framed mirror covers a doorway that originally led from the technical and projection booth. It is not known what the image at the top of the photograph is. It may be a photo-processing error, but theater people prefer to think it may be one of their spirits who inhabits the building. As no historic building tale is complete without its ghost story, this photograph reflects that the Keswick Theatre has its own. The presence is felt at house right, on the stairs, where there has been a sighting, and backstage, where there has also been a sighting. The sightings have both been of men, one in early-20th-century dress. No mischief has been performed, however, and this is believed to be a good sign.

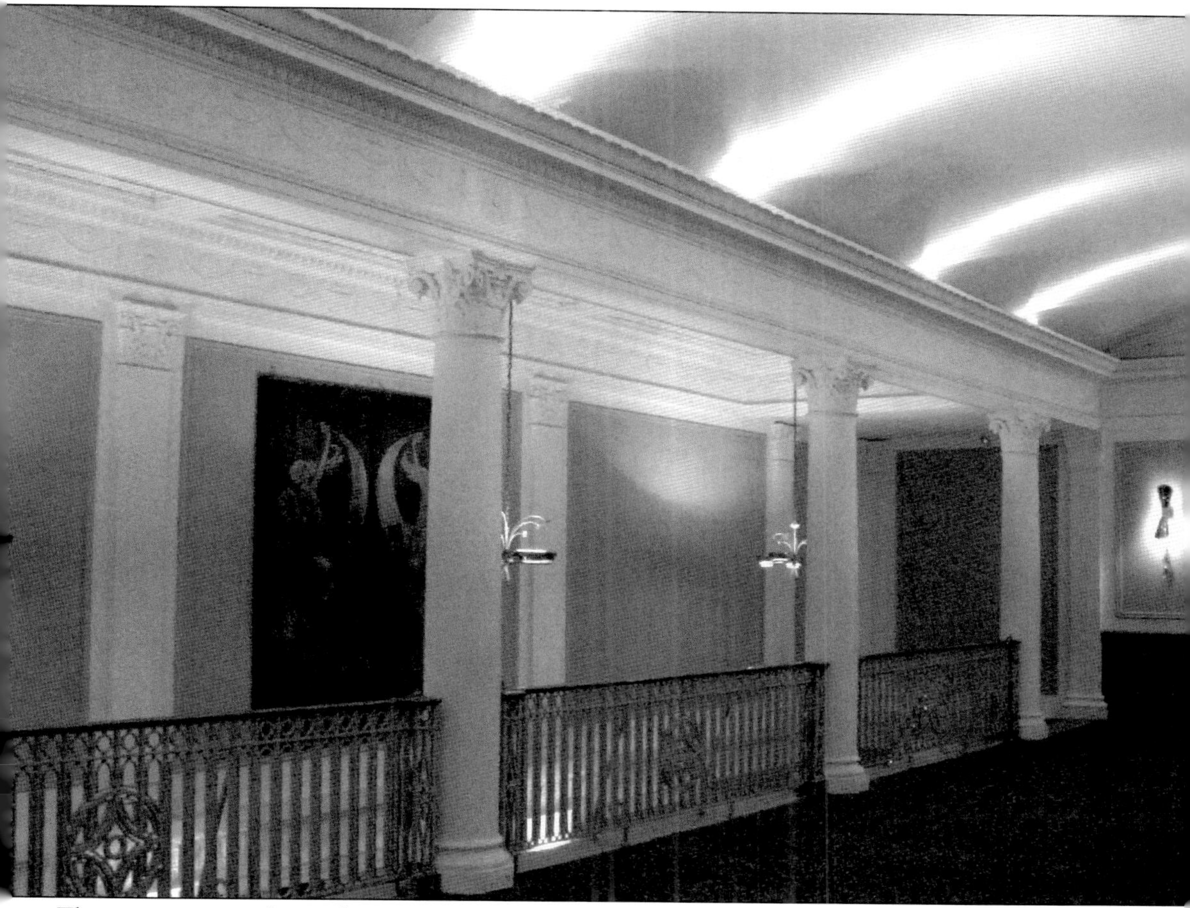

The mezzanine is shown here as it is today. The photograph reflects the cove lighting and the restored plasterwork, as well as the ornamental screen in place. The balustrade is original. Where the lighting fixtures are now located on the wall, there was originally art glass work, but as no original drawings, photographs, or plans exist, it will be hard to reconstruct this detail in the future. Horace Trumbauer originally included 65 separate drawings of the venue. Copies of six known drawings have been donated to the Philadelphia Athenaeum by Keswick Entertainment Group, but the remaining items are believed lost, as neither the collectors of Keswick, Trumbauer, nor Turner Construction have reported any. Proof that 65 drawings existed is found in the records at the Athenaeum of Philadelphia, which has Trumbauer's original account books.

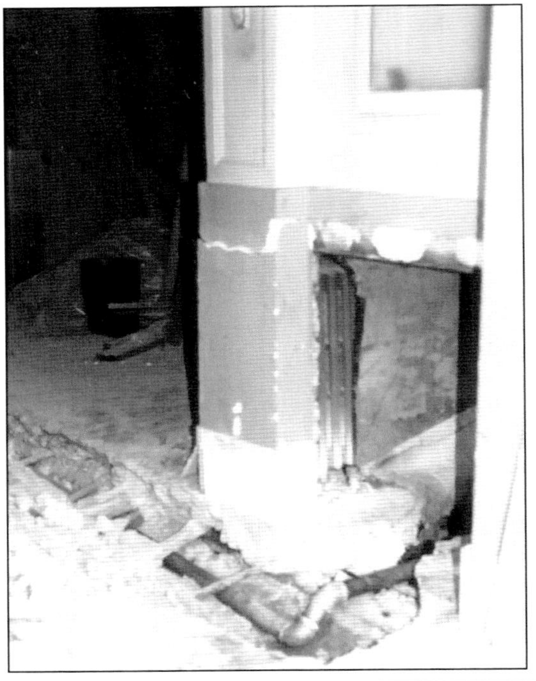

This photograph shows the excavation of the main lobby to satisfy code needs for a sprinkler and plumbing. A portion of the terrazzo floor was lost during this work and previous work to the floor (specifically rug installations). Portions of this floor have been sighted under layers of paint, concrete, and floor covering, but it would be massively expensive to unearth or redesign. The floor is said to have been of red terrazzo and covered by a rug designed especially for the room. Small portions of the black terrazzo floor in the mezzanine do exist, but remain covered by rugs, except in the hall to the offices by the men's room. When this work was done, some rubble may have been put in the tunnels under the auditorium aisles, thus blocking them.

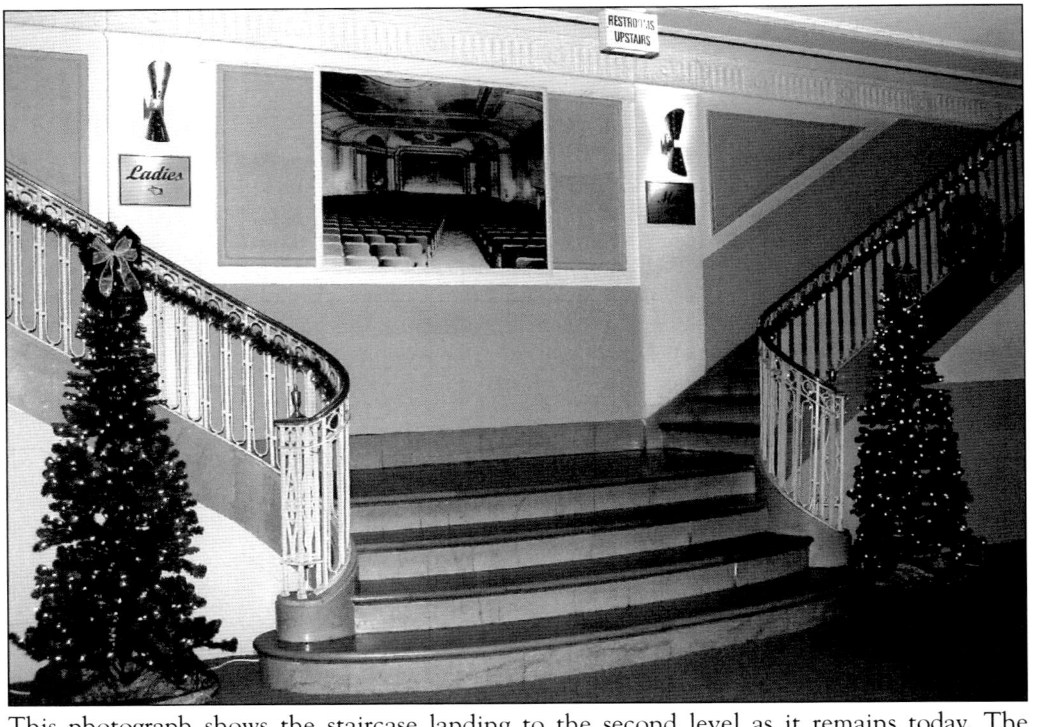

This photograph shows the staircase landing to the second level as it remains today. The lighting is c. 1950–1960. The photographs are of the original auditorium, but the balustrade remains the same. The Granox marble staircase has had all of the carpeting removed, and is as it was in 1928.

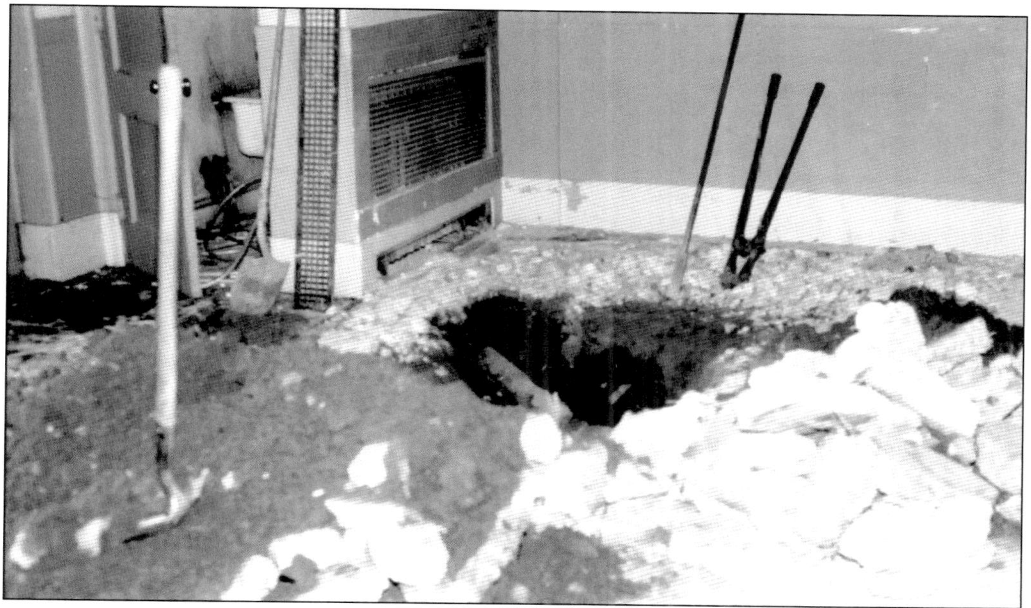

Shown in these photographs is the construction of the handicapped bathroom in the first-floor lobby. Construction of the bathroom was required before G. B. M. Wharton could reopen the building in 1988. This excavation and the tie-in to the waste disposal line at the other end of the building further damaged the terrazzo flooring. The area to the right is the bar setup. The company did not want to install any more areas around the original architecture, so the bar is completely mobile and free standing. The exit signs are believed to be from the 1950s; those shown are original. When they are broken, damaged, or missing, Tom Killeen reconstructs these signs personally.

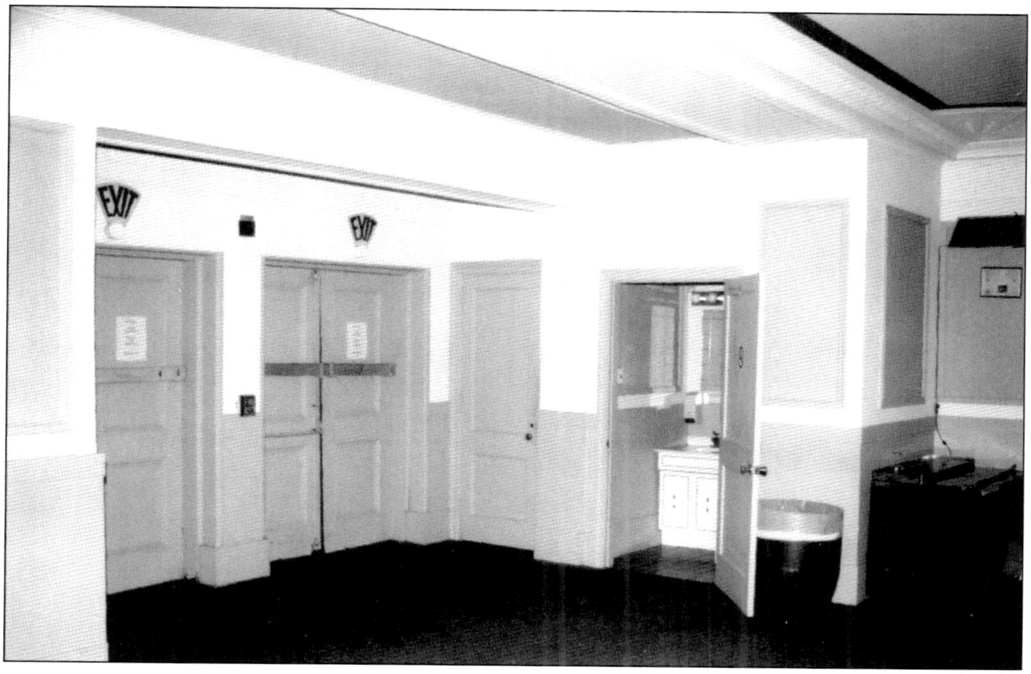

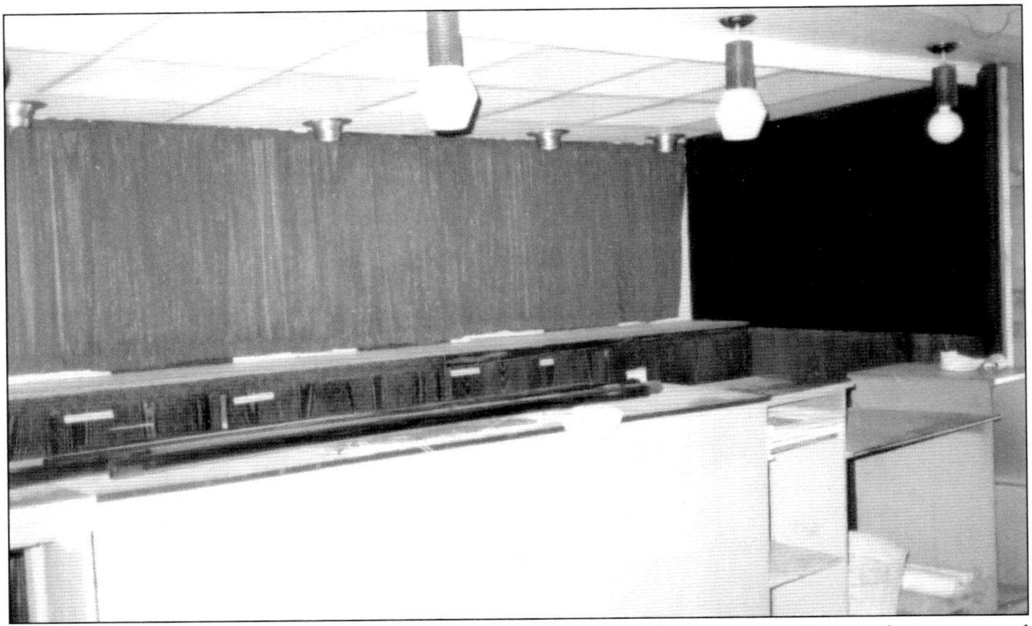

The concession stand is shown here in the main lobby in the process of being deconstructed before the venue reopened in 1988. This stand was put in sometime during Melvin Koff's stewardship of the building. Oral history speaks of the concession stand being in the auditorium foyer by the staircase at the time of the fire.

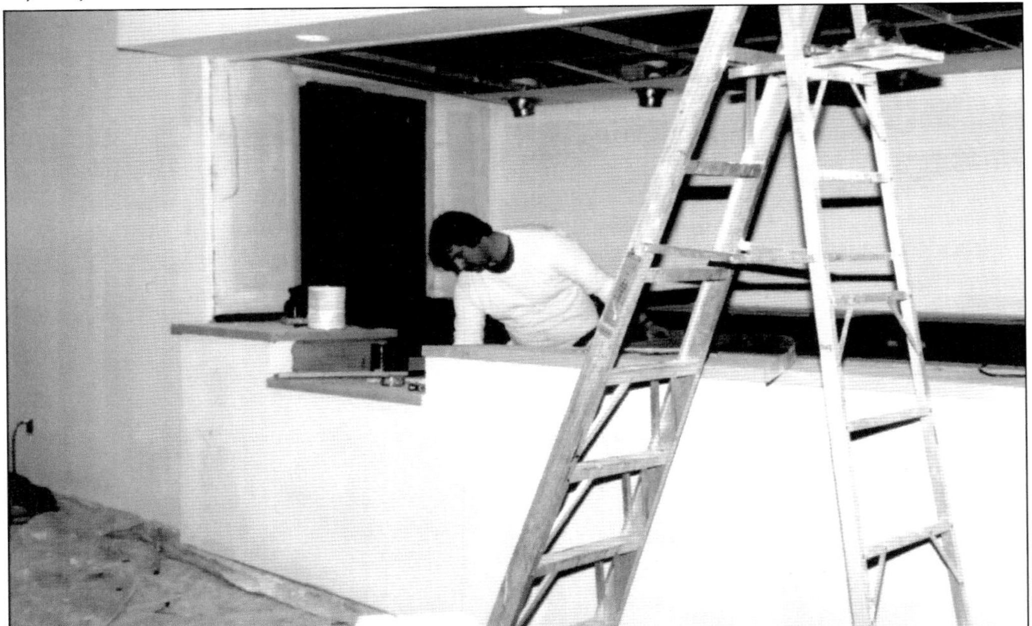

The concession stand remains beside the office and hides part of the original wall of the main lobby. The Moravian tile floor is visible. Records show the purchase of another stand in the early 1990s. At one time, standard fluorescent lights were recessed much higher into the ceiling of this area. Portions of the original lobby can still be seen behind the walls.

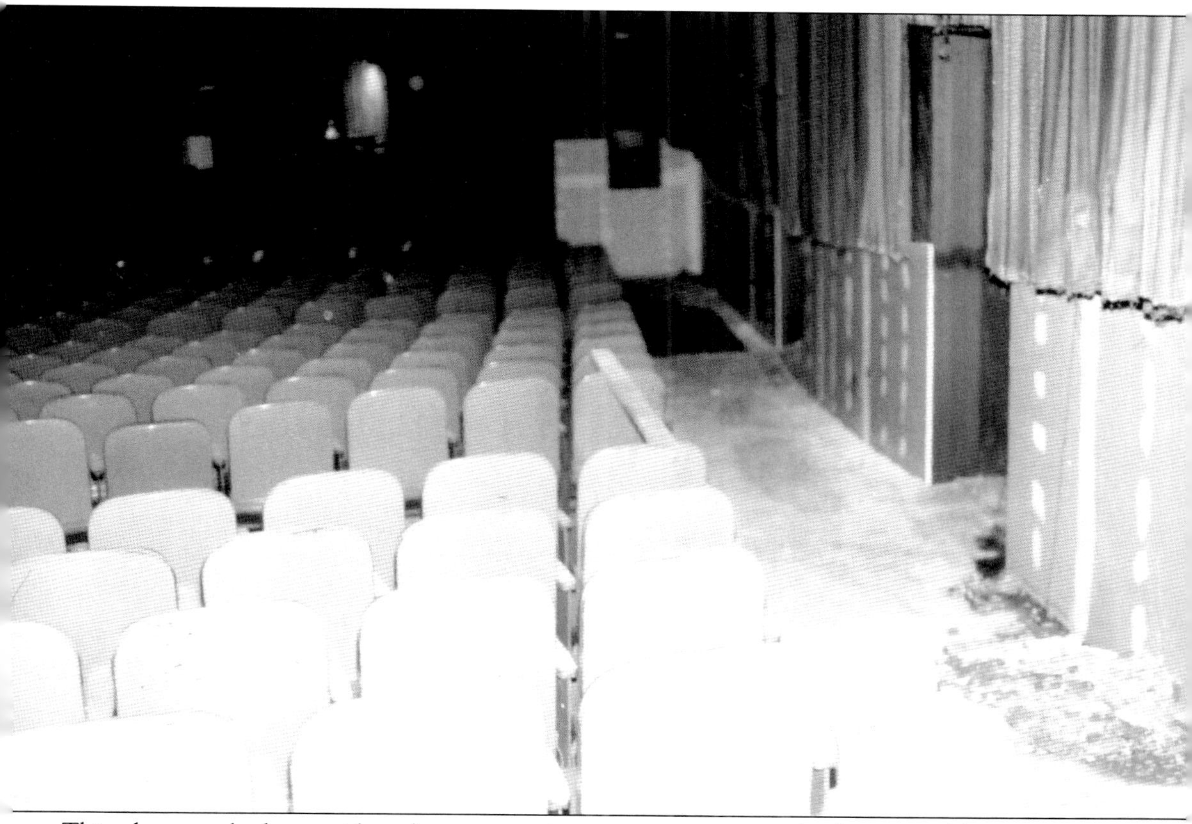

This photograph shows either the construction or reconstruction (perhaps to add or restore insulation) of the auditorium walls. Water had flowed through the walls of the venue for many years. This flooding, coupled with the damage done during the fire of 1952, destroyed large portions of the original walls of the auditorium. In the 1955 reopening photographs, the walls had received some type of paneling treatment, which appears to be a vinyl or leather insert (no records have been found regarding the paneling). Sometime between 1955 and the 1980s, curtains replaced the paneling. Reports are that during the last days of both the movie house era and the nonprofit eras, the auditorium was extremely cold. It appears that efforts were under way here to insulate the room and make use of the existing curtains.

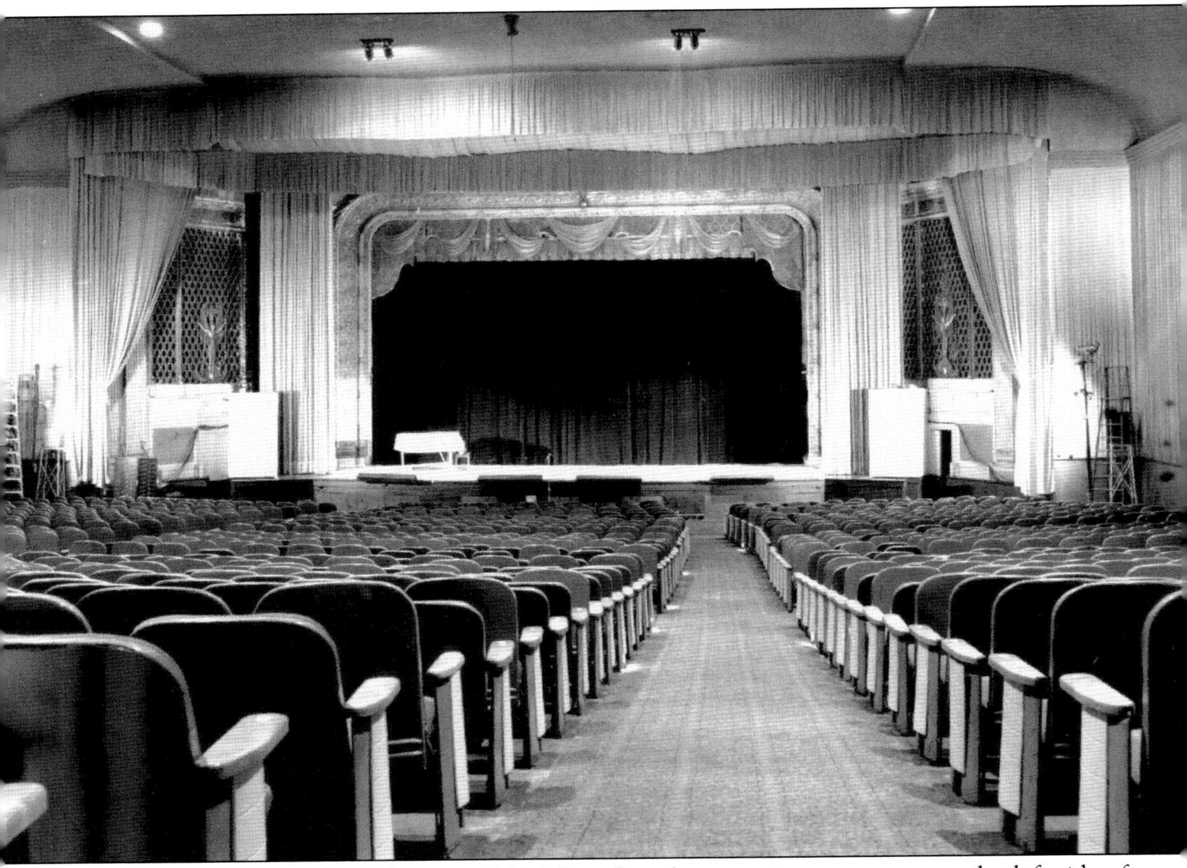

The auditorium is shown here in 1982. Note that the organ is not present on the left side of the stage. The stage has been extended on this side to accommodate the organ. The curtains and wainscoting are present, and the proscenium is draped. There are more valances in this photograph than currently exist. Unknown is whether any of the original ceiling may exist under the valances. This portion of the ceiling would have contained grilles and glass, as well as plasterwork, as shown in the next photograph. The room will need to be carefully studied before restoration work so that its current acoustical balance can be maintained. A closeup of the proscenium is featured on page 70.

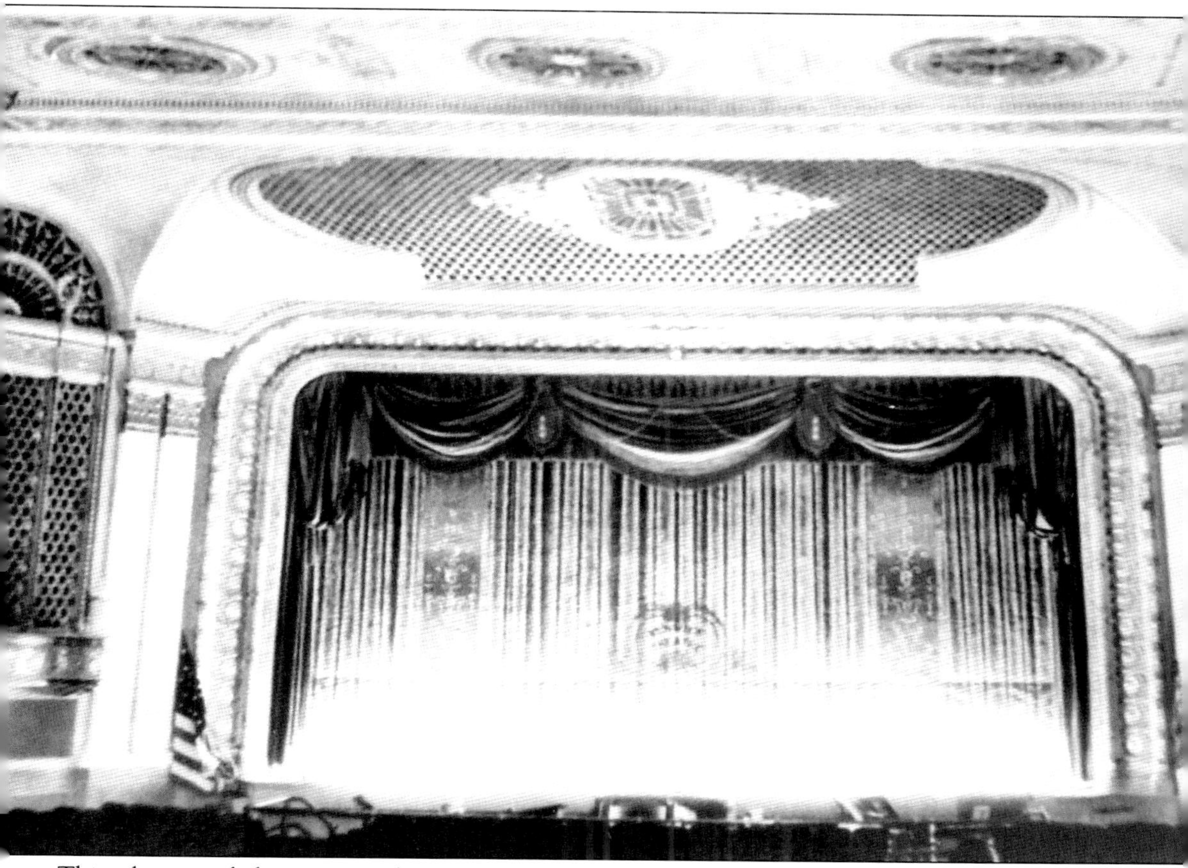

This closeup of the stage and pit area *c.* 1929 provides insight into the original details surrounding the stage. The doors on either side still exist. The right side accesses backstage and the left is behind the current organ. The balcony-like objects were never used for seating and appear to have some type of fixture attached to them. The original orchestra pit, including the base to raise the organ, still exists under the stage thrust built on top of it. However, the brass poles are gone. Much of the stage's detail work remains on the right and left sides. Robert Harper, author of an article on local theaters for the Old York Road Historical Society, says this work remains "like a coy beauty hidden behind a fan."

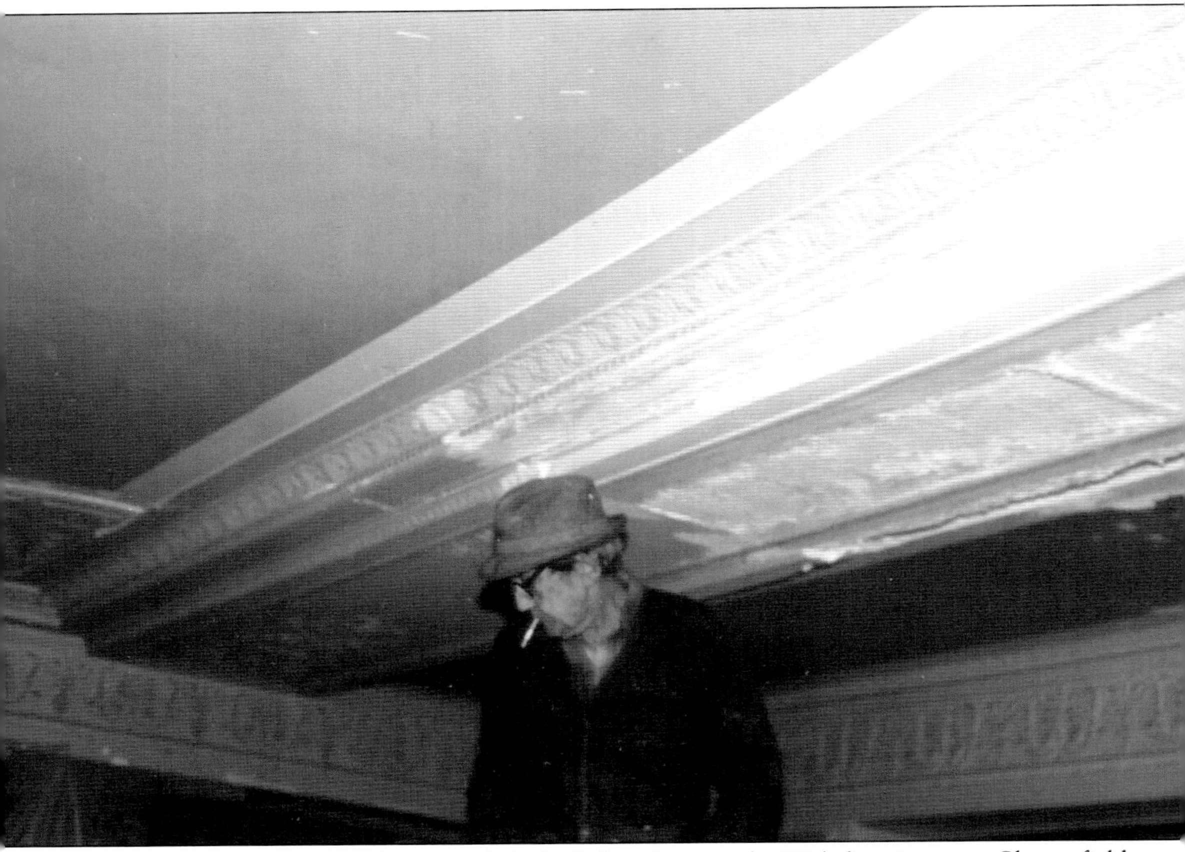

Earle Felber, famous craftsman, refurbished the plasterwork. With his signature Chesterfield hanging from the side of his mouth, Felber did not grace the stage but graced the building with the contributions of his work. Felber apprenticed with the Voigt Company that did the original plasterwork of the building. He went on to achieve fame in his own right, working on many historic buildings in the country. After his death, subsequent maintenance of the plaster was necessary. As the plaster molds remain the property of the artist unless otherwise indicated by contract, it is necessary to have these recreated each time they need to be replaced.

These closeup images of the plasterwork at the Keswick Theatre are historic restorations of the original Voigt designs as seen in the Voigt catalog of 1928. The designs have been painstakingly recreated and are maintained by masters. It becomes increasingly hard to find craftspeople for this work. Currently, Thomas Hennelly & Sons maintains the Keswick plasterwork, coming in about once a year to check its condition and make any necessary repairs or maintenance. Support from organizations like the League of Historic American Theatres and other historical societies make finding these tradespeople and artists more meaningful. The information on Earle Felber was found at the Old York Road Historical Society, and the Voigt Company information was available at the Historical Society of Pennsylvania.

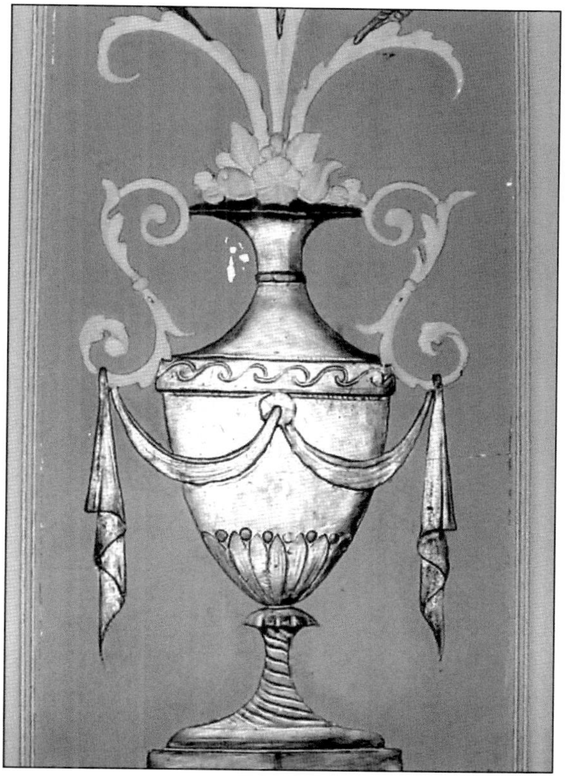

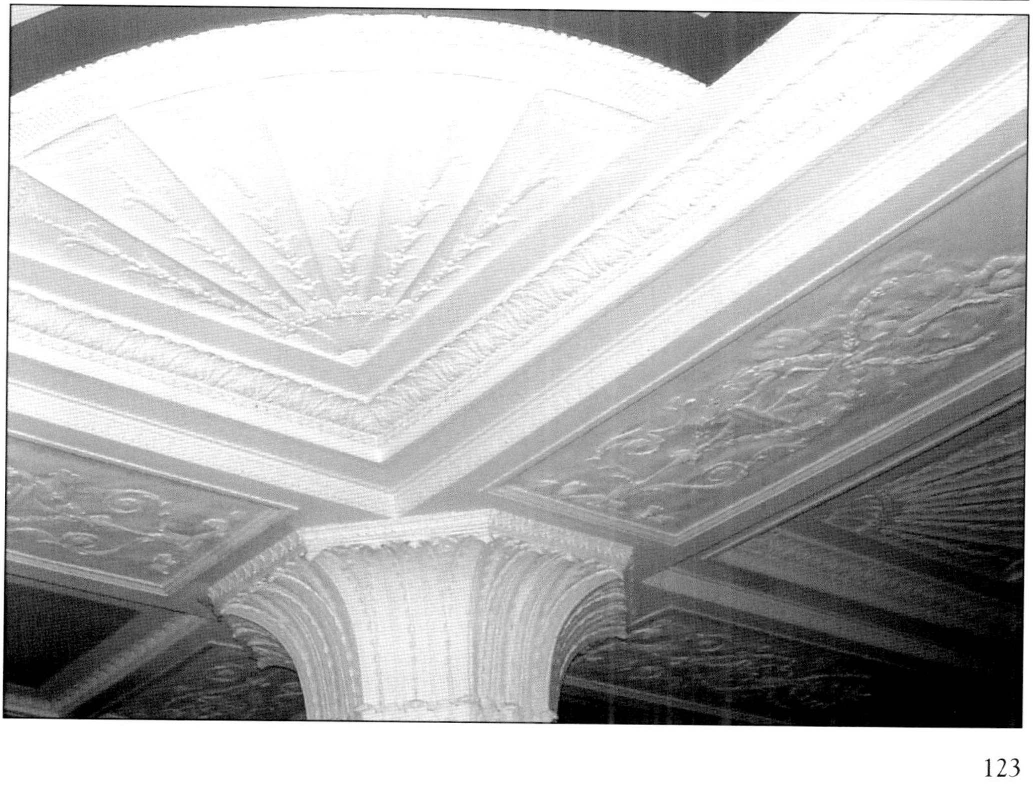

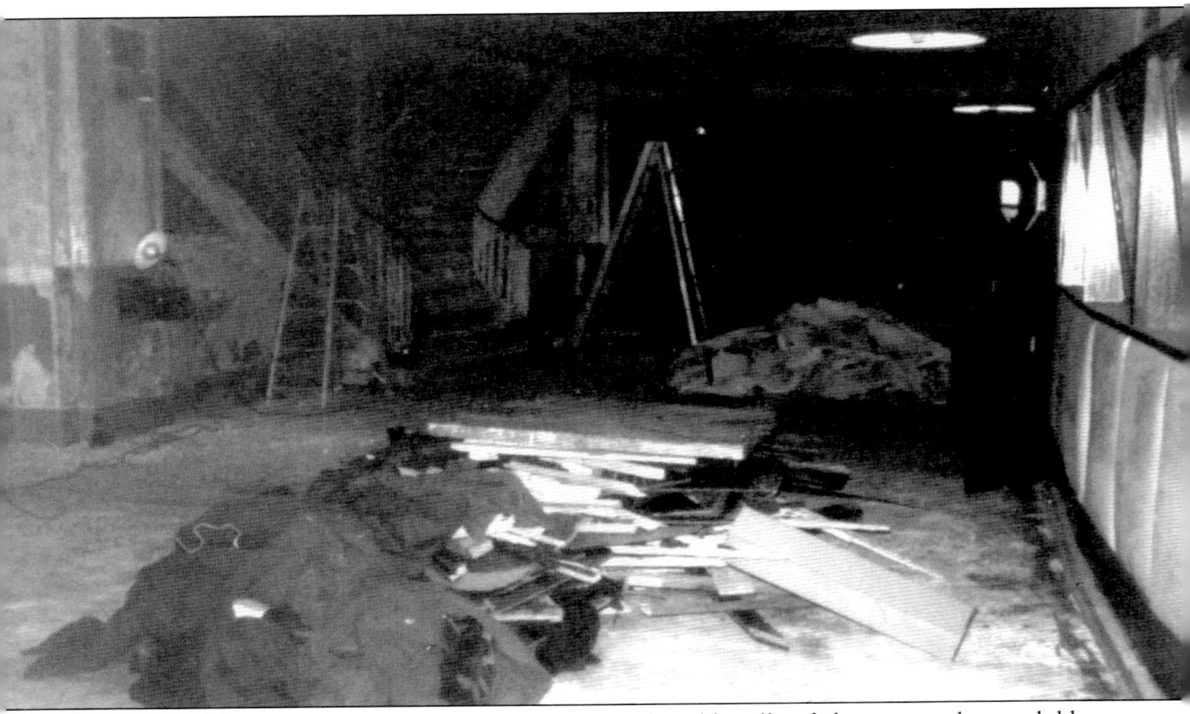

This photograph is the only known closeup of the old walls of the movie theater lobby as designed by Melvin Koff's architects, David Supowitz and Shander Berger. The clean lines, the use of vinyl or leather, wood, and glass typify the hip, modern 1950s of Hollywood, California. It is not known whether the drapery fabric on the floor covered this structure or the area between the glass and poles now part of the restored lobby. Most individuals who recall coming to the theater specifically for the movies say they have no recollection of ever seeing the columns or glass. The rest of the lobby shows areas of other discoveries, and portions of the red terrazzo floor are barely visible under the construction.

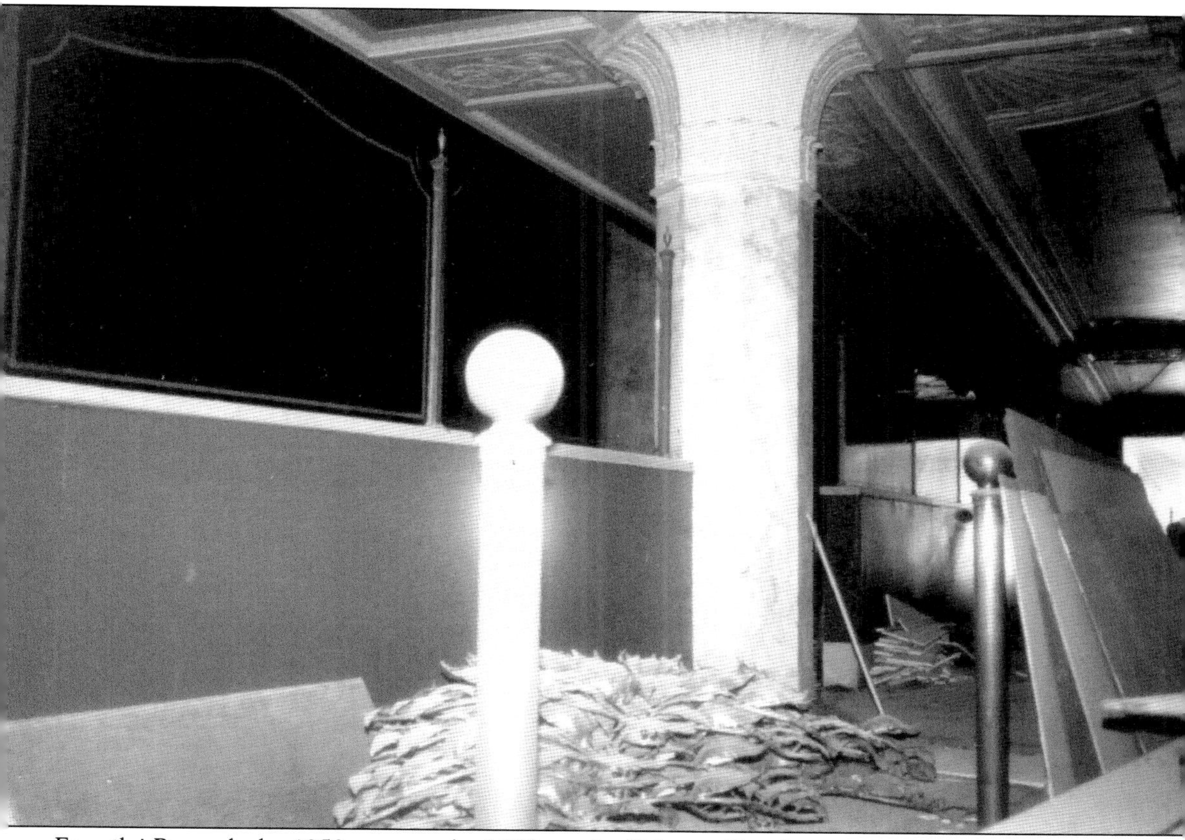

Et voila! Beneath the 1950s returns the 1920s work of Horace Trumbauer, awaiting restoration. The columns still had gold-leaf gilding and scagliola finishes; the leaded-glass windows and brass stands were all intact, waiting quietly for rediscovery. Today, patrons come out and stand on the steps directly across the lobby to see the stage. The brass stanchions are the same design as the ones that are seen at the midway point of the auditorium. Despite the beauty of the restorations, there is still some wistful feeling for the 1950s architectural style.

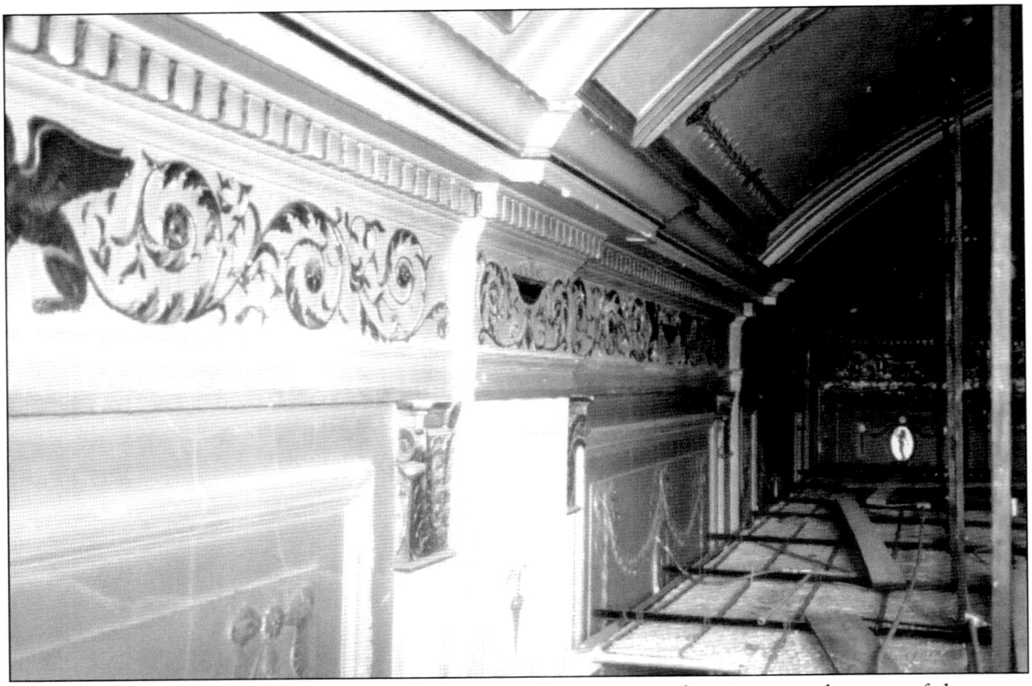

These photographs, taken in order to help obtain historic certification, are closeups of the areas that still remain above the false ceiling in the outer lobby. The griffins, scrolls, and capstans await the day when they, too, are uncovered. Each photograph shows images of the famous cameos, one of which is now missing. The colors of this area also remain very close to the original and are being used to slowly move the building back toward its original color scheme. This treasure is priceless in the continued efforts to restore the venue.

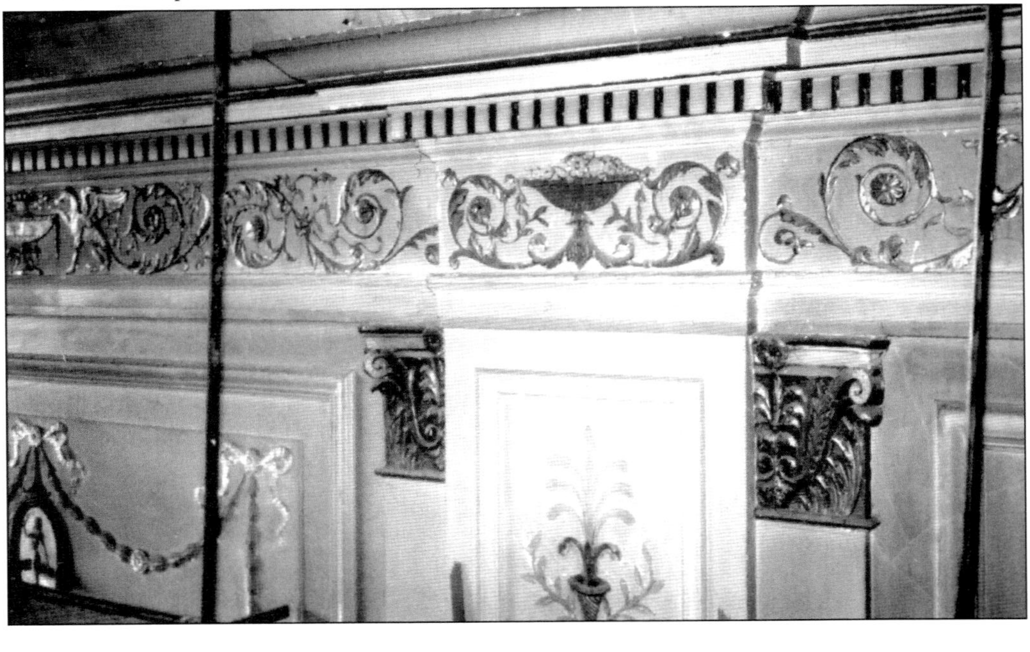

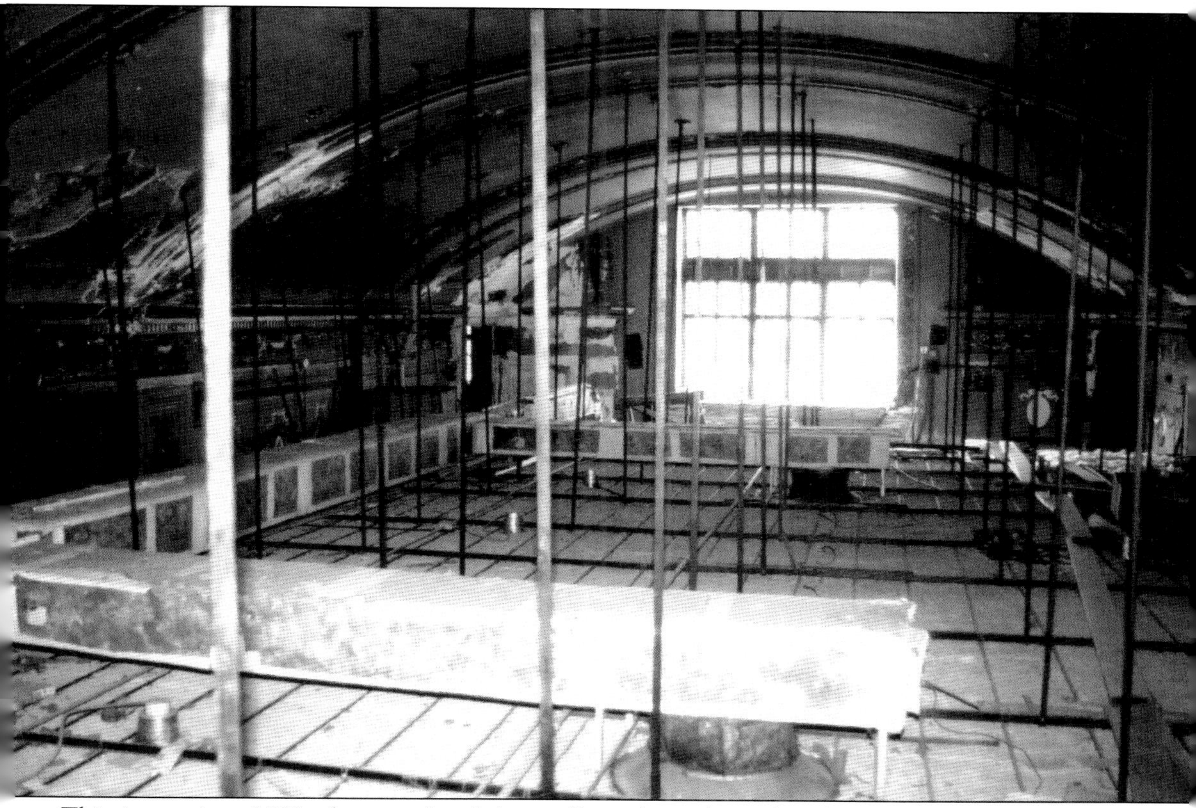

This image is a 1982 photograph of the mullioned windows that look out onto Keswick Village. This is the next area under consideration for renovation. The area has access through the two turret towers via a spiral metal staircase that leads up to a platform, which once had a balustrade and was used as an observation deck or for access to the marquee roof. Making the area accessible will enable people to see the vaulted ceiling, although it is in disrepair. Also visible from this area will be the doors leading to the original ladies' lounge and out onto Keswick Avenue. Visitors will be able to see the view that the building has had for the past 75 years—a view of the community.

PHOTOGRAPH CREDITS

American Seating Company: 20 below.
Brandywine Museum collection: 23 above.
Delaware Valley Organ Society: 78 below, 79.
DeMarco family: 54, 62.
Don Neiman: 71 above, 72 below, 73, 76 above.
Edith Brackinridge and Isabella Barthelmeh: 37, 38 below, 87 below.
Free Library of Philadelphia theater collection: 11, 20 above, 24, 98, 121. Reproduction by Joseph Checcia.
George Bodman: 80 above.
Glenside Kiwanis Club: 40 above.
Glenside Weldon Fire Company photograph collection: 6, 9, 12–13, 16, 33–34, 35 below, 45 above, 46–48, 52, 57 below, 58, 59 below, 60–61, 64, 65 above, 66 above, 67.
Harry Barbin restoration collection: 21 below, 72 above, 74, 76 below, 77, 78 above, 80 below, 81–82, 83 above, 84 above, 92 below, 94 below, 95–97, 99–104, 106, 108–111, 113 above, 116 above, 117–119, 122, 124–127.
Historical Society of Pennsylvania, vol. 7: 1917: cover.
Joseph Checcia: 85 below.
Keswick Theatre and Philadelphia Athenaeum: 18.
Melvin Koff family (Dr. Sklar and Mrs. Sunshine): 53, 57, 59 above, 66 below.
Old York Road Historical Society: 2–3, 14–15, 17, 26–28, 31, 35 above, 36 above, 38 below, 39, 42–43, 44 above, 45 below, 51, 65 below, 71 below, 87 above.
Paley Library, Temple University Urban Archives: 68.
Paul Bunting: 19, 55 above, 56 above, 69, 75, 114, 120.
Robert Harper theater collection: 29–30, 36 above, 44 below, 49, 63 above.
Roy Snyder: 14 below, 84 below.
Times Chronicle/Richard Gerding: 55 below, 56 below.
Virginia Killeen: 85 above.

The balance of photographs are from the Keswick Theatre photograph collection. Special thanks go to Patricia Taddei for photographic and scanning assistance on this project.